Calvin@500

Calvin@500

Theology, History, and Practice

Edited by

RICHARD R. TOPPING *and* JOHN A. VISSERS

☙PICKWICK *Publications* · Eugene, Oregon

CALVIN@500
Theology, History, and Practice

Copyright © 2011 Wipf and Stock Publishers. All rights reserved. Except for brief quotations in critical publications or reviews, no part of this book may be reproduced in any manner without prior written permission from the publisher. Write: Permissions, Wipf and Stock Publishers, 199 W. 8th Ave., Suite 3, Eugene, OR 97401.

Pickwick Publications
An Imprint of Wipf and Stock Publishers
199 W. 8th Ave., Suite 3
Eugene, OR 97401

www.wipfandstock.com

ISBN 13: 978-1-49825-929-3

Cataloging-in-Publicationdata:

Calvin@500 : theology , history, and practice / edited by Richard R. Topping and John A. Vissers.

xiv + 182 p. ; 23 cm. Includes bibliographical references.

ISBN 13: 978-1-61097-131-7

1. Calvin, Jean, 1509–1564. I. Topping, Richard R., 1960–. II. Vissers, John A. III. Title.

BX9418 T66 2011

Manufactured in the U.S.A.

For the World Communion of Reformed Churches

"So powerful is participation in the church that it keeps us in the society of God. In the very word 'communion' there is a wealth of comfort because, while it is determined that whatever the Lord bestows upon his members and ours belongs to us, our hope is strengthened by all the benefits they receive."

Calvin, *Institutes* I.iv.3

Contents

List of Contributors / *ix*

Introduction and Acknowledgements—John A. Vissers / *xiii*

1　"The First-Born in God's Family": Calvin and the Jews
　　—*William Klempa* / 1

2　Scripture Funded: Reforming Reformed Imagination
　　—*Richard R. Topping* / 23

3　The Holy Spirit in the Thoughts of John Calvin
　　—*Gerard Booy* / 38

4　A Reformed Culture of Persuasion: John Calvin's "Two
　　Kingdoms" and the Theological Origins of the Public Sphere
　　—*Torrance Kirby* / 52

5　Calvin as Apologist—*Jason N. Zuidema* / 67

6　John Calvin and the "Still-born" Third Option in the French
　　Reformation—*Axel Schoeber* / 86

7　Pilgrimage: Calvin and the Rehabilitation of a Reformation
　　Renegade—*Lynne McNaughton* / 98

8　Calvin and the Preaching of the Lively Word
　　—*Stephen Farris* / 113

9　John Calvin, Refugee—*R. Gerald Hobbs* / 128

10　A Comment on Calvin's *The Necessity of Reforming the Church*
　　(1543)—*Victor Shepherd* / 146

11　"Everyone's a Part of the Line of Production"
　　—*Stephen Allen* / 162

Bibliography / 173

Contributors

STEPHEN ALLEN serves as Associate Secretary for Justice Ministries with The Presbyterian Church in Canada in Toronto, Ontario. Justice Ministries cooperates with and assists congregations and courts of the church to respond faithfully to the justice imperatives of the gospel by encouraging theological reflection and action on faith and justice issues.

GERARD BOOY is the minister of Haney Presbyterian Church in Maple Ridge, British Columbia. He holds a DD degree in Old Testament from the University of Pretoria and serves on the Board of Management of St. Andrew's Hall, Vancouver. He is a regular contributor to the "Acts of Faith" column in the *Maple Ridge News* and has written several articles in the *Woordwyser* series of the Dutch Reformed Church, Eastern Synod.

STEPHEN FARRIS is Dean of St. Andrew's Hall and teaches preaching in the Vancouver School of Theology. He is a former President of the Academy of Homiletics, the international society of teachers of preaching. His most recent book is *Grace: A Preaching Commentary Press* (Abingdon, 2003).

R. GERALD HOBBS is Professor Emeritus of Church History and Music at Vancouver School of Theology. A specialist on Martin Bucer and the Strasbourg Reformation, he is the author of numerous studies on the Bible in the early modern period, with particular reference to the Psalms.

TORRANCE KIRBY is Professor of Ecclesiastical History and Director of the Centre for Research on Religion at McGill University. He is the author of *The Zurich Connection and Tudor Political Theology* (Brill, 2007) and several books on the thought of Richard Hooker including *Richard Hooker, Reformer and Platonist* (Ashgate, 2005).

x   *Contributors*

WILLIAM KLEMPA is Principal Emeritus of The Presbyterian College, Montreal, and Adjunct Professor in the McGill Faculty of Religious Studies. He is the author of *Exploring the Faith: Essays in the History and Theology of the Reformed Tradition* (Presbyterian College, 2011) and a former Moderator of The Presbyterian Church in Canada.

LYNNE MCNAUGHTON, for thirteen years on the faculty of Vancouver School of Theology teaching Christian Spirituality, is presently serving on a team developing a new model for Anglican ministry in North Vancouver. She leads spiritual heritage pilgrimages and has written on pilgrimage as a spiritual practice and model for church leadership in change.

AXEL SCHOEBER is Associate Professor of Supervised Ministry at Carey Theological College in Vancouver, Canada, with twenty-seven years of pastoral experience. In addition to holding a DMin degree, he is a PhD candidate at the University of Victoria, and is writing a dissertation on Gérard Roussel: An Irenic Agent of Religious Change (1520s–1540s in France).

VICTOR SHEPHERD is Professor of Theology at Tyndale University College & Seminary; Professor *Ordinarius* at the Graduate Theological Foundation, University of Oxford, UK; and Adjunct Professor, Trinity College, University of Toronto. His publications include *The Nature and Function of Faith in the Theology of John Calvin* (Regent, 2008), *Interpreting Martin Luther: An Introduction to His Life and Though* (Regent, 2004), *A Ministry Dearer Than Life: The Pastoral Legacy of John Calvin* (Clements, 2009), and *Mercy Immense and Free: Essays on Wesley and Wesleyan Theology* (Clements, 2010).

RICHARD R. TOPPING holds the St. Andrew's Hall Chair of Studies in the Reformed Tradition in Vancouver, Canada, where he teaches at the Vancouver School of Theology and lectures at Regent College. He is the author of *Revelation, Scripture and Church: Theological Hermeneutic Thought of James Barr, Paul Ricoeur and Hans Frei* (Ashgate, 2007).

JOHN A. VISSERS is the Principal of Presbyterian College in Montreal, Quebec, and Adjunct Professor of Christian Theology, McGill Faculty of Religious Studies. He is widely published in the area of Reformed thought and history; he is the author of *The Neo-Orthodox Theology of W. W. Bryden* (Pickwick, 2006).

JASON N. ZUIDEMA is a full-time lecturer in Christian Spirituality at Con-cordia University in Montreal. He is author of *Peter Martyr Vermigli (1499–1562) and the Outward Instruments of Divine Grace* (Vandenhoeck & Ruprecht, 2008) and co-author of *Early French Reform: The Theology and Spirituality of Guillaume Farel* (Ashgate, 2011).

Introduction and Acknowledgements
Calvin@500

Aᴠꜰᴛᴇʀ 500 ʜᴜɴᴅʀᴇᴅ ʏᴇᴀʀꜱ John Calvin continues to bedevil us. He was, as Bruce Gordon notes, "the greatest Protestant reformer of the sixteenth century, brilliant, visionary, and iconic."[1] He was also ruthless, manipulative, and domineering. He wrote one of the greatest theological treatises in history, *Institutes of the Christian Religion*, but he was complicit in the execution of Michael Servetus. He had a prodigious intellect and a troubled conscience. He was an inspiring writer, confident in his own positions, yet was always conscious of his plight as a refugee, vulnerable as an exile in Geneva. He was, in short, a complex figure who continues to elicit admiration and scorn, within and outside the Christian tradition.

The essays in this book explore various aspects of Calvin's complicated legacy. They were originally delivered at two conferences organized by Canadian Presbyterians to celebrate the five hundredth anniversary of John Calvin's birth (1509) in the fall of 2009. The first was held in September at St. Andrew's Hall, Vancouver, and the second in October at The Presbyterian College, Montreal. These two conferences gathered people from across Canada and North America, many with international reputations as Calvin scholars, historians of the Reformation, and Reformed theologians. The editors of this volume wish to thank Professor Bruce Gordon of Yale University and Professor Randall Zachman of Notre Dame University for their participation in these conferences and for their encouragement of this publication. Both gave excellent plenary addresses and both were generous with their time and involvement.

The range of essays in this book reflects the diversity of Calvin's legacy. Those who delivered papers came neither to praise nor persecute Calvin. The conferences were not exercises in historical or theological hagiography, meetings where Calvinist church leaders preached to the

---

1. Gordon, *Calvin*, vii.

xiii

xiv *Introduction and Acknowledgements*

choir. They were exercises in appreciative criticism. Each of the speakers worked with the assumption that Calvin left an enduring legacy which, when critically appropriated, has continuing significance. This book is intended, then, for those who have an interest in Calvin's thought and its relevance for church and society. The essays presuppose a basic knowledge of Calvin's life, ministry, and theology and each seeks to engage Calvin's legacy critically and constructively. The essays reflect the depth and breadth of Calvin scholarship from the sixteenth century to the present, primarily in English and French, but also in German and Latin, as found in the footnotes.

The collection begins with William Klempa's very fine essay on Calvin and the Jews, whom Calvin called "the first-born of God's family." This plants the Calvin legacy squarely in the middle of contemporary religious dialogue and world politics. Klempa shows how Calvin's emphasis on the "one covenant of grace" ought to cultivate a positive disposition by Christians towards Jews. In the next essay, my co-editor Richard Topping sets out to rehabilitate the role of imagination in Reformed biblical interpretation by positing a Calvinist use of Paul Ricoeur's hermeneutics. Imagination, he argues, like reason and will and affection, has a role in our reading the Bible as long as it is continually "funded and shaped and strengthened by the Word of God in the power of the Spirit."

Gerard Booy treats the important topic of the Holy Spirit in Calvin's thought from a pastoral perspective. Churches which stand in the Reformed tradition, he reminds us, have often forgotten the significance of Calvin's pneumatology. Torrance Kirby makes an important contribution to our understanding of the origins of the public sphere and its place in a secular age by looking at John Calvin's "two-kingdoms" doctrine. Jason Zuidema sketches Calvin's work as an apologist and asks critically whether Calvin's polemical theology has any role in contemporary theological formulation.

Axel Schoeber argues that Calvin's campaign against Nicodemism in France was perhaps his biggest mistake, with greater consequences than Calvin's consent to the execution of Michael Servetus for heresy. Lynne McNaughton explores how the meaning and practice of pilgrimage shifted during the Reformation and how Calvin figured into this change. Stephen Farris revisits Calvin's theology and practice of preaching with an eye to contemporary homiletics. Calvin believed that Christian preaching is meant to deliver a life-giving word as a means through which the Living

Introduction and Acknowledgements xv

Word—Jesus Christ, is mediated. Professor Farris carefully examines the role of the preacher, the hearer, and the sermon in Calvin's preaching. He concludes by reminding us that Calvin is dead but the Word to which he committed his life as a preacher endures forever.

Gerald Hobbs recasts the image of Calvin as "settled tyrant of Geneva" to Calvin as "refugee in the world." Calvin, argues Hobbs, should be understood as he probably understood himself: "as a permanent refugee in the world, having no homeland save perhaps the childhood France to which he could never return in safety." Calvin knew the truth of Hebrews 13:14 as an existential reality: "For here we have no lasting city." Victor Shepherd delivers a careful reading of Calvin's 1543 tract *The Necessity of Reforming the Church* by setting this document in its historical context and expounding its main themes: doctrine, catholicity, worship, sacraments, and spirituality. The book concludes with an essay by Stephen Allen on Calvin's concept of justice and its significance for Reformed churches in an era of globalization.

Several institutions and people are to be thanked for their contributions to this book. As noted above, the two conferences in which the essays were originally delivered as papers were sponsored by The Presbyterian College, Montreal, and St. Andrew's Hall, Vancouver. Both theological schools are owned and operated by The Presbyterian Church in Canada and are affiliated with ecumenical consortia located in public universities (The Montreal School of Theology, McGill University; and The Vancouver School of Theology, University of British Columbia). The boards, faculties, staffs, and students of both theological schools are to be acknowledged for their support and participation in the original conferences. Funds from the General Assembly of The Presbyterian Church in Canada earmarked for the Calvin 500 celebration enabled us to employ James Dickey and Joel Coppieters to do the copyediting, proofreading, and formatting. In addition to contributing an essay, my co-editor Richard Topping did most of "the heavy lifting" on this project by collecting and collating the essays and working with the publisher.

As editors, we should also like to thank the supporting cast at Wipf and Stock Publishers with whom it has been a privilege to work. Our editor, Dr. Robin Parry, the Assistant Managing Editor, Christian Amondson, and the typesetter, Patrick Harrison, provided excellent guidance and assistance in making the book better and bringing it to publication.

xvi *Introduction and Acknowledgements*

As a theologian and biblical expositor John Calvin often marveled at the grace and majesty of the divine presence which he believed was encountered in God's Word. Calvin used various images and concepts to describe this experience. Because of human weakness, Calvin argued, God accommodates to human capacity so that we may understand God. God stoops to our level as a mother stoops to her child, and speaks in language we can understand. Or, because we are bleary-eyed people with weak vision who cannot see and read correctly without the aid of eyeglasses, God has given us Scripture as spectacles to see aright and gather up the confused knowledge of God in our minds. Or, the splendor of God's countenance is like an inextricable labyrinth unless we are led into it by the thread of God's Word.

Of all the ways in which Calvin speaks of Scripture, however, the most compelling may well be a quote Calvin borrowed from Augustine: "it is better to limp along the path of God's word than to dash with all speed outside it."[2] Despite a complicated legacy, there is still something inviting about pursuing that path alongside Calvin, even after 500 years.

John A. Vissers
Epiphany 2011

2. Calvin, *Institutes of the Christian Religion,* I.6.3.

1

"The First-Born in God's Family"

Calvin and the Jews

WILLIAM KLEMPA

THE CONDITION OF JEWISH people in Europe, on the eve of the Reformation, can be accurately described by the word "miserable."[1] For centuries Jewish communities and individual Jews had been persecuted by Christians. Jews were regarded as rejected by God for crucifying Jesus and were blamed for plagues, natural disasters and various misfortunes. They were accused of the ritual murder of Christian children, charged with desecrating the Eucharistic host and were generally resented for their money lending practices.

A new chapter in the persecution of the Jews began with the preaching of the First Crusade by Pope Urban II in 1095. This crusade ignited a series of murderous attacks against Jews, first in France and then along the Rhine in Germany, in what has been called "the first holocaust." The German church opposed this torrent of racial and religious hatred and violence since canon law did not condone the victimization of the Jews and prohibited forced conversions. Yet for the most part the Pope and the bishops reacted as in earlier times and would later. They simply looked on and did little.[2]

---

1. Oberman, *The Roots of Anti-Semitism in the Age of Renaissance and Reformation*, 95. He points out that the word "misery" in High German is equivalent to the word "exile."

2. See Asbridge, *The First Crusade: A New History*, 84–89.

Bernard of Clairvaux promoted the Second Crusade in 1146. To guard against any anti-Jewish fervor, he warned: "Whoever touches a Jew to take his life is like one who harms Jesus himself . . . for in the book of Psalms it is written of them, 'Slay them not, lest my people forget.'" Bernard was, of course, simply repeating, as Paula Fredriksen has pointed out,[3] Augustine's justly famous "witness doctrine" found in his *The City of God* and elsewhere in his writings.[4] I will enlarge upon this doctrine later, but in brief, Augustine stated that through their possession and preservation of the ancient Scriptures, and as a result of their dispersion among all nations, the Jews, in spite of themselves, were witnesses that the Christian church had not fabricated the prophecies about Christ. The effect of this preaching was that there were no similar murderous attacks on the Jews during the Second Crusade. The teaching of these two theologians—John Calvin's favorite and the two he quoted most— definitely curbed but, of course, did not put an end to persecution of the Jews. Jews were expelled from England in 1290; from France in 1306; from Spain in 1492 and from Portugal in 1497. Many found asylum in the Low Countries and Turkish lands.

LUTHER AND THE JEWS

Jewish hopes were aroused and then dashed by Martin Luther's initial break with the medieval church and its anti-Jewish legacy. As a biblical scholar Luther placed a high value on the Old Testament Scriptures and in his lectures on the Psalms (1513–15) he laid the exegetical foundations for a christological interpretation of the Old Testament. In 1523, he published his tract, *That Jesus Christ was born a Jew*, in which he argued that the Jews are blood-relatives of Christ. "We are aliens and in-laws," Luther wrote, [they] "are actually nearer to Christ than we are." They ought therefore, to be treated in a kindly manner.[5] This was a rare exhibition of philo-Semitism in an age in which there were few friends of the Jews,[6] but alas, it did not last. When Jews failed to convert to Christianity, which was always Luther's main motive for Christian friendship, he turned against them in his virulent tract, *On the Jews and*

3. Fredriksen, *Augustine and the Jews*, xi–xii.

4. Augustine, *The City of God*, xviii, 46, and 657.

5. *Luther's Works*, Vol. 45, 200–201.

6. Andreas Osiander and Justus Jonas are rare exceptions. See Oberman, *The Roots of Anti-Semitism*, 101.

Their Lies (1543).[7] In it he called for the destruction of their homes, synagogues, and books, as well as the abrogation of any civil rights they still had. In his later years, Luther was feverishly focused on the apocalyptic struggle with the Anti-Christ—and Jews, along with the Pope, the Turks, and false Christians, represented what we would call today the four Axes of evil. It has been said in his defense that his animus toward the Jews was theological and not racist. Yet Luther cannot be exonerated so easily. His anti-Judaism became in fact anti-Semitism by virtue of the harsh measures he demanded the state to enact. It was a pre-figurement for Hitler's "final solution"—the Holocaust and the Nazis did not hesitate to use Luther's hateful tracts[8] for their evil purposes. Rabbi Josel of Rosheim, his friend Philip Melanchthon and his Nuremberg disciple, Andreas Osiander, expressed their deep shock but Luther ignored them. He continued his venomous tirade against the Jews to the end of his life in 1546.

JOHN CALVIN AND THE JEWS

John Calvin was twenty-six years younger than Luther and twenty-five younger than Zwingli and belonged to the second generation of reformers. What was his stance toward Jews and Judaism? Unquestionably, Calvin was a faithful follower of Martin Luther's theology. Did he share Luther's attitude to the Jews? Whether or not he was familiar with Luther's essay *That Jesus Christ was born a Jew,* like the early Luther, Calvin emphasized that Christ proceeded from the Jewish race. According to Calvin, this gave Jews a pre-eminence in the divine economy. Thus, commenting on Rom 9:5, Calvin stated, "for it was not a thing to be lightly esteemed, to have been united by a natural relationship with the Redeemer of the world; for if he had honored the whole human race, in joining himself to us by a community of nature, much more did he honor them, with whom he had a closer bond of union." But Calvin added that this favor, if not connected with godliness, far from being an advantage leads to a greater condemnation.[9]

---

7. *Luther's Works,* Vol. 47, 268–72.

8. Luther published two more tracts, "On the *Shem Hamphoras*" and "The Last Words of David" in which he railed against the Jews.

9. Calvin, Comm. *Romans* 9:5; in the Corpus Reformatorum edition, cited hereafter as *CO; CO* 49, 174; Calvin, *Romans and Thessalonians,* 197 in *Calvin's New Testament Commentaries,* cited hereafter as *CNTC.* See also *Institutes* 2.13.1 & 3.

The crucial question, however, is; did Calvin share Luther's later views expressed in his infamous tract of 1543, *On the Jews and their Lies*? It is very likely that Calvin did not know Luther's later views, although he must have known Martin Bucer's negative views. In May, 1561, Ambrosius Blaurer, pastor at Biel and Winterthur, wrote to Calvin to ask him his opinion on the toleration of the Jews. In his letter he stated, "I know you are not unfamiliar with what Luther wrote in 1543 in a thoroughly sharp way against the Jews" and then added in the margin of the letter that perhaps Calvin had not read it since it was written only in German without a Latin translation.[10] Calvin's answer to this letter is unfortunately no longer extant. But we can surmise that Calvin gave a nuanced answer to Blaurer's question since in a subsequent letter Blaurer thanked Calvin for his "opinion on the toleration or non-toleration of the Jews."[11]

In the same year that Blaurer asked Calvin for his views, Calvin had written in his Daniel commentary: "I have often spoken with many Jews. I never saw the least speck of godliness, never a crumb of truth or honesty, not even discerned any common sense in any Jews whatsoever."[12] This is the only direct statement that we have from Calvin about meeting Jews. Certainly, he did not meet them in Noyon, Paris, or Geneva. When, where, and with whom did Calvin come into contact? These questions are difficult to answer. While most scholars assume that Calvin had no direct contact with Jews, Achim Detmers has argued persuasively that we can learn indirectly that Calvin met a number of Jews during his sojourn in Strasbourg from 1538–41. It was also during this period that he traveled to Frankfurt-am-Main, Hagenau, Worms, and Regensburg. Calvin spent six weeks in Frankfurt where there was a large Jewish ghetto of around 400 Jews. It is also probable that he was familiar with the question of the toleration of Jews since this issue was debated at the Frankfurt princes' assembly. At a public disputation at which Calvin may have been present, Rabbi Josel of Rosheim countered the anti-Jewish views of Luther and Bucer. Detmers thinks it is likely that Calvin met

10. *CR* 46, *CO* XVIII: 421, 41–45 (no. 3371) quoted by Detmers, "Calvin, the Jews and Judaism," 209.

11. *CR* 46, *CO* XVIII: 537–38 (no. 3430), quoted by Detmers, "Calvin, The Jews And Judaism," 210.

12. "Ego saepe loquuntus sum cum multis Judaeis: nunquam vidi guttam pietatis, nunquam micam veritatis vel igenuae naturae, imo nihil communis sensus in ullo Judaeo unquam deprehendi" *CR* 68 *CO* 40: 605 on Dan 2: 455. I have used T. H. L. Parker's translation in *Calvin's Old Testament Commentaries*, Vol. 20, *Daniel* I, 103.

Rabbi Josel of Rosheim either in Strasbourg or in Regensburg where he was a representative of the German Jews. At the same time while Detmers credits Calvin with adopting the Upper German-Swiss covenant theology and formulating enduring views about the election of the Jewish people, he holds that "the late Calvin confronted Judaism and its scriptural interpretation exceedingly negatively."[13] The previously cited passage from the Daniel commentary is for Detmers a clear indication of this negative attitude to contemporary Judaism. Yet this one remark made in the polemical context of refuting Isaac ben Judah Barbinel, a Spanish Jewish commentator on Daniel, cannot be taken as indicative of the complexity of Calvin's stance towards Jews and Judaism. Calvin was not uniformly negative, as Detmer seems to imply of the later Calvin, in his use of Jewish interpreters; for example, he regarded David Kimchi (1160–1235) as a most reliable Jewish exegete.[14]

To determine Calvin's stance, we need to attend to the main thrust of his writings, in his *Institutes*, commentaries, particularly his commentary on Romans, and his sermons. In a 1990 essay, entitled, "Calvin and the Jews: A Textual Puzzle," Mary Potter Engel, after reading Calvin's interpretation of Paul's view of "the church and Israel" in Rom 9–11, stated: "It seemed to me that Calvin's interpretation was just as full of contradictions as Paul's text."[15] To try to solve the puzzle she turned to Calvin's sermons to see if she could discover some interpretative clues. On the basis of this research, she wrote: "My conclusions . . . fall somewhere between pardon and condemnation," for "we cannot conclude simply that Calvin was an enemy of the Jews and Judaism"[16] and "we also cannot conclude simply that he is a friend to the Jews and Judaism."[17]

In favor of Professor Engel's even-handed conclusion is the fact that Calvin's writings contain a rather broad spectrum of statements about Jews and, of course, Jews as they are met almost solely on the pages of the Bible. On the one hand, there are strong comments echoing the denunciation of the prophets and apostles regarding Jewish obstinacy, pride, ingratitude, hypocrisy, blindness, and unbelief. On the other hand, there are statements stressing the continuity of the one church made up of

13. Detmers, "Calvin, the Jews and Judaism," 217.

14. See on Ps 112:5; *CO* 32, 174.

15. Engel, "Calvin and the Jews: A Textual Problem," 106.

16. Ibid., 119.

17. Ibid., 120.

6   CALVIN@500

both faithful and unfaithful Jews and faithful and unfaithful Christians and the continuing role of Jews in God's plan of salvation. While appreciating her careful scholarship and her judicious conclusion, I propose to argue that there are other considerations that may serve as weighty-enough material and I hope, that the effort will not be seen as placing a proverbial thumb surreptitiously on the scales to tip Professor Engel's evenly-balanced scales, to lead us to conclude that Calvin's theology was a theological defense of the Jews and the Old Testament faith. Although of little immediate effect in sixteenth century Western Europe in the few places where Jews still resided, it could not but have positive consequences for these communities in the following two centuries.

THREE WEIGHTY CONSIDERATIONS

I want to propose three considerations that should be taken into account and the three are intimately related: first, Calvin's use of Augustine's "witness doctrine" to defend the role of Jews in God's economy of salvation; secondly, his doctrine of the one covenant of grace in which Israel's honor as "the first-born in God's family" is preserved; and thirdly, his exposition of Rom 9–11 giving a continuing role to the Jewish people.

1. Calvin's Use of Augustine's "Witness-People Doctrine"

In her important 2008 book, *Augustine and the Jews: A Christian Defense of Jews and Judaism*, Paula Fredriksen—herself a Jew and a Professor of Ancient Christianity at Boston University—has set forth Augustine's "witness doctrine" as an extraordinary defense of the Jews and Judaism. In her view, it is his enduring theological legacy to the Christian church. Her book, she tells us, arose out of a conference for which she was preparing. She stayed up late skimming Augustine's work *Contra Faustus* for anti-Jewish quotations and to her surprise she found none. Instead she discovered a strong defense of things Jewish against Faustus, an anti-Jewish Manichean and Marcionite. Augustine defended the Old Testament, Jewish law and ritual, and Jewish fleshliness, for they all prepared the way, he believed, for God's coming to save us in the Word made flesh. This was part of his "witness doctrine," namely his teaching that God's gracious providence has so arranged it that Jews, whether they reject or defy Christianity, actually promote it. By killing Christ (Augustine did not speak of deicide for Jews did not recognize Jesus Christ as God) the

Jews brought about the founding of the church and the redemption of the Gentiles. Moreover, God has scattered the Jews to punish them for the death of his Son. Their dispersion among the nations means that they serve as witnesses to the prophecies which were promulgated before the coming of Christ. They testify that the church did not invent them but that they were published and preserved by the Jewish nation. Jewish unbelief increases rather than lessens the authority of these books. The whole people exist as librarians or as "a guardian of the books for the sake of the church bearing the Law and the prophets, and testifying to the doctrine of the church, so that we honor in the sacrament what they disclose in the letter."[18]

John Calvin was not only familiar with, but also made use of this, "witness doctrine." In his *Institutes of the Christian Religion*, I.8.10, where he discusses the credibility of Scripture and the marvelous way God has preserved the Law and the Prophets, Calvin refers to Augustine's teaching by asking: "And through whom did God preserve for us the doctrine of salvation embraced in the Law and the Prophets, that Christ in his own time might be made manifest [Matt 22:37–40]?" He answers: "Through the Jews, Christ's most inveterate enemies, whom Augustine justly calls the 'bookmen' of the Christian church, because they have furnished us with reading matter of which they themselves do not make use."[19] Though they are "the most inveterate enemies" they perform this most valuable service for the church.

Calvin echoed Augustine in holding that the Jews continue to suffer "merited punishment for despising and opposing Christ."[20] Of all nations, he noted, "none has suffered greater misery."[21] Again like Augustine, he held that the nation was collectively responsible for the death of Christ. Commenting on Peter's words at Pentecost in Acts 2:23, "him have you slain" Calvin says: "not that they crucified him with their own hands, but because the people with one voice, desired to have him put to death." He adds that while all the hearers may have not consented to Jesus' death, "yet does he justly impute the same to the nation; because all of them had defiled themselves either with their silence, or else through their

---

18. Augustine, *Contra Faustus* 12: 11, quoted by Fredrikson, *Augustine and the Jews*, 276. See also ibid., 265.

19. Calvin, *Institutes of the Christian Religion*, Vol. XX, 90.

20. Calvin, "Remarks on the Letter of Paul II" in *Calvin's Tracts and Treatises*, 274.

21. Calvin, "To the Emperor Charles V" in *Calvin's Tracts and Treatises*, Vol. I, 247.

carelessness."[22] But later—in reference to Peter's words, "I know that you did it through ignorance as did your rulers"—Calvin says "This therefore, is Peter's meaning, that they did it rather through error and a blind zeal, than through any determined wickedness."[23] Like Augustine, Calvin never charged the Jews with deicide. Again following Augustine, Calvin states that the dispersion of the Jews among the nations has worked providentially: "But we must know," Calvin says, commenting on Acts 17:4 about certain Greeks in Thessalonica believing the gospel, "that whither soever the Jews were exiled, there went with them some seed of godliness, and there was some smell [savor] of pure doctrine spread abroad. For their miserable scattering abroad was so turned unto a contrary end by the wonderful counsel of God, that it did gather those unto the true faith who did wander in error."[24]

In connection with Augustine's "witness doctrine" Calvin also spoke of Jews being mirrors in which Christians can see themselves. There is a striking instance of this in his *Sermons on Jeremiah*:

> We see, then, that we are like the Jews. They are our mirror to show us our own rebellion against God. When God severely chastises us, will we say that He has not paid close enough attention to us, that we are not totally corrupt through and through. When we read today's passage, let us not condemn the Jews, but ourselves. Let us know that we are no more worthy than they. If there was such brutality among them that they did not serve the Word of God, today we are equally, if not more brutal.[25]

Calvin goes on to emphasize this point. The Jews are the sacred line; we are only miserable specimens. They are the blessed root God chose. Yet God punished them so severely and he will punish us also. "We know that we are not more precious than the Jews and that Geneva is not more privileged than Jerusalem."[26] When Calvin castigates the Jews, commenting on the prophetic denunciations of Jewish pride and obstinacy,

---

22. Comm., on Acts 2:23, *CO* 48, English translation, Calvin Translation Society (Grand Rapids: Eerdmans, 1948) cited hereafter as CTS, vol. 1, 95.

23. Comm., on Acts 3:17; *CO* 48, 70; CTS, vol. 2,148.

24. Comm., on Acts 17:4; *CO* 48, 395; CTS, vol. 2, 133.

25. Calvin, *Sermons on Jeremiah*, (chapter 16), Texts and Studies in Religion, Vol. 46, 95. See Karl Barth for a strikingly similar use of Augustine's teaching: *Church Dogmatics*, III/3, 222: "the Jew is a mirror in which we immediately recognize ourselves."

26. Ibid., 235.

ingratitude and unbelief, he is equally harsh on Christians. Augustine's "witness doctrine" provides an interpretative framework in which Jews serve as witnesses both as "mirrors of total purity"[27] and as noted earlier, as a mirror of Christian rebellion against God.

If Paula Fredriksen is right in her positive evaluation of Augustine's "witness doctrine" as a defense of Jews and Judaism, then Calvin's use of this doctrine, I believe, can be construed as a similar defense.

2. One Covenant of Grace and One People of God

The second factor which must be taken into account as possibly also tipping the scales is Calvin's teaching of "one covenant of grace" embracing believing Jews and Christians. This teaching is more familiar but it still needs to be set out. In the opening chapter of Book IV of the *Institutes* on "The True Church" Calvin states: "we must hold that from the creation of the world there was no time when the Lord did not have his church (*ecclesiam*); and even until the consummation of the age, there will be no time when he will not have it."[28] Calvin's use of the word "ecclesia" here is usually seen as an instance and example of Christian co-option and even of Christian triumphalism. But not so. "Ecclesia" is the term the Septuagint employs and Calvin follows this usage. In his *Commentary on the Psalms,* Calvin notes that David spoke of God's nation.[29] Calvin speaks instead of God's church and it is his way of emphasizing the close binding of the New Testament church with the people of Israel. In this one church of God the Jews have the chief place: "For though Christ reconciled the world to his Father, yet they were former in order, who were already near unto God, and of his family."[30] The church has not replaced Israel. It is Calvin's consistent teaching that "the fellowship of the Gentiles did not take from the Jews the right of the first-begotten, but that they were always the chief in the church of God."[31] I have used the phrase, "the first-born in God' family" in the title of my paper because Calvin employs it again and again. Commenting on Acts 2:39—"for the promise belongs to you"—he says that the promise was first made to the Jews, then to their children and last of all to the Gentiles and he adds:

27. Sermon on 1 Tim. *CO* 53 627.

28. *Institutes* 4.1.17.

29. Introduction; *CO* 31, 52. See on Ps 12:1, *CO* 31, 126; Ps 14:1, 135. I am indebted to Selderhuis, *Calvin's Theology of the Psalms*, 237–38, for these references.

30. Commentary on Acts 13:46, *CO* 48, 311; CTS, vol. 1, 551.

31. Ibid.

"We know the reason why the Jews were preferred before other people; for they are as it were, the first begotten in God's family, yea they were then separated from other people by a singular privilege."[32] This pre-eminence, Calvin was always careful to point out, was not because of their own worthiness but by reason of God's gracious adoption.[33]

Calvin's hermeneutical presupposition informing the above statements is the indissoluble unity which exists between the Old Testament Israel and the New Testament church. Calvin had inherited from Irenaeus the concept of a single economy of salvation from Adam to Christ, and its corollary of God's covenants with Adam, Noah, Moses and Christ being one in substance but differing in accidents.[34] He had also appropriated Augustine's classic statement of the relation of old and new "In the Old Testament the New is concealed, in the New the Old is revealed."[35] This "one covenant of grace" theology became the hallmark of the Upper German-Swiss theologians. Calvin's statement of it is well-known: "The covenant made with all the patriarchs is so much like ours in substance and reality that the two are actually one and the same. Yet they differ in the mode of dispensation."[36] Achim Detmers claimed: "Calvin even saw himself forced—in order to maintain the continuity of the covenant—to hold on to the permanent 'natural' privilege of the Jews."[37] If by "forced," Detmer means constrained by the witness of Scripture and if by the word "natural" he means, as he appear to mean, that the covenant made with Abraham was fulfilled in "the fleshly seed of Abraham" (*Inst.* 4.16.15) that is, Jesus Christ, then, of course, he is correct. The unity of the covenant implies that the patriarchs "participated in the same inheritance and hoped for a common salvation with us by the grace of the same Mediator."[38] Calvin spells this out in three ways. The unity of the covenant means first that the hope of immortality rather than earthly prosperity was the goal set before the Jews; secondly, that the covenant was based solely on God's grace rather than their merits; and thirdly, that they had and knew Christ as Mediator through whom they were joined

32. Comm., on Acts 2:39, *CO* 48, 55; CTS, vol. 1, 122.

33. Comm., on Acts 10:15; *CO* 48, 207; CTS, vol. 1, 423.

34. Irenaeus, *Against Heresies* in *The Ante-Nicene Fathers*, II, xi 8, 429.

35. Augustine, *The City of God*, 16.26, 549.

36. Calvin, *Institutes*, 2.10.2, 429.

37. Detmers, "Calvin, the Jews and Judaism," 212.

38. Calvin, *Institutes* 2.10.1, 429.

to God.[39] Mary Potter Engels regards this grounding of the one covenant of the one God in the pre-existent Christ as an indication of Calvin's anti- Judaism.[40] Yet one wonders how she can continue to speak of "the one covenant of the one God" without holding on to one Mediator of the covenant of grace. Is she not then obliged to speak of two covenants, one for Jews, one for Christians and supposedly, a third one for Muslims, to meet and satisfy the objectives of contemporary religious pluralism?

The unity of the covenant meant for Calvin that there was no deficiency in either the law or the sacraments of the Old Testament.

A. One Covenant of Grace Means No Deficiency in the Law

Calvin emphasized that there is no deficiency in the Old Testament law. The law is a large topic in Calvin but I shall limit myself only to a few points. According to Calvin, God gave the law through Moses as an integral part of the covenant, a seal of his grace and the revelation of his will. Calvin defined the law as "not only the Ten Commandments, which set forth a godly and righteous rule of living, but the form of religion handed down by God through Moses."[41] With this broad view of the law as expressed by the Hebrew word "Torah" meaning instruction, teaching—the "teaching of God himself," Calvin sought to avoid the charge of legalism but not successfully as we shall note. The law, Calvin said, did not wipe out the promise made to the Jews but reminded them of it and renewed it.

Calvin devoted two chapters—chapters six and seven—in Book II of the *Institutes* to remind the reader that "Fallen Humanity Ought to Seek Redemption in Christ" and that "The Law was given not to restrain the folk of the old covenant under itself, but to foster hope of salvation in Christ until his coming." Following tradition, Calvin divided the law into moral, ceremonial and judicial laws.[42] The ceremonial and judicial laws have been abrogated. The moral law has been set down in the two tables of the law. It is virtually identical with natural law which has been engraved on the human mind. Moral law is unchangeable and is not abrogated; it has a continuing validity for Christian believers. As is generally known, Calvin emphasized the third use of the law, which is its

39. Ibid., 2.10.2.

40. Engel, "Calvin and the Jews: A Textual Problem," 120.

41. 41 Calvin, *Institutes*, 2.7.1, Vol. 1, 348.

42. Ibid., 4.20.15.

principal use, to teach us perfect righteousness. Along with Zwingli, the father of the Swiss Reformation, Calvin gave the evangelical reformation an ethical turn, strongly emphasizing moral uprightness and the sanctification of the community.

The moral law was given by a gracious and faithful God to the people of Israel and it has a continuing force and validity for Christians. From the law we learn that God is our Father, that God is merciful and holy and that in loving kindness, God requires our obedience.[43] To use it properly, Torah has to be spiritually understood and interpreted by always looking at God the Lawgiver. God is concerned not simply with outward appearance but also with purity of heart. Thus God in his law, unlike a king in promulgating civil law, prohibits not only the outward actions of fornication, murder and theft but also the inward ones of lust, anger and hatred. It is this inward, spiritual understanding of the law that Christ came to restore when he taught over against the Pharisees, for example that to glance unchastely at a woman is to be guilty of adultery. Calvin comments: "Those who did not comprehend these teachings fancied Christ another Moses, the giver of the law of the gospel which supplied what was lacking in the Mosaic law. Whence that common saying about the perfection of the law of the gospel, that it far surpasses the old law—in many respects a most pernicious opinion!"[44]

The common error to which Calvin refers and which he calls "pernicious" (*perniciosissimum*) is the view that Jesus' new "evangelical law" (*lex evangelicae*) completed and supplied the deficiency which was present in the Jewish Torah. Such a view, Calvin believed, disparages the Torah. It insinuates that the sanctity of the fathers under the Old Testament was hypocritical and lures us away from the "sole and everlasting rule of righteousness." "It is very easy to refute this error," Calvin says. "They have thought that Christ *added* to the law when he only *restored* (*restituit*) it to its integrity in that he freed and cleansed it when it had been obscured by the falsehoods and defiled by the leaven of the Pharisees [cf. Matt 16:6, 11, and parallels]."[45]

This emphasis on *restoration* rather than *addition*, on *fulfillment* rather than *abolition* strikes at the very root of a false Christian supersessionism. As Bernard Cottret, the French historian and biographer of

43. See Calvin, *Institutes*, 2.8.3.

44. Ibid., 2.8.7.

45. Ibid., 2.8.7—Emphasis added.

Calvin, has commented perceptively: "Calvin's Christ was a reformer of Judaism. Now a reformer in the sixteenth-century sense was not exactly an innovator or a revolutionary; on the contrary, he fought against novelties. Similarly, the Jesus Calvin presented entered into conflict with the Pharisees in the name of the original authenticity of the Jewish law. He wanted to restore it to its purity. Jesus was not a second Moses; he did not promote a new law, nor did he abolish the old one."[46] Jaroslav Pelikan, the historian of doctrine, has expressed it well when speaking of the relation of the gospel and the Jewish faith: the gospel is "new, but not brand-new"; that is, it is something *restored* and *fulfilled*.[47]

B. One Covenant of Grace Means the Sacraments of the Law Were Not Deficient

Secondly, if the Old Testament Law was in no way deficient the same holds true of the sacraments of the Law. They have the same spiritual power and efficacy as the sacraments of the Gospel. Calvin bases this view on Paul's words in 1 Cor 10:3–4: "and all ate the same spiritual food, and all drank the same spiritual drink. For they drank from the spiritual rock that followed them, and the rock was Christ." Here Paul teaches, Calvin said, "that the ancient Sacraments of the Law had the same virtue as ours have at this day."[48] They were not bare emblems but imparted what they represented "for God is not a deceiver to feed us with empty fancies." Calvin presumably had the Anabaptists in mind when he spoke of "bare emblems." Yet he also wanted to refute the Scholastics who held that the ancient sacraments were only emblems of grace while the Christian sacraments actually conferred God's grace. "This passage," Calvin said, "is admirably suited for refuting that error, for it shows that the reality of the Sacrament was presented to the ancient people of God no less than to us."[49] Calvin, however, grants that since the coming of Christ the sign is clearer. Yet the difference is only a matter of degree, simply "more and less."

This teaching was of critical importance to Calvin. A deficient Law and deficient Sacraments would mean a deficient church. Calvin insisted that the true church existed among the Israelites:

46. Cottret, *Calvin: A Biography*, 315–16.

47. Pelikan, *The Christian Tradition*, Vol. 1, 13.

48. Comm., on 1 Corinthians 10:3; *CO* 49, 453–54; CTS, vol. 1, 316.

49. Ibid., *CO* 49, 454; CTS, vol. 1, 317. See also *Institutes* 4.14.23.

Their condition represented ours in such a manner that there was at the same time, even then, a proper condition of a church. The promises given to them shadowed forth the gospel in such a way that they had it included in them. Their sacraments served to prefigure ours in such a way that they were nevertheless, even for that period, true sacraments, having a present efficacy. In fine, those who at that time made a right use, both of doctrine and of signs, were endowed with the same spirit of faith as we are.[50]

Christians, therefore, must not think that because they have Baptism and the Lord's Supper that they are better than the Jews. "Paul," Calvin says, "means to disabuse Christians of thinking that they are superior to the Jews through the privilege of baptism."[51] When the Jews abused their privileges, they did not escape punishment. Nor will we escape with impunity the hand of God which punished them.[52]

C. The Charge of Judaizing

It is not at all surprising that Calvin was criticized as a Judaizer. As Augustine was accused by his contemporary Jerome of Judaizing, so Calvin was reproached in his lifetime and afterwards of being guilty of a similar fault. Servetus, the anti-Trinitarian, made such an accusation as we can infer from Calvin's letter to him. "You reproach me," Calvin said, "that I judge in fleshly and in Jewish ways regarding the corporeal race of Abraham."[53] Apparently some Anabaptists had also accused him of being too Jewish in his theology and of minimizing the "newness" of the gospel. Calvin responded in the *Institutes* to both Servetus and the Anabaptists, by accusing them of holding derogatory views of the Old Testament people: "Indeed, that wonderful rascal Servetus and certain madmen of the Anabaptist sect regard the Israelites as nothing but a herd of swine."[54] Evidently, Calvin had nothing but disdain for this attitude of Christian superiority.

Calvin was reproached in 1595 by the Hessian Lutheran, George Nigrinus, for being an "intercessor of the Jews" and of aligning himself with Jewish rabbis rather than Christian teachers." Nigrinus charged that

50. Comm., on 1 Corinthians 10:11; *CO* 49, 460; CTS, vol. 1, 328.

51. Calvin, *Institutes*, 2.10.5, 432.

52. Calvin, Comm., on 1 Corinthians 10:1; CO; CTS I, 432.

53. CO 8, 491. Calvin responds that he distinguished the spiritual from the fleshly sons of Abraham.

54. Calvin, *Institutes*, 2.10.1.

Calvin interpreted "many passages in the Old Testament just as the rabbis interpret them ... as if he would follow them rather than the established holy teachers of the Church."[55] Similar accusations appear in the polemical work, *Calvinus Judaizans* by Aegidius Hunnius also in 1595.

Hand in hand with the charge of "Judaizing" is the charge of Jewish legalism. Reinhold Seeberg, the Lutheran historian of dogma, has charged that in Calvin's system law controls all life and its ramifications. "Calvin's legalism," he says, "results in a tendency to blur the boundaries between the Old and New Testaments."[56] Paul Wernle makes a similar allegation: "In his moral zeal, Calvin utterly denies the difference between the Old and the New Testaments, closes his eyes to all the new values which Jesus brought into the world and degrades Him to the position of an interpreter of the ancient lawgiver Moses. How much more clearly the Baptists saw the truth in this respect."[57] The anti-Judaic character of these criticisms is most evident in Georgia Harkness' study of Calvin's ethics: "Calvin's system of doctrine," she wrote, "is more Hebraic than Christian. It rests more upon the Old Testament than the New."[58] These accusations seem to come from a dualist opposition of law and gospel and the view of a strongly contradictory relationship of Judaism and Christianity.

3. The Continuing Role of Jews in God's Plan of Salvation

The third consideration is Calvin's understanding of the continuing role of the Jews in God's plan of salvation. The *locus classicus* on the relationship of Christianity and Judaism is undoubtedly Rom 9–11, and specifically, Rom 11:25–26: "a hardening has come upon part of Israel, until the full number of the Gentiles come in, and so *all Israel will be saved*" (my italics). This is a notoriously difficult passage and it has led to different interpretations in both ancient and modern times.[59]

---

55. Cited in Friedrich Müller, "Georg Nigrinus in seinen Streitschriften: 'Jüdenfeind, Papistische Inquisition und Anticalvinismus" in *Wihelm-Diehl-Festschrift*, 115 cited by Detmers, "Calvin, The Jews and Judaism," 198.

56. Seeberg, *Texbook of the History of Doctrines*, Vol. II, 416.

57. Wernle, *Der evangelische Glaube*, III, *Calvin*, 13 quoted by Wilhelm Niesel, *The Theology of Calvin*, 104–5.

58. Harkness, *John Calvin: The Man and his Ethics*, 72.

59. See Fitzmyer, *Romans*, 618–24.

A full discussion of Calvin's interpretation of Rom 9–11 is not possible here. Again I will need to limit myself to one or two points. I will begin by referring to a fine essay by Dr. Daniel Shute, "*And All Israel Shall Be Saved*: Peter Martyr and John Calvin on the Jews according to Romans, chapters 9, 10, and 11." In it Dr. Shute notes that unlike Zwingli, Bucer, and Peter Martyr, Calvin interpreted "all Israel" to mean "all the people of God."[60] First, Dr. Shute calls Calvin's interpretation "eccentric." It is, of course, "eccentric" in relation to Zwingli, Bucer, and Martyr but not in regard to the long tradition of interpretation before and following Calvin. A number of patristic writers including Irenaeus, Clement of Alexandria, Origin, and Augustine (the latter two were ambivalent, speaking sometime of ethnic Israel and sometime of spiritual Israel), held this view. Moreover, the majority of fifth to twelfth century commentators also followed this interpretation. Yet it has its difficulties. Paul's line of argument appears to be that first, the remnant of Israel will be saved, then the Gentiles, and finally Israel as a whole. Calvin appealed to Gal 6:16 to support his interpretation where by "the Israel of God" Paul meant believing Jews and Gentiles. His given reason for this exegesis is that the consummation of the kingdom of Christ cannot be confined to the Jews but includes the whole world. Calvin's interpretation cannot be excluded for it accords with Paul's use of "all" in 11:32: "God has imprisoned all in disobedience in order that he may have mercy on all" where "all" clearly refers to both Jews and Gentiles.

Secondly, Dr. Shute goes on to state that "Calvin managed to avoid any meaningful notion of the Jews' continuing special status, while Martyr made statements that were harbingers of a philo-Semitism that was to fascinate some Reformed students of scripture in the next generation."[61] Dr. Shute is, of course, correct in what he says about Peter Martyr but is he right in what he says about Calvin?

---

60. See Calvin, Romans, CTS, 437: "26. *And so all Israel, &c.* Many understand this of the Jewish people as though Paul had said that religion, would again be restored among them as before: but I extend the word *Israel* to all the people of God, according to this meaning—"When the Gentiles shall come in, the Jews also shall return from their defection to the obedience of faith; and thus shall be completed the salvation of the whole Israel of God, which must be gathered from both; and yet in such a way that the Jews shall obtain the first place, being as it were the first-born in God's family."

61. See Dr. Shute's essay in *Peter Martyr Vermigli and the European Reformations: Semper Reformanda,* 160.

Did Calvin fail to give Jews a "continuing special status" in the divine economy of salvation? There can be no question that in his view they had a special status before Christ's coming. Do they continue to have a special status after his incarnation and crucifixion? It almost seems as if they do not. Calvin speaks in the bleakest and most forbidding way of God's vengeance, rejection, and destruction of the Jewish nation as a consequence of the crime of putting Jesus to death. Commenting on Jesus' words in Matt 24:21 "For there will be great tribulation," Calvin speaks of the Jews breaking God's covenant through obstinate malice and of the nation's desperate wickedness reaching its height. "The most destructive plague inflicted on the Jews," Calvin writes, "was that the light of heavenly doctrine was extinguished among them and that they were rejected by God; but they were compelled to feel the evil of their rejection by sharp and severe chastisements."[62] Christians need to learn from their punishment that nothing is more heinous in God's sight than obstinacy in despising his grace. Yet lest we think that Calvin's final word is judgment, "end of story," Calvin finds consolation in verse 22: "And if those days had not been cut short, no one would be saved; but for the sake of the elect those days will be cut short." The calamities which God brought against the Jews would be sufficient "to exterminate the very name of the Jews, if God did not look to *his elect,* and on their account grant some alleviation." God remembers his gracious covenant and spares his elect. In punishing the Jews, God's wrath burned to an extent which was awful and yet, contrary to human expectation, he restrained it so that not one of the elect perished. In words that are again reminiscent of Augustine's "witness-doctrine," Calvin continues: "And it was a miracle which almost exceeded belief, that as salvation was to proceed from Judea out of a few drops of a fountain which was dried up God formed rivers to water the whole world; for, in consequence of the hatred of all nations which they had drawn upon themselves, they narrowly escaped from being murdered in all places, by a preconcerted signal, in one day."[63]

Calvin believed that Titus, the Roman emperor who captured and destroyed Jerusalem in 70 A.D., was restrained by God from giving permission to his soldiers utterly to destroy the whole nation. As Calvin was fond of repeating, this was on account of the elect: "It was because his grace dwelt in the people whom he had adopted; and, that his cov-

62. John Calvin, Comm., on Matthew 24:21; *CO* 45, 661; CTS vol. 3, 136.

63. Comm., on Matthew 24:22; *CO* 45, 662; CTS 3, 138.

enant might not fail, some were *elected* and appointed to salvation by his eternal purpose." Isaiah's teaching in 1:9 and Paul's teaching in Rom 11:5, about a remnant, were determinative for Calvin: "Let us know then that, wherever the Scripture denounces eternal death against the Jews, it excepts a *remnant*, (Isa 2:9; Rom 11:5) that is, those in whom the Lord *preserves some seed* on account of his free *election*."[64]

It is because of the elect that God set a limit to the calamities "so as not utterly to destroy the Jews." Calvin, of course, sees everything through the lens of his doctrine of double predestination. Yet it is an aspect of his doctrine that the identity of the elect and the reprobate is known only to God. Calvin is fully aware that it may be objected that many of those who were saved were reprobate. To this, Calvin says, the reply is easy: "A part of the nation was preserved that out of them God might bring his elect, who were mixed with them, like the seed after the chaff has been blown off."[65] Temporal safety was bestowed on both the reprobate and elect, "yet, as it was of no advantage to the reprobate, it is justly ascribed to *the elect* alone, for it was to their benefit that the wonderful providence of God was elected."[66] Clearly the Jews have a continuing role in God's plan of salvation even though Calvin interpreted "all Israel" in Rom 11:26 to refer to the whole people of God, Jewish and Gentile believers in Jesus Christ.

Without a doubt, Calvin's understanding of the relationship of the church and Israel was shaped by his close reading of Paul's *Letter to the Romans*, specifically, chapters 9–11. Calvin's commentary on Romans was the first one he wrote. It was published in 1540 and revised in 1551 and then again in 1556 and in terms of importance it occupied a place next to the *Institutes*. In concluding this section, I want to refer to a few places where Calvin emphasizes the continuing role of the Jews.

In his outline of Romans, in the *argumentum*, referring to Rom 11, Calvin writes that Paul asserts: "that the covenant remains even in the physical descendants of Abraham but only in those whom the Lord has predestinated by his free election."[67] Gentiles must not, however, exult over the Jews "as though they had been rejected." Then Calvin goes on

---

64. Comm., on Matthew 23:34; *CO* 45, 670–71; CTS 3, 102.

65. Comm., on Matthew 24:22; *CO* 45, 662; CTS, 3, 139.

66. Ibid.

67. Comm., on Romans, "The Theme," *CO* 49, 5; *Romans and Thessalonians*, 10; hereafter CNTC.

to affirm: "God's covenant has not wholly departed from the seed of Abraham, for the Jews are at length to be provoked to jealousy by the faith of the Gentiles, so that God may gather all Israel to Himself."[68] The same point is made in Calvin's comments on 9:3 where Paul emphasizes that adoption belongs to the Jews:

> The intention of the whole of Paul's discourse is that, although the Jews had blasphemously separated themselves from God by their defection, yet the light of the grace of God had not wholly been extinguished among them, as he has said in Romans 3:3. Although they were unbelievers and had broken His covenant, yet their perfidy had not rendered the faithfulness of God void, not only because He preserved for Himself some seed as a remnant from the whole multitude, but also because the name of a church still continued among them by the right of inheritance.[69]

Similar comments are made on Rom 11:11: where Paul asks, "Have they stumbled that they should fall?" "He [Paul] asks the question whether the Jewish nation had so stumbled at Christ that it was all over with them universally and no hope of repentance remained. Here he justly denies that the salvation of the Jews was to be despaired of, or that they were so rejected by God, that there was to be no future restoration, or that the covenant of grace, which he had once made with them, was entirely abolished, since there had ever remained in that nation the seed of blessing."[70]

Calvin did not exclude the restoration of the Jews to the obedience of faith. This is his interpretation of Rom 11:26: "When the Gentiles shall come in, the Jews also shall return from their defection to the obedience of faith; and thus shall be completed the salvation of the whole Israel of God, which shall be gathered from both; and yet in such a way that the Jews shall obtain the first place, being as it were the first born in God's family."[71]

In Calvin's view, the covenant which God made with the Jewish people continues to be valid and cannot made void. A whole section was devoted to this point in the 1559 *Institutes* where Calvin defended the practice of baptizing infants over against the Anabaptists:

68. Ibid.

69. Comm., on Romans 9:4; *CO* 49, 72; *CNTC*, 194.

70. Calvin, *Commentary on Romans* 11:11, *CO* 49, 218; *CTS*, 421.

71. Calvin, *Commentary on Romans* 11:26, *CO* 49, 226; *CTS*, 437.

Nevertheless, when Paul cast them [i.e., the Jews] from vain confidence in their kindred, he still saw, on the other hand, that the covenant which God had made once for all with the descendants of Abraham could in no way be made void. Consequently, in the eleventh chapter he argues that Abraham's physical progeny (*carnalem Abrahae cognationem*) must not be deprived of their dignity. By virtue of this he teaches that the Jews are the first and natural heirs of the gospel, except to the extent that by their ungratefulness they were forsaken as unworthy—*yet forsaken in such a way that the heavenly blessing had not departed utterly from their nation. For this reason, despite their stubbornness and covenant-breaking, Paul still calls them holy* [Rom 11:16], such great honor does he give to the holy generation whom God had held worthy of his sacred covenant; but he calls us (if we are compared with them), as it were, posthumous or even abortive children of Abraham (*velut posthumus, aut etian abortivos Abrahae filios*)— and that by adoption, not by nature—as if a sapling broken from its tree were grafted upon the trunk of another [Rom 11:17]. Therefore that they might not be defrauded of their privilege, the gospel had to be announced to them first. For they are, so to speak, like the first-born in God's household (*in Dei familia velut primogeniti*). Accordingly, this honor was to be given them until they refused what was offered and by their ungratefulness caused it to be transferred to the Gentiles. *Yet, despite the great obstinacy with which they continue to wage war against the gospel, we must not despise them, while we consider that, for the sake of the promise God's blessing still rests among them. For the apostle testifies that it will never be completely taken away: "For the gifts and the calling of God are without repentance"* [Rom 11:29. Vg.][72]

CONCLUSION

Calvin's use of Augustine's "witness doctrine," his emphasis on one covenant of grace and one People of God, and his affirmation of the continuing role of the Jews in God's economy of salvation are, I believe, weighty-enough considerations to tip the scale in favor of contending that Calvin's stance to Jews was basically positive. Unquestionably, he inherited aspects of medieval anti-Judaism and a certain animus against the Jews keeps appearing when he deals with Jewish exegetes of the Old Testament Scriptures, especially when they deny christological prophe-

---

72. Calvin, *Institutes*, 4.16.14—Emphasis added.

cies. Yet he appears largely to have overcome that legacy when he befriended a converted Jew, Immanuel Tremellius, who taught Hebrew at Sturm's Academy in Strasbourg and sought to help him to obtain a teaching position, albeit unsuccessfully, in Berne, Lausanne and in Geneva where anti-Semitic views still seemed to flourish. Calvin appears to have distanced himself from the later Luther and Martin Bucer's negative attitude and yet there is no evidence that he embraced Wolfgang Capito's view of the toleration of the Jews. Yet it is not without significance that in the seventeenth century Jews were granted new civil rights in countries influenced by the Calvinist reformation.

It is now conventional wisdom that a straight line runs from Renaissance humanism to the vanguard of Locke, Hume, and Voltaire and then to the breakthrough of the toleration of the Jews during the period of the European Enlightenment.[73] This wisdom is questionable on two counts: first, its rosy view of Renaissance humanism's attitude to the Jews. Erasmus and other humanists showed a deep hostility to Jews. Secondly, it ignores the heritage of the Calvinist Reformation or more accurately that of the work of the Upper German-Swiss reformers. In spite of many negative elements, they were responsible for sowing seeds that came to fruition decades later and these seeds were Augustine's "witness-people doctrine", the one covenant of grace and the continuing role of the Jews.

I know of no prayer of Calvin for the Jews but there is a prayer by Theodore Beza, Calvin's friend and successor, who was a faithful disciple of Calvin's theology. It appears in connection with his exposition of Rom 11. After lamenting the guilt of Christians in relation to "the holy nation of the Jews" which they have maltreated in so many ways, Bèze wrote:

> I pray daily with all my heart for the Jews in this manner: "Lord Jesus, truly you judge in your righteousness that one not scorn you and this ungrateful people deserves to be severely punished. But, Lord I pray that you will have regard for your covenant and look with kindly eyes on this forsaken and unfortunate people for your name's sake. But with regard to ourselves, the most unworthy of all humankind, whom you have nonetheless made worthy by your great mercy, grant in your grace that we may so grow in understanding that we may not be instruments of your anger, but instead be enabled to call them back to the right way, through knowledge of your Word and by the example of a holy

---

73. See for example, Gay, *The Enlightenment*, 297.

life through the power of your Holy Spirit, so that you may be unanimously glorified by all nations and people to eternity. Amen."[74]

In an age of racial bigotry and religious intolerance, it's a remarkable prayer, recognizing as it does, to use Calvin's words, that the Jew is "the first-born in God's household," and that we Gentiles are, "posthumous or even abortive children of Abraham—and that by adoption, not by nature."

---

74. See Locher, "Calvin spricht zu den Juden," 193–94, to whom I am indebted for this quotation from Théodore de Bèze, *Nouveau Testament* (4. éd.,1589) on Romans 11:18.

2

Scripture Funded

Reforming Reformed Imagination

RICHARD R. TOPPING

IN THIS PAPER TWO Magisterial Protestant thinkers on biblical interpretation and revelation are brought into conversation. They are
the sixteenth century Reformer John Calvin and the twentieth century
hermeneutic philosopher, Paul Ricoeur.[1] The conversation revolves
around a category that has become so very important for contemporary
theology, biblical and liturgical studies, and hermeneutics: imagination.

Calvin, as far as I know, never makes a positive reference to "imagination" as a human faculty in the service of God. This does not mean that
his work and exegesis were unimaginative or that he did not inspire a
particularly Reformed imagination.[2] It is just that he does not speak well
of the human capacity to imagine and there was a salutary "mimetic"

---

1. Ricoeur affirms that in his writings the interests of a hermeneutical philosopher
and one who belongs to the Christian tradition (the French Reformed Church) confront one another: on the basis of these two "affiliations" he enters the world of biblical
interpretation. See Ricoeur, *Critique and Conviction*, 139ff.; Ricoeur, "Two Essays by
Paul Ricoeur: The Critique of Religion and the Language of Faith," and Reagan, *Paul
Ricoeur*, 125–26.

2. See Dryness, *The Reformed Imagination and Visual Culture*; Matheson, *The
Imaginative World of the Reformation*; and Brown, *Singing and the Imagination of
Devotion*. Brown notes that even when imagination acquires a more positive valuation
in Reformed thinking, as it does in seventeenth-century England, it remains "a weaker
sister of sorts among the faculties, one unfortunately susceptible to the direct blandish-
ments of the devil" (ibid., 80).

CALVIN@500

sense of it available to him.[3] Calvin seems to understand imagination, as does much of early modern Protestantism, as strictly akin to fantasy, a lesser faculty. Understanding is the featured human cognitive register where it comes to the knowledge of God—all the rest (particularly the will and the heart) follow the lead of understanding as it is either captive to sin or regenerated and sanctified at the hearing of the Word through the agency of the Holy Spirit.

Ricoeur, on the other hand, deploys imagination as a faculty central to text and biblical text interpretation. For Ricoeur, imagination (not reason or will) is the primary anthropological site to which "revelation" makes its non-violent appeal.[4] Revelation, which is generated in the act of reading by genric friction, projects a possible world to imagination (ethically brokered by conscience) that readers might inhabit.[5]

While initially it seems that there is a wide variance between Calvin and Ricoeur on the role of imagination relative to the knowledge of God and the interpretation of Scripture, there are positive features that arise from this conversation. The interaction with Ricoeur might enable a more positive valuation of the faculty of imagination for the Reformed tradition. There are resources in Calvin, particularly in his theology of Word and Spirit, that could render Ricoeur's largely poetic account of revelation, as appeal to the imagination, more serviceable to Christian theology.

MIND THE GAP: IMAGINATION THEN AND NOW

There are perils in this venture of comparison, perhaps the greatest of which is that the meaning of "imagination," is not stable through time. Imagination from biblical and classical worlds through the Enlightenment

---

3. See Kearney, *The Wake of Imagination*, 1–33.

4. See Ricoeur, "Toward a Hermeneutic of the Idea of Revelation," 73–118. Ricoeur identifies this essay as seminal for his thinking about revelation and biblical interpretation. See also Ricoeur, *Critique and Conviction*, 148–49 and Topping, *Revelation, Scripture and Church*, 31–53.

5. Ricoeur, "The Summoned Subject in the School of the Narratives of the Prophetic Vocation," 271–75. See also Ibid., Wallace, "Introduction," 28–30. Imagination, as the point of contact between the word of God and humans is supplemented, in this later work of Ricoeur, by conscience, which is the moral capacity to select which figure presented by imagination best enables eccentric expression of the self in the care of the other.

and into our post-modern world has become an increasingly inventive faculty.

For Homer and the classical world, imagination aims at forming a copy of the way the world is, the truth of existence. The "craftsperson" obediently copied the transcendent plan using imagination. That this sort of imagination is operative but not named in Calvin's corpus of writings comes through in his preference for realism in the fine arts. Imagination has a "mimetic" or representing function and so in classical thought is strongly connected with memory.[6] Imagination plays the role of the screen on a digital camera where images stored in memory are displayed through recall.

During the Enlightenment, however, the imagination acquires a more synthetic role in working with the material given to it through the senses: the "craftsperson" gives way to the "inventor."[7] "The imagination," says Kant, "is namely very powerful in creating, as it were, another nature, out of the material one gives it. We entertain ourselves with it when experience seems too mundane; we transform the latter."[8] One can always listen to a speaker and do an improvisation or embellishment on the material presented. In any case, in Kant (and others), imagination is a capacity for pleasurable improvisation on what comes into consciousness through the senses; imagination starts to move in a productive and constructive direction.[9] Imagination performs a synthetic "photoshopping" of impressions into a composite "reality."

Finally, in late modernity and post-modernity, imagination does even more work. Wherever that prophet of post-modernism, Nietzsche, is followed—"there are no facts, only interpretation"—imagination is Promethean: it is world and meaning making. Imagination performs not the more modest "mimetic" or "embellishment" function; it constructs

6. Kearney, *The Wake of Imagination*, 6–12.

7. Ibid., 12–13.

8. Kant, *Critique of the Power of Judgement*, 5:314, 192. Cited in Dyrness, *Reformed Theology*, 3.

9. George Schner maintained that the prominence of imagination in constructive theologies finds its roots not so much in Kant as in developments in nineteenth-century thought. However, he does note in commentary on *Critique of Pure Reason* that: "Human freedom and imagination, as two aspects of human self-transcendence, come to function as surrogates for the transcendent itself. In sum, construction as radical invention sets aside the receptive and habitual in the Christian way of life, whether understood as faith, as tradition or as experience." Schner, "Metaphors in Theology," 21.

reality (sometimes with persuasive and persuaded others in a social/ cultural imaginary). Where it comes to text interpretation, one interpretation displaces another not so much by plausibility on the basis of what the text will bear, but rather by means of imaginative genius; like musical styles displace each other through more compelling performance. The post-modern imagination, as Kearney has it, is the "parodic" imagination of the "*bricoleur*."[10] The best that it can do is to parody, to play games with, to construct and propose a world that seduces because there no is "text" or "world." In some ways, the real world is the world inside your head. It is all interpretation. It is *mimesis* in reverse—image and reality are inverted, even subverted. "Like a character in a Pynchon novel or Wenders film, the postmodern artist wanders about in a labyrinth of commodified light and noise, endeavoring to piece together bits of dispersed narrative."[11]

William Dyrness, however, identifies a fundamental continuity in the understanding of imagination from the Middle Ages to the present. The common thread is slender, but threads always are: "Imagination is," he writes, "the ability to shape mental images of things not present to the senses."[12] And so while imagination is not conceived of by Calvin and Ricoeur in the same way, and while there is certainly a great deal more positive attention paid to the faculty post-enlightenment, there is still some overlap in our understanding of it as a shaping, even inventive piece of human cognitive equipment.

That brings us to the second potential peril in the comparison between Calvin and Ricoeur on imagination. This peril has to do with the relative value they each assign to it as a representing and/or inventive human faculty. My guess is that much of the current interest in imagination as an important faculty for theological and biblical studies has to do with our unmitigated praise for creativity. Moderns and post-moderns almost universally praise human creativity and inventiveness, the source of which is imagination. While thinkers from the Middle Ages to our own time recognize our capacity to conjure up and tinker with mental

---

10. Kearney, *The Wake of Imagination*, 13.

11. Ibid. Mary Warnock in her *Imagination and Time*, renders a similar genealogy of imagination. She notes the critical eighteenth-century movement from imagination as "mirror" reflecting reality to imagination as "lamp" casting light on the world by its own "inner brilliance," ibid., 2. See also Abrams, *The Mirror and The Lamp*.

12. Dyrness, *Reformed Theology and Visual Culture*, 4.

images through recall or invention, there is no unanimity as to the value of it. The human mind has imaginative prowess; it is generative and creative. Like Kant, we late moderns find pleasure in such mental dexterity and ingenuity; the sixteenth century Reformers, especially where it comes to the knowledge of God, render a negative judgment on this root of human creativity.[13]

CALVIN ON IMAGINATION

1. Interposed between the Sense of the Divine and Piety

Listen to Calvin: "In seeking God, miserable men do not rise above themselves as they should, but measure God by the yardstick of their own carnal stupidity, and neglect sound investigation; thus out of curiosity they fly off into empty speculation. They do not therefore apprehend God as God offers himself, but imagine him as they have fashioned him in their own presumption" (*sed qualem pro sua temeritate fabricati sunt, imaginantur*).[14] Both in this passage and in his commentary on the first chapter of Romans, Calvin is trying to establish at least two things: first, that there is a natural awareness of God, a seed of religion, in all people. While this impression of God as creator is not sufficient for salvation, it is clear and sufficient enough to render us culpable before God. Human beings cannot blame God for a lack of awareness of God since human beings do not cultivate to fruition that sense of the divine implanted in them. "No real piety remains in the world," writes Calvin.[15]

And that brings us to the second related point: Calvin uses the term "piety" to wed the affective and cognitive domains. In our thought world, we think knowledge and affective response apart. This dichotomy is not a part of Calvin's intellectual world. Knowledge for Calvin is not head knowledge—"what flits around in the brain"—but includes commitment, affective involvement and experiential response. He says that piety

---

13. In their treatments of Romans 1 both Calvin and Luther find human inventive capacity (imagination) at the root of idolatry, which is the source of sinful disorder. The fundamental human problem is doxological, we ascribe glory to a god of our own imaginative making, and so life is disordered. See Calvin's New Testament Commentaries, *The Epistles of Paul to the Romans and Thessalonians*, 31–34 and Martin Luther, in *Luther's Works*, vol. 25: *Lectures on Romans: Glosses and Scholia*, 158–60.

14. Calvin, *Institutes*, I.iv.1. All citations from the Institutes are from the Library of Christian Classics edition.

15. Ibid., I.iv.1.

is "that reverence joined with the love of God which the knowledge of his benefits induces."[16]

It is important for us to remember this when we address the topic of imagination. For Calvin, we don't move from an implanted awareness of God to true knowledge of God (piety) as we ought because something interposes itself. That something is sin in the form of human mental activity, in a word, imagination. Like reason (indeed all human faculties), human imagination corrupted by sin asserts its autonomy, and ventures out on its own, speculating about God, projecting idols more suited to immanent causes and egocentric need. The imagination "choke[s]" "the seed of true knowledge ... before it grow[s] to maturity."[17] Impiety is therefore the human condition because of sin. The seed of the divine planted in the human creature is not cultivated toward piety; instead imagination, fertilized by presumption and carnal stupidity, yields idols.[18]

2. Perpetually Churning Out Gods

Listen to Calvin again: "Man's mind, full as it is of pride and boldness, dares to imagine a god according to its own capacity (*deum pro captu suo imaginari audet*): as it sluggishly plods, indeed is overwhelmed with the crassest ignorance, it conceives an unreality and an empty appearance as God."[19]

In this section of the *Institutes*, Calvin searches out the origin of images in the desire of the flesh to take solace in a visible and tangible figure of the divine, an image. People are ensnared in idolatry, says Calvin, because of this carnal need. What begins as veneration ends up as idolatry/image worship since we transfer something of the divinity to the representations we construct.

---

16. Ibid., I.ii.1.

17. Calvin, *Romans*, 33.

18. Calvin's tendency to conflate image and idol is at the root of his entirely negative account of imagination. Dyrness, *Reformed Theology*, 14. Susan Brown notes that in cultures where Reformation ideals were influential, creative energy was focused on the more abstract arts—singing and literature. She attributes this preference to the fear of idolatry, which "elicited an enormous amount of attention during this era." Brown, *Singing and the Imagination of Devotion*, 24.

19. Calvin, *Institutes*, I.xi.8.

What is particularly important about this treatment of images-become-idols is the sense of inevitability and spontaneity that surrounds the role of the imagination in the production of them. The imagination, says Calvin, "begets an idol," inwardly, and the hands produce it outwardly in the form of an image. It is as if the imagination cannot but play its role in the ongoing assembly line of image manufacture. The mind, made audacious by pride and boldness, together with the flesh, yearning as it does after tangibility, press imagination into drafting blue prints for the "factory of idols,"[20] which the hands dutifully manufacture.

In all of this there is an uncontrollably slavish quality to the imagination. Alongside this metaphor of the "perpetual factory," Calvin sets the spring or fountain of water: "Just as waters boil up from a vast, full spring, so does an immense crowd of gods flow forth from the human mind."[21] The imagination, in this section of the *Institutes*, is fecund and cannot, of its own accord, cease from churning out gods who are "unrealities," "empty appearances"[22] and in the Romans commentary "insubstantial phantoms."[23] We might say that the imagination is not free to do anything but conceive of mental idols: the imagination is frenetic at the drafting board of divinity. To borrow a phrase from Luther, we might speak here of the bondage of the imagination, set as it is among fallen human faculties that press it perpetually into the service of idolatry and dead image making. The wayward idolatrous imagination perpetually misdirects the sense of the divine implanted in the human creature away from its proper end in pious fruition.

3. A Humanist Caveat

A short caveat before we continue. Calvin's theological account of imagination in the early part of the *Institutes* and in his commentary on *Romans* is just that: a theological account. Calvin is writing about the spiritual function of imagination as a faculty estranged from God in the fallen human creature. Calvin was an Augustinian. Sin thoroughly corrupts the human capacity properly to know God. Imagination goes awry because of pride and carnality and it presses into new wickedness when

20. Ibid., I.xi.8.

21. Ibid., I.v.12.

22. Ibid., I.xi.8.

23. Calvin, *Romans*, 32.

CALVIN@500

it provides the blueprints for manufactured and visible representations of God.

However, Calvin was also a Humanist, and so it ought not to be said that he was a Philistine. As is suggested by Lucy Bregman, we need to be careful not to take "the Renaissance out the Reformer."[24] Calvin was a not an enemy of creative endeavor and the arts (at the level of "things below"); and so he does not write and speak as an outsider to them. He was, it must be said, a realist in the plastic arts. "Therefore it remains that only those things are to be sculptured or painted which the eyes are capable of seeing."[25] Calvin regarded sculpture and painting, as gifts of God which had "a pure and legitimate use."[26] Artists, like philosophers and poets and lawyers, do search out the truth in "earthly things"[27] and we ought not to be surprised if we find some echoes of the truth about God in their work since they and their enterprises are animated by the Spirit, "who fills, moves and quickens all things."[28] Calvin acknowledges, "One can read competent and apt statements about God here and there in the philosophers"[29] and by analogy, we might add, in the work of artists.

However, because of "giddy imagination" (*vertiginosam quandam imaginationem*) these momentary glimpses vanish swiftly, are not reliable and "do not direct them to the truth [about God], much less enable them to attain it."[30] They are like flashes of lightning by which sight is momentarily given, "but the sight vanishes so swiftly that he is plunged again into the darkness of the night before he can even take a step—let alone be directed on his way by its help."[31] Again in book two of the

---

24. Bregman, "Religious Imagination," 47.

25. Calvin, *Institutes*, I.xi.12.

26. Ibid. In his Geneva Catechism the question is asked concerning the second commandment: "Does this prohibit us entirely from painting anything or sculpting likenesses?" The answer is: "No; but it does forbid two thing (sic): that we make images either for representing God or for worshipping him." Once again we get both a mimetic understanding of imagination, hovering but unnamed, and Calvin's artistic realism. "The Catechism of the Church of Geneva that is a Plan for Instructing Children in the Doctrine of Christ," in *Calvin: Theological Treatises*, 109.

27. Calvin, Institutes, II.ii.13.

28. Ibid., II.ii.16.

29. Ibid., II.ii.18.

30. Ibid.

31. Ibid.

Institutes momentary insight about God gets estranged from piety by the interposing of, in this case, "giddy" (*vertiginosam*) imagination.

RICOEUR: REVELATION AND IMAGINATIVE APPEAL

Paul Ricoeur, an elder in the French Reformed church in the late twentieth and early twenty-first centuries, may well be called a philosopher of the imagination. At least, where his work touches on biblical interpretation and the knowledge of God, the faculty of the imagination is featured. Ricoeur's seminal essay, one he returned to again and again in his writings on scripture—"Toward a Hermeneutic of the Idea of Revelation"—features imagination as the human correlate of a modulated poetic understanding of revelation.

There is, of course, a great difference between Ricoeur and Calvin in terms of polemic context. For Calvin, hovering in the not so distant background is the specter of images and superstition and idolatry he found in the Roman Catholic Church of his own time. Imagination is complicit in the breaking of the second commandment.

Ricoeur, on the other hand, engages with the faculty of imagination over against the Kantian concern with heteronomy.[32] Ricoeur always said that Kant was his favorite philosopher of religion. Throughout the whole of his life, Ricoeur returns to this theme of revelation and heteronomy, trying to articulate some sense of revelation which is not implicated in commanding. It means that Ricoeur is particularly allergic to any understanding of revelation and scripture interpretation that involves primacy of appeal to the will for obedience. Ricoeur's deployment of imagination as the human faculty that corresponds to revelation needs to be seen in this apologetic context.

We should also note that Ricoeur articulates his understanding of imagination and revelation over against Bultmann, who Ricoeur thought rushed too quickly to "inauthentic existential signification." On Ricoeur's view, Bultmann was so driven by the question of relevance in

---

32. See, for instance, Ricoeur, "Philosophical Hermeneutics and Biblical Hermeneutics," 89–101; Ricoeur, "Toward a Hermeneutic of the Idea of Revelation"; Ricoeur, *Critique and Conviction*, 149; Ricoeur, "Thou Shalt not Kill," 124. and Ricoeur, "Theonony and/or Autonomy," 284ff. For the case that Ricoeur renders his case for imagination apologetically, in the light of Kantian notions of autonomy, see Topping, *Revelation, Scripture and Church*, 39–51.

Scripture interpretation, that at times he "moves too fast" to get there.[33] Ricoeur's hermeneutic councils a slower pace in which the objectivity of the text in its generic diversity is carefully considered. Ricoeur deploys poetics to slow us down in our consideration, not only of the thing—the subject matter—of the Bible, but also of the literary genres in which the subject matter of the Bible is presented. Ricoeur insists that authentic appropriation of Scripture by imagination is patient upon what he calls "explanation."

A final distinction: all the genres of literature in the Bible, on Ricoeur's view, have a poetic function. By poetic function Ricoeur means to point to the way in which biblical texts refer in a manner that is different from scientific texts. The texts of the Bible not only refer to rocks and trees and people and things of everyday experience, they refer to what might be—"a possible world." What comes from a serious reading of the Bible is a world unfolded in front of the text that we might inhabit, new ways of being in the world that we might take up. Ricoeur maintains that the texts of the Bible project a possible world, one I can inhabit if I leave behind aspects of what and who I am at the moment. In reading the Bible and following the itineraries it proposes to imagination, "I exchange me, the *master* of itself, for self, *disciple* of the text."[34]

Now to draw the threads together: for Ricoeur, this projecting and proposing capacity of the Bible when read as a poetic text is revelation. The solicitous possible world I might inhabit through self-divestment is the appeal of revelation to the reader of the Bible. And that appeal, says Ricoeur, is to my "creative"[35] imagination, which is invited to extend and prolong the itineraries of meaning opened up by the Bible. Whether or not this movement is taken up depends on the vivacity of appeal to imagination, the solicitousness of the possible world projected by the text. However, this appeal is resolutely not, or at least not first of all, a command to the will for obedience. Ricoeur writes—speaking of the anthropological site to which poetic texts make their appeal: "I am indeed speaking here of imagination and not will. For the power of allowing oneself to be struck by new possibilities precedes the power of

33. See Ricoeur, "Preface to Bultmann," 49–72. See also Lowe, "Hans Frei and Phenomenological Hermeneutics," 134–35.

34. Ricoeur, "Phenomenology and Hermeneutics," 113. Ricoeur's emphasis.

35. Ricoeur, "The Bible and the Imagination," 50.

making up one's mind."[36] To live out or within a proposed possible world projected by the Bible is to wager that its texts contain the "figures of my liberation." This wager Ricoeur calls faith. To sum up: "Encountering biblical discourse in its poetic function, one responds with the imagination, that part of ourselves that can encounter revelation no longer as unacceptable pretention, but a nonviolent appeal."[37]

WHAT CALVINISTS MIGHT TAKE FROM RICOEUR

While it is regrettable that Calvin does not directly speak of imagination in positive terms, it is not hard to understand Calvin's negative judgment on the imagination given his polemic context and his Augustinian (Pauline) anthropology. Imagination, a fallen human faculty, gets deployed in the service of sin in human creatures. Imagination interposes itself so that the sense of the divine is not fulfilled in full blown piety: it is the whereabouts within which idols are conjured up, the site at which blue-prints for superstitious dead images are generated. It is at the root of the violation of the second commandment.

However, similar negative judgments about the whole variety of human faculties might be found in Calvin. Because of sin, reason is an unreliable guide to the knowledge of God, the will unable to long for the good and the heart, even at the hearing of the Word alone, unable to trust and remain constant in the promises of God. All human faculties share in the economy of salvation: creation, fall and redemption is the story of the whole set of human endowments where it comes to the knowledge and love of God. For Calvin there is no innocent region of the human creature that stands outside the need of God's renewing grace. "The whole man is overwhelmed—as by a deluge—from head to foot, so that no part is immune from sin."[38]

And yet, Calvin will speak of the Word and Spirit regenerating other fallen human faculties. Blind reason, the mind, is illumined by the Word and taught by the Spirit and so lead to Christ.[39] The will is informed and liberated by Word and Spirit to the right and grateful conduct of life, not

---

36. Ricoeur, "Philosophical Hermeneutics and Biblical Hermeneutics," 101.

37. Ricoeur, "Toward a Hermeneutic of the Idea of Revelation," 117.

38. Calvin, *Institutes*, II.i.9.

39. Ibid., III.i.1–3; III.ii.33.

just once but over and over again, as the prayers of the Psalmist teach.[40] The heart is assured of the truth of the Gospel through the promises of the Word, which are sealed on the heart of the one engrafted into the saving work of Christ by the Spirit.[41]

Could we not extend Calvin's thinking here and speak of regenerated, redeemed and sanctified imagination? Ricoeur encourages us to think of imagination not as an autonomous generative faculty, but rather as evoked and shaped by the thing—the subject matter—of the Bible. This generated and scripture-shaped imaginative capacity for perceiving the world could be spoken of as the faithful imagination (Garrett Green),[42] the scriptural imagination (Luke Timothy Johnson),[43] or the paradigmatic imagination (David Kelsey).[44] Here we might retrieve another aspect of the human creature brought into correspondence with the world disclosed in the Bible such that we begin, as disciples, to imagine the world scripture imagines.

We might even push Calvin a little harder, with Ricoeur's help, and propose paradigmatic imagination as that capacity patterned by the Word and guided by the Spirit which enables Christians to perceive the world in the light of the knowledge and glory of God. After all, isn't this what Calvin does in the second half of his sermons and elsewhere? From exposition (looking *at* the text as part of a canon, the *scopos* of which is Christ) he moves to application (looking *through* the text).[45] And so what

40. Ibid., II.iii.6–14.

41. Ibid., III.ii.33–36.

42. See Green, *Imagining God:* 126–52 and Green, *Theology, Hermeneutics and Imagination*, 187–206. In both works Green's final chapter is entitled, "The Faithful Imagination."

43. Johnson, "Imagining the World Scripture Imagines," 3–18.

44. Kelsey, *Imagining Redemption*, 97–106. Kelsey draws heavily on Garrett Green's work. Kelsey notes helpfully that in the West "imagining has been defined in contrast to knowing" so that "the standard case of imagination" is "fantasy," "the imaginary." Such would seem to be the case with Calvin. Paradigmatic imagination as Kelsey articulates it has two roles: interpretative, i.e., a retrospective seeing of concrete events as included within Jesus' story, and perceptive, i.e., a learning to imagine (spiritual formation) the world as redeemed by means of creed, liturgy, Scriptures, and the narratively rendered identity of Jesus. Some account of how these two dimensions of imaginative formation are related to the work of the Spirit would strengthen Kelsey's account as a theological one.

45. See Zachman, *John Calvin as Teacher, Pastor, and Theologian*, 163–72. Zachman argues for three parts to Calvin's preaching—exposition, retention and application to use and practice. Exposition is practiced with a view to making the congregation feel

is application but tracing the trajectory of the passage into the world, an imaginative rereading of our life and times and challenges in the light of Scripture. Here imagination has less of a "picturing" and more of a 'patterning' function.[46] And so faithful imagination would not in this case be a faculty that interposes itself and leads us from God (with images); but rather one (re)patterned by the scriptural witness (the spectacles) by means of which we see the world.

Ricoeur's lucid depiction of imagination as anthropological correlate to revelation might also be a means to re-envision what has been an intellectualist bent in the Reformed Tradition. Listen to Calvin (the good Platonist): "The understanding is, as it were, the leader and governor of the soul; and . . . the will is always mindful of the bidding of the understanding, and its own desires await the judgment of the understanding."[47] Ricoeur's depiction of the function of the imagination has Pelagian tendencies and it is rendered much too generic to be transposed easily into a Reformed doctrine of revelation; but it might be worth the effort given Reformed cerebral predilections. Could reformed doctrine take into itself a theological anthropology in which sanctified imagination were "the leader and governor of the soul?" followed by understanding and will? I think it's an option worth reckoning with, not least for its affective and empathic aspects. Regenerated reason may absorb a deeper and broader understanding of scripture but might not imagination formed by the Spirit and patterned by the Word help us lovingly to identify with and so to interpret and apply scripture at affective, emotional and dispositional levels.[48]

---

the force of teaching so that fruit is born in the hearer. Zachman is careful to relate this preacherly goal to the work of the Spirit all the way through the homiletic endeavour. "Calvin addresses his congregation as fellow scholars of God in the school of Christ, studying to learn the meaning of Scripture under the guidance of a pastor skilled in the exposition of Scripture, and praying for the guidance of the Holy Spirit." See ibid., 158–59 and Pitkin, "John Calvin and the Interpretation of the Bible," 352.

46. The distinction is Greens'. See Green, *Imagining God*, 93–125 and Kelsey, *Imagining Redemption*, 99–102. Patterned by the story instantiated in scripture imagination seems less bedevilled by "picturing" where it comes to God.

47. Calvin, *Institutes*, I.xvii.7.

48. See Hedley, *Living Forms of the Imagination*. Hedley resists the impoverishment of reason by invoking imagination without setting the two against each other.

WHAT RICOEURIANS MIGHT TAKE FROM CALVIN

There is simply no question that Calvin would find Ricoeur's depiction of imagination and its function as the anthropological correlate of revelation insufficient, even presumptuous; lacking as it is in theological density. To speak the criticism most generally: Ricoeur renders generic what Calvin would serve up name brand.

Perhaps the most problematic aspect of Ricoeur's proposal is that his poetic reconfiguration of revelation with its attendant discussion of imagination is an entirely naturalized account of text interpretation. Most telling in this regard is the answer we get to the compound question: *who* reveals by means of the Bible and *whom* is revealed by means the Bible?

First of all, Ricoeur seems to ascribe agency to the texts of Scripture themselves—they project possible worlds, they unfold realities before the text, sparks of meaning fly up from them when they are read cross-genre.[49] Calvin writes of God's agency by means of the text or, more specifically, of the work of the Spirit, who regenerates the reader to be a true hearer of the Word of God. It is the work of the Spirit to credential the Bible as having come from God, and also to open our ears to hear, our minds to understand, our hearts to love and our wills to follow the way to the kingdom of God that is open. It may be quite possible to extend the regenerating work of the Spirit from mind and heart and will to imagination, but on a Calvinist account, imagination would be opened up by the Spirit to envision the possible world of the kingdom of God within which Jesus Christ and his benefits are central.

And this leads us to the question of what or whom is revealed in the Bible. For Calvin what the Spirit, by means of the Word of God, illumines and teaches and unites us to is Christ. It is not just any possible world disclosed to the reader by means of the Word and Spirit; nor is revelation *primarily* a matter of disclosing to the imagination ways in which we might dispose our own subjectivity. Here, I think, Ricoeur makes primary what Calvin would make secondary. God is the primary subject of revelation, not us.[50] Imaginative modes of being in the world continuous

---

49. See Ricoeur, "Philosophical Hermeneutics and Biblical Hermeneutics," 96ff. and Ricoeur, "Toward a Hermeneutic of the Idea of Revelation," 102–3. Nicholas Wolterstoff maintains that Ricoeur's account of revelation is "agentless"; that is, it is granted self-generating independence from the action of God. Wolterstorff, *Divine Discourse*, 62.

50. See Ricoeur, "Biblical Hermeneutics," 127–28. In this essay Ricoeur maintains

with the God revealed in Scripture are disclosed but are always adjunct to, generated by, the God who is the subject of the scriptural witness and the agent of his own identification. It is a fundamental theological move properly to prioritize the generative (God the Holy Spirit by means of the scriptural witness) over the generated (ways of being in the world). On this matter, Ricoeur's account could be theologically reordered by borrowing from Calvin.

In sum then: To make Calvinist use of Ricoeurian imagination we would need to say that imagination, like reason and will and affection, "needs continual" funding and shaping and strengthening by the Word of God in the power of the Spirit. Where such sanctification is taking place, imagination may, like reason and will and affection, become a servant of the gospel especially in the role of the proposing, inhabiting and living toward the kingdom that is coming. Like other human faculties imagination can, by the sanctifying grace of God, function in a manner conducive to and resulting from true Christian piety.

Luke Timothy Johnson in his "Imagining the World Scripture Imagines" provides a fitting conclusion:

> The life of faith in the community is generated and guided by the power of the Holy Spirit given by the resurrected Lord Jesus. The faith community therefore imagines itself in a world filled with the power of that resurrected life, and in the constant presence of the Living One through word, sacrament, fellowship, prayer and solidarity with the suffering ... A community of readers committed to transformative practices of Christian piety allows for the imaginative reading of Scripture while holding in check the human potential for misguided fantasy and projection ... A community grounded in practices derived from Scripture and constantly nurtured by the wisdom communicated through the complex images and symbols of scripture can be trusted [imaginatively] to read [the world] with discrimination and discernment according to the mind of Christ.[51]

that what Scripture reveals is "the religious dimension of *common* human experience." See also Placher, "Paul Ricoeur and Postliberal Theology: A Conflict of Interpretations?" 42.

51. Johnson, "Imagining the World Scripture Imagines," 18.

3

The Holy Spirit in the Thoughts of John Calvin

GERARD BOOY

AS A PASTOR, MY life's work is to give witness to God, to raise awareness of God's work in all of life, and more specifically to witness to God's work of salvation in Jesus Christ. Day by day I concern myself with how the life of Christ is formed in believers and how the Scriptures—read, proclaimed, and studied—contribute to their spiritual formation. I believe and know from experience that ministry is not simply a matter of technique or eloquent words (even though I would like to think it is). Spiritual growth and transformation do not merely result from the innovation and persuasiveness of the preacher or the compassion and hard work of the pastor. Most of the time I just stand humbly by as the Holy Spirit transforms the hearts and minds of people and communities. Thus my interest in Calvin's pneumatology.

To give an account of the Holy Spirit in John Calvin's theology is a daunting task. Very little, if anything, in his theology is not influenced by his theology of the Holy Spirit. Princeton theologian Benjamin B. Warfield reminds us that Calvin related the whole experience of salvation specifically to the Holy Spirit's work of applying salvation to the soul. He goes so far to consider the *Institutes* "just a treatise on the work of God the Holy Spirit in making God savingly known to sinful man, and bringing sinful man into holy communion with God."[1] Warfield therefore calls Calvin the theologian of the Holy Spirit.

---

1. Warfield, *John Calvin the Theologian*, Electronic Edition by ReformationInk.

Whereas the Holy Spirit plays a central role in the thoughts of Calvin, the same cannot be said of many subsequent theologians and the church. In an article in the Presbyterian Record, John Vissers calls the Holy Spirit the Cinderella of the Trinity.[2] And he is right. Students of Scripture know the Spirit as the "shy" or elusive member of the Trinity. The problem however is that in the church the Spirit all too often becomes the neglected and forgotten member of the Trinity.[3] Let me share two examples.

A friend recently showed me a copy of the findings of a nationwide survey of adult's spiritual beliefs done by the Barna Group in 2008.[4] It reveals the diverse set of beliefs that Americans who consider themselves to be Christian adhere to. This is not surprising, but one finding stands out with regards to this topic. Most of the 1,871 self-described Christians who participated in the survey do not believe that the Holy Spirit is a living being. When asked to comment on the statement that the Holy Spirit is "a symbol of God's power or presence but is not a living entity," 38 percent strongly agreed and 20 percent agreed somewhat. Only 34 percent disagreed to varying degrees with the statement. Those who were unsure were 9 percent.

I come from a Reformed church in South Africa that has a unique tradition of celebrating Pentecost. Since the 1860s, congregations nationwide have been holding special series of services, prayer meetings, and mission fests annually during the ten days between Ascension and Pentecost. This church has a wonderful tradition of teaching and preaching about the Holy Spirit. The same church however used to be very critical and suspicious of people's experiences of the Holy Spirit and of movements that emphasize the gifts of the Spirit.

This is not unique. "The institutional church has always looked on the experience of and appeal to the Spirit as potentially subversive and in need of control," writes Daniel L. Migliore. He cautions that, "routine neglect and suspicion of the work of the Holy Spirit has damaging effects on both Christian life and Christian theology," saying that "when the work of the Holy Spirit is forgotten or suppressed, the power of God is apt to be understood as distant, hierarchical, and coercive; Christocentric faith

2. Vissers, "The Forgotten God," 37.

3. Snodgrass, "Introduction," v.

4. The Barna Group, Ltd. "Most American Christians Do Not Believe that Satan or the Holy Spirit Exist," April 10, 2009.

deteriorates into Christomonism; the authority of Scripture becomes heteronomous; the church is seen as a rigid power structure in which some members rule over others; and the sacraments degenerate into almost magical rites under the control of a clerical elite."[5]

Faith and life is bent out of shape where the work of the Spirit is neglected. Fortunately, the tide seems to be turning. A rapidly growing body of literature by both biblical and systematic theologians suggests a renewed interest in the person and work of the Holy Spirit.[6] But where does this come from?

One factor is undoubtedly the contemporary interest in spirituality. While many people are dissatisfied with the institutional church and with faith experiences where form and structure dominate over vitality and purpose, people continue to have a deep hunger for God, for an authentic faith, for genuine love and lasting relationships, and for spiritual resources to deal with the crises of our time.[7]

Another reason has to do with the authority of Scripture. The Christian community has always accepted the Scriptures as revelation, but little consensus exists regarding the interpretation of Scripture. In addition, we have seen in recently years a cultural shift from modernism to post-modernism. Modernist questions and answers no longer suffice. These include modernist views on the authority of Scripture. New formulations are required. Brueggemann, for instance, suggests that the authority of Scripture has to be reformulated in terms of authorization, i.e. how the biblical literature as voice of the Holy God, authorizes the faith community's obedience and praise.[8]

A third contributing factor is the reality we all experience of living in a pluralist world where we continually rub shoulders "with people of other religions who already have a faith."[9] In a pluralist world we have to consider the work of the Spirit beyond the Christian community. This

---

5. Migliore, *Faith Seeking Understanding*, 224.

6. Further evidence is a number of assemblies, colloquiums, and symposiums with the Holy Spirit as theme: The seventh Assembly of the World Council of Churches gathered in Canberra under the theme "Come Holy Spirit—Renew the Whole Creation"; the 6th Colloquium of the Calvin Studies Society devoted itself to "Calvin and the Holy Spirit"; the 1996 North Park Symposium on the Theological Interpretation of Scripture met to discuss the work and person of the Holy Spirit as is evidenced in their publication *Ex Auditu* 12 (1996).

7. Migliore, *Faith Seeking Understanding*, 224.

8. Brueggemann, *The Book that Breathes New Life*, 3–19

9. Vissers, "The Forgotten God," 38

begs the question about the work of the Holy Spirit in the world. How is the work of God the Spirit related to the realities of our time, our work, science, politics, and art? How is the work of the Spirit related to people who do not belong to the Christian community?

Given the indispensable role that the Holy Spirit plays in the theology of John Calvin, I believe that his thoughts can make a significant contribution to the current discussion. I therefore intend to look briefly at three aspects of Calvin's pneumatology under the headings: Spirit and Word; Spirit, Salvation and Christian Life; and Spirit in the World.

SPIRIT AND WORD

Calvin's use of and adherence to Scripture is one of the main features of his theology. Warfield, in calling Calvin the Biblical Theologian among the Reformers, writes, "Whither the Bible took him, thither he went: where scriptural declarations failed him, there he stopped short."[10] As an exegete, Calvin sets out to follow the goals to which Chrysostom aspired, namely to "never stray from a clear elaboration and explanation of the text," and to "speak with common people in mind."[11]

An integral part of this commitment to the Word is his concern with piety. This comes out clearly when he writes in an address to King Frances I (1536): "My intention was only to furnish a kind of rudiments, by which those who feel some interest in religion might be trained to true godliness." For Calvin piety has to do with knowledge; more specifically with knowledge of God and knowledge of ourselves. We can only know ourselves, he maintains, in relation to God. We think we know ourselves, but we cannot trust our image of ourselves. "We always seem to ourselves just, and upright, and wise and holy, until we are convinced by the clear evidence of our injustice, vileness, folly, and impurity."[12] In order to know ourselves more correctly, we have to know God first. He makes his point with this striking metaphor: "If at midday we either look down to the ground, or on the surrounding objects which lie open to our view, we think ourselves endued with a strong and piercing eyesight; but when we look up to the sun, and gazed at it unveiled, the sight which did

10. Warfield, *John Calvin the Theologian*.

11. Greidanus, *Preaching Christ from the Old Testament*, 127.

12. Calvin, *Institutes of the Christian Religion* (Henry Beveridge) 2008, 1.1.2.

CALVIN@500

excellently well for the earth is instantly so dazzled and confounded by the refulgence, as to oblige us to confess that our acuteness in discerning terrestrial objects is mere dimness when applied to the sun."[13] Knowledge of God precedes and gives birth to our knowledge of ourselves.

But how do we know God? Calvin follows the distinction made in Ps 19. We know God in creation and in Scripture. God wants people to know him. And all people can know God, Calvin insists, because God has naturally planted in all human minds a sense of his Godhead.[14] He constantly renews and enlarges this by holding out to us a mirror of his Deity in his works.[15] "Those blessings which unceasingly distil to us from heaven are like streams conducting us to the fountain," he writes.[16] By contemplating God's works in creation and the continuing government of the world, we know God as Creator. But we are sinful and therefore unable to receive a pure and clear knowledge of God simply by contemplating his works in creation. Not only are we forgetful, we are inclined to all kinds of error, and we are bent on worshiping the fabrications of our own hearts instead of God. We see a myriad of God images in the creation mirror, but they often are out of focus. God's revelation in creation, marvelous and wondrous as it is, is not sufficient for a clear knowledge of God.

This is where the Scriptures come in. God comes to our aid by giving the Word to lead us to knowledge of God as Redeemer in Christ. Scripture, in revealing Christ to us, functions like a pair of glasses: "For as the aged, or those whose sight is defective, when any book, however fair, is set before them, though they perceive that there is something written are scarcely able to make out two consecutive words, but when

13. Ibid., 1.1.2.

14. Ibid., 1.3.1.

15. Ibid., 1.6.1.

16. Ibid., 1.1.1. The following quotes are also noteworthy: God "doth manifest his perfections in the structure of the whole universe, and daily place himself in our view, that we cannot open our eyes without being compelled to behold him" (ibid., 1.5.1). "On each of his works his glory is engraved in characters so bright, so distinct, and so illustrious, that none, however dull and illiterate, can plead ignorance of their excuse" (ibid., 1.5.2). "There is no portion of the world, however minute, that does not exhibit at least some sparks of beauty; while it is impossible to contemplate the vast and beautiful fabric as it extends around, without being overwhelmed by the immense weight of glory" (ibid., 1.5.2). "None who have the use of their eyes can be ignorant of the divine skill manifested so conspicuously in the endless variety, yet distinct and well-ordered array, of the heavenly host" (ibid., 1.5.2).

BOOY—*The Holy Spirit in the Thoughts of John Calvin* 43

aided by glasses, begin to read distinctly, so Scripture gathering together the impressions of Deity, which, till then, lay confused in our minds, dissipates the darkness, and shows us the true God clearly."[17]

Calvin first establishes the necessity of Scripture as a guide and teacher to God, and then continues by asking the essential question, how do we know that we can trust the Scriptures? He does some of his best work as he explains the relationship between Spirit and Word. He is very practical about it, holding that there can be no faith in the Scriptures unless we are convinced that God is the author. He makes it clear that "the truth of Scripture must derive from a higher source than human conjectures, judgments, or reasons." This higher source he finds in the "secret testimony of the Spirit."[18] Through the testimony of the Spirit, God bears witness to his own words to give credibility to it and to seal it upon the hearts of believers. "Scripture carries its own evidence along with it," he says, "and deigns not to submit to proofs and arguments, but owes the full conviction with which we ought to receive it to the testimony of the Spirit."[19] Any certainty we have of the Word comes from the inner testimony of the Spirit, "for the Lord has so knit together the certainty of his Word and his Spirit, that our minds are duly imbued with reverence for the Word when the Spirit shining upon it enables us there to behold the face of God."[20]

The importance of this doctrine in Calvin's time has to do with two views of scriptural authority which he disputed. The Roman Catholic Church claimed that the authority of Scripture is derived from the church, and Anabaptists on the other hand made claims of specific, private revelations of the Spirit. Both, Calvin maintains, make the fatal mistake of separating Word and Spirit. Word and Spirit belong together like the sun and the light that radiates from it.

Not only the authority of the Scriptures, but also the effect of the Word on our minds and hearts, depend solely on the illuminating work of the Spirit. The Spirit illuminates the Word and impresses it on our hearts in order to exhibit Christ. Calvin maintains that all of Scripture

17. Ibid., 1.6.1.

18. Ibid., 1.7.4. Calvin elaborates on the inner secret witness of the Spirit in Book 1 chapters 7 and 9.

19. Ibid., 1.7.5.

20. Ibid., 1.9.3.

points to Christ[21] and the one covenant of grace that runs through the Scriptures. This covenant is like the rising sun that progressively increases in light.[22] As the Spirit exhibits Christ, we are enabled through the Word to appropriate the blood of Christ and to respond in faith and reverent love. Both our minds and hearts are touched. Here Calvin interestingly puts more emphasis on the heart than on the mind, the reason being that "there is more distrust in the heart than blindness in the mind"; that it is "more difficult to inspire the soul with security than to imbue it with knowledge."[23]

Calvin maintains that the Word has no effect if the Spirit of God does not engage our hearts and minds. Without the Spirit, the letter is dead (1 Cor 2). He makes his point with another marvelous metaphor: "The Word is, in regard to those to whom it is preached, like the sun which shines upon all but is of no use to the blind . . . the Word cannot penetrate our mind unless the Spirit, the internal teacher, by his enlightening power makes an entrance for it."[24]

The matter of the authority of Scripture is once again on the forefront of theology with "battles for the Bible" being fought in various parts of the church.[25] Calvin's contribution, the doctrine of the inner testimony of the Spirit, is a breath of fresh air. It is a gift to the church. It is original[26] and as relevant today as it was in Calvin's own time.

SPIRIT, SALVATION AND CHRISTIAN LIFE

I referred earlier to the contemporary interest in spirituality. As much as this excites us, we also have to acknowledge that much of what is presented as spirituality today has little, if anything, to do with Holy Spirit. I recently attended a presentation on "spiritual care" at our local hospital. Nothing in the material referred to Christ or Holy Spirit, nor was any mention made of God in a more generic sense. This is just one

21. Opitz, *Calvin's Appeal to Scripture*, online: www.calvin09.org.

22. Calvin, *Institutes* 1.3.1.

23. Ibid., 3.2.34.

24. Ibid.

25. See N. T. Wright, *The Last Word*, 3f and Brueggemann, *The Book That Breathes New Life*, xiiif.

26. Hesselink, "Calvin, the Holy Spirit, and Mystical Union," 16 and McLeod, "A Taste of Pure Religion," 31–32. Calvin was the first to formulate the doctrine of the inner testimony of the Spirit.

BOOY—*The Holy Spirit in the Thoughts of John Calvin*   45

example of the way in which spirituality is viewed simply as an aspect of our inner selves. Calvin's thoughts on the other hand provide the strong christological and pneumatological roots necessary for a Christian understanding of and approach to spirituality.

Let me explain. Having talked in Book I of the *Institutes* about the "knowledge of God the Creator" and in Book II about the "knowledge of God the Redeemer in Christ," Calvin turns his attention in Book III to the "mode of obtaining the grace of Christ" and in Book IV to "the external means by which God invites us to fellowship with Christ and keeps us in it." Book III, and especially chapter 1, is the *locus classicus* of Calvin's work on the Holy Spirit. Hesselink reminds us that "nowhere is Calvin more obviously the theologian of the Holy Spirit than in his understanding of Christian life."[27] His purpose is pastoral because Calvin is convinced that God's Word is not given for mere knowledge, but for the benefit of believers.[28] He wrestles with the question of how the benefits of Christ become available to us. How do we obtain the grace of Christ? How do we come to possess "the blessings which God has bestowed on his only begotten Son . . . to enrich the poor and needy"?[29]

Calvin's reason for asking is simple: "So long as we are without Christ and separated from him, nothing which he suffered and did for the salvation of the human race is of the least benefit to us."[30] How can anyone benefit from Christ's work unless he/she is united with him? Christ must become ours and dwell in us. Calvin makes an enormous contribution in this regard. As Joel Beeke writes, "Calvin's doctrine of union with Christ is one of the most consistently influential features of his theology and ethics."[31]

How then does Christ become ours and dwell in us? The answer is already given in the title of chapter 1: "The benefits of Christ made available to us by the secret operation of the Spirit" (Notice how the wording here corresponds with the way he speaks about the inner secret witness of the Spirit with regards to the Word.) Referring to Rom 5:5, Calvin concludes that communion with the Holy Spirit is the only way to taste the love of the Father and the benefits of Christ. The Holy Spirit draws

27. Hesselink, "Calvin, the Holy Spirit, and Mystical Union," 16.

28. Rogers, "The Mystery of the Spirit in Three Traditions," 247.

29. Calvin, *Institutes* 3.1.1.

30. Ibid., 3.1.1.

31. Beeke, *Calvin on Piety*, 127.

us to Christ and in doing so gives us minds and hearts far above our own understanding. "It is only when the human intellect is irradiated by the light of the Holy Spirit that it begins to have a taste of those things which pertain to the kingdom of God; previously it was too stupid and senseless to have any relish for them."[32]

Calvin assigns the highest ranking to the union between Christ and believers, but what does he mean by it? Union with Christ through the Spirit means that Christ makes us one with himself by the Spirit. We now have a fellowship of righteousness with him. He grafts us into his body so that we enjoy all his gifts. Calvin calls this *the* "residence of Christ in our hearts"[33] and uses the term mystical union to describe it. This term may sound strange to us, but Calvin makes it abundantly clear that the mystical union between Christ and believers never includes a mingling or a mixing of substance between us and Christ. He fiercely combats and refutes the thoughts of Osiander who taught an "essential righteousness" that issues in a mixture of substance "by which God, transfusing himself into us, makes us as it were a part of himself."[34] Union with Christ through the Spirit does not mean absorption into the sphere of divine being.[35] The mystical union with Christ is historical, ethical, and personal, but it is not a union of essence.[36]

The principal work of the Spirit in uniting us to Christ is faith.[37] Calvin defines faith as "a firm and sure knowledge of the divine favor toward us, founded on the truth of a free promise in Christ, and revealed to our minds and sealed on our hearts by the Holy Spirit."[38] In his understanding, faith, produced in us by the Spirit, is knowledge of Christ. Faith embraces Christ as he is offered by the Father, and it grafts us into the death of Christ so that we "derive from it a secret energy as the twig does from the root."[39] This knowledge of Christ, Calvin insists, leads to obedience to the gospel (Rom 1:5). Faith is therefore grounded in the Word of which the Holy Spirit is the inner teacher. The relationship

---

32. Calvin, *Institutes* 3.2.34.

33. Ibid., 3.11.10.

34. Ibid., 3.11.5.

35. Ibid., 3.11.10.

36. Beeke, *Calvin on Piety*, 128.

37. Calvin, *Institutes* 3.1.4.

38. Ibid., 3.2.7.

39. Beeke, *Calvin on Piety*, 129.

BOOY—*The Holy Spirit in the Thoughts of John Calvin*

between Word and Faith is consequently inseparable. "Take the Word away," Calvin states, "and no faith will remain."[40]

The Holy Spirit not only originates faith, but also increases it in our lives.[41] A characteristic of Calvin's thoughts in this regard is that faith leads to a double grace—the grace of justification and the grace of sanctification[42]—because Christ is being offered by the Father for both our justification and our sanctification. "Christ confers upon us, and we obtain through faith, both free reconciliation and newness of life."[43] Justification and sanctification are united in Christ, and cannot be separated just as we cannot divide Christ into two parts. The connection is mutual and undivided, even though each has distinct properties.[44]

In Calvin's understanding, justification is the work of the Holy Spirit who extends the righteousness of Christ to us, on the basis of which God considers us righteous.[45] Justification comes to us; it does not come from us.[46] The testimony of the Spirit seals the cleansing and sacrifice of Christ and engraves it on our hearts;[47] it seals the forgiveness of sins in the elect.[48]

Justification by faith is the central doctrine for both Luther and Calvin, but Calvin goes beyond Luther in emphasizing sanctification, the process by which the believer is gradually conformed to the image of Christ. Beeke calls it the "re-making of the believer by the Holy Spirit."[49] The Spirit is the Spirit of sanctification, the "seed and root of heavenly life in us."[50]

40. Calvin, *Institutes* 3.2.6.

41. Ibid., 3.2.33.

42. Ibid., 3.11.1, 3.3.19, and 3.2.8.

43. Ibid., 3.2.1.

44. Ibid., 3.11.6, 3.3.1 "holiness of life . . . is inseparable from the free imputation of righteousness."

45. Ibid., 3.11.2.

46. Vial, *The Importance of the Holy Spirit and Its Role in Salvation*, www.calvin09 .org. The term foreign grace has been used to explain that justification comes to us, not from us.

47. Calvin, *Institutes* 3.1.1.

48. Ibid., 3.2.11.

49. Beeke, *Calvin on Piety*, 130.

50. Calvin, *Institutes* 3.1.2.

In talking about sanctification or regeneration, we have to discuss repentance.[51] Repentance follows faith and is produced by it. Calvin defines repentance as "a real conversion of our life unto God, proceeding from sincere and serious fear of God, and consisting in the mortification of our flesh and the old man, and the quickening of the Spirit."[52] God destroys the dominion of sin by supplying the agency of the Spirit,[53] but although we are purged by the Spirit from iniquity, there still remain in us many vices and weakness.[54] It is not true, Calvin argues, that those who are under the guidance of the Spirit do not sin, because we do not return to a state of innocence. The Christian life is a "constant study and exercise in mortifying the flesh until it is slain and the Spirit of God obtains dominion in us."[55] We have to be smitten by the Sword of the Spirit and annihilated, Calvin says.[56] It makes sense then that Calvin views self-denial as the summary of Christian life.[57] He understands the entire Christian life in terms of the working of the Holy Spirit in uniting us to Christ and in effecting justification and sanctification.

SPIRIT IN THE WORLD

Calvin's thoughts on the Holy Spirit make a tremendous contribution to the discussion about salvation and the Christian life. Of equal significance are his thoughts on the work of the Spirit in the world. We are facing enormous ecological, social, and political challenges—climate change, poverty, world hunger, conflict, tension, religious intolerance. The world is hurting and broken. Christians today also live, as I have indicated before, in a pluralist world. We are in need therefore of a robust theology that can relate the work of God with the dire realities of our time.[58] Such a theology, I believe, can be found in Calvin's thoughts on the work of the Spirit in the world.

51. Ibid., 3.3.

52. Ibid., 3.3.5.

53. Ibid., 3.3.11.

54. Ibid., 3.3.14.

55. Ibid., 3.3.20 and 3.3.5.

56. Ibid., 3.3.8.

57. Ibid., 3.7.

58. Rice, *Reformed Spirituality*, 162.

Douglas K. Harink points out in an article entitled "Spirit in the World in the Theology of John Calvin"[59] that Calvin had a broader understanding of the Spirit's work than is often accredited to him. References to the Spirit's work in all spheres of creation, culture, and society are implicit in his theology. These affirm that the Spirit works beyond the Christian community and lives of individual Christians.

In order to understand Calvin's thoughts on the Spirit in the world, one has to begin with Gen 1. Calvin asserts that the Spirit was at work in "cherishing the confused mass" even before the beauty of the world existed.[60] He explains in his Genesis commentary how the world was an "indigested mass" before God perfected it, and that the power of the Spirit was necessary in order to sustain it.[61]

Not only was the Spirit at work before creation, but the Spirit continues to work in all spheres of creation "sustaining, invigorating, and quickening all things in heaven and on earth."[62] He writes that God fills, and animates all things by virtue of the Spirit, each according to its peculiar nature.[63] The work of the God in creation is superbly celebrated in the fifth chapter of book 1, where Calvin talks about the knowledge of God in creation. Oliver Rice puts it like this, "The creation theatre buzzes with activity and shines with the glory of God, not merely because of natural processes, but because of the ceaseless activity and grace of the Holy Spirit, the life-giver, within it."[64] Without the work of the Spirit in preserving creation, the world will not be able to sustain itself and will consequently degenerate into chaos.

The Spirit also works in human history where the Spirit's work is evident in the fruits of human knowledge, art, and labor. Art, literature, technology, policy-making, economy, science, philosophy, medicine, and music all give evidence to the work of the Spirit.[65] Calvin sees skill, knowledge, and intelligence as blessings which the Spirit "dispenses to whom he will for the common good." Yang-en Cheng aptly reminds us of Calvin's view that common grace and natural gifts are bestowed on

59. Harink, "Spirit in the World in the Theology of John Calvin," 61–81.

60. Calvin, *Institutes* 1.13.14.

61. Calvin, *Genesis 1:2* in *Commentaries on the First Book of Moses called Genesis*.

62. Calvin, *Institutes* 1.13.14.

63. Ibid., 2.2.16.

64. Rice, *Calvin's theology of the Holy Spirit*, online: www.e-n.org.uk.

65. Calvin, *Institutes* 2.2.13–16.

all people, even on those who lack faith.[66] Calvin consequently insists that we avail ourselves of the fruits of human skill and intelligence, because "the Lord has been pleased to assist us by the work and ministry of (even) the ungodly in physics, dialectics, mathematics, and other similar sciences."[67] He does not want us to neglect these spontaneous and natural gifts of the Lord.

Continuity of truth plays an important role in Calvin's thoughts on the Spirit in the world. He calls the Spirit the "only fountain of truth." In talking for instance about unbelieving authors, he points out that truth in their works shows that their fallen minds are still adorned and invested with admirable gifts from their creator.[68] The same can be said about truth as expressed in the work of scientists, philosophers, mathematicians, biologists, psychologists, and physicians. We cannot deem it noble and praiseworthy, Calvin maintains, without tracing it to the hand of God. *Living Faith* echoes these sentiments when it says about the church's mission and other faiths, "We recognize that truth and goodness in them are the work of God's Spirit, the author of all truth."[69] Another document of the Presbyterian Church in Canada, *A Catechism For Today*, expresses the same sentiment.

Is the pursuit of science incompatible with faith in God? No. We believe that God created a universe with its own order which we can explore by scientific investigation. Yet scientific investigation and the Christian faith differ in their goals and approaches. While science proceeds by theorizing about and testing the universe, the Christian faith is primarily concerned with knowing God who exists above and beyond creation. The Christian faith values all efforts to understand the universe that God has made. We are guided by the conviction that all truth comes from God.[70]

The Spirit is at work in the world; in the Christian community, and also beyond the Christian community; in nature and also in human history. This has ecological, social, and ethical implications for the church. The Spirit who works beyond the church is always ahead of the church,

66. Yang-en Cheng, "Calvin on the Work of the Holy Spirit and Spiritual Gifts," 186–87.

67. Calvin, *Institutes* 2.2.16.

68. Ibid., 2.2.15.

69. Calvin, *Living Faith*, 9.2.1.

70. *Catechism For Today*, Sunday 2, Question 4.

calling the church to fulfill its mission to the world. The Spirit's work in bringing believers to Christ is aimed not just at the personal growth of the believer, but at the transformation of the world through works of service and love. The church is called in this regard to solidarity with the poor and oppressed, and to an ecological concern that echoes God's concern for creation.[71]

Awareness that the Spirit is preservingly and re-creatingly at work in every society and culture, also has implications for the way Christians engage in dialogue in a pluralist world. We learn to engage in dialogue with a sense of gratitude for all the good gifts of the Spirit that are already displayed among other people, listening for signs and words of truth, pointing to the truth of Christ in which other people live already, and realizing at all times that the Spirit, not us, works transformation.[72]

CONCLUSION

Having covered a lot of ground, we have nevertheless not nearly exhausted the contribution of Calvin's thoughts on the Holy Spirit to our understanding of the work of God and the current situation of the church in the world. We have just scratched the surface.

But I would like to offer the following short prayer by Calvin as a summary and a reminder of the ongoing work of the Spirit in sanctifying us and the faith communities of which we are part:

> Almighty God, thou hast seen fit to take us to be priests, and hast chosen us while we were not only in a lowly condition but even profane and strangers to holiness, and hast dedicated us to thyself by the Holy Spirit. Grant now that we may offer ourselves to thee as a holy sacrifice.[73]

---

71. Chung, "Calvin and the Holy Spirit," 49–53.

72. Harink, "Spirit in the World in the Theology of John Calvin," 73–81.

73. Rice and Williamson, *A Book of Reformed Prayers*, 19. Calvin apparently prayed this prayer as part of a lecture on Mal 1:9.

4

A Reformed Culture of Persuasion

John Calvin's "Two Kingdoms" and the Theological Origins of the Public Sphere

TORRANCE KIRBY

THE CONSPICUOUS GROWTH OF a popular "culture of persuasion" fostered by the Protestant Reformation contributed in no small part to the genesis of the early-modern public sphere.[1] Whereas in his well-known account of the "structural transformation" of the public sphere Jürgen Habermas placed a primary emphasis upon the commercial activity of global mercantile companies, our purpose is to draw closer attention to changes in religious assumptions as a source of explanation of this phenomenon, specifically through an exploration of the theological anthropology of John Calvin.

By the end of the sixteenth century, and largely owing to this cultural shift, the "moral ontology" which defined religious identity had come to be radically transformed for both the evangelical avant-garde and the Catholic reformers newly energized by the Council of Trent.[2] While at a certain level the distinction between the primary ontological "orders" of the divine and the human—between eternal and temporal

---

1. Habermas, *The Structural Transformation of the Public Sphere*, 14–26.

2. The language of "moral ontology" as it is employed here is borrowed from Charles Taylor, *Sources of the Self,* 5–8, 9, 10, 41, *passim*. According to Taylor, the concept of moral ontology refers to the essential objectivity of the deepest assumptions concerning human spiritual identity and our place within the cosmic order. In this respect the argument of *Sources of the Self* has been interpreted as an effort of metaphysical "retrieval." See, e.g., Kerr, "The Self and the Good: Taylor's Moral Ontology," 84–104.

planes of reality, between soul and body, grace and nature, immortality and mortality—was jointly affirmed by both Protestant reformers and Catholic defenders of traditional religious identity, the impulse towards comprehensive Reformation of the doctrine and practice of the church, as well as the reinterpretation of the principles underlying secular political life, was based upon a deep-seated theological difference on how to interpret the precise disposition of these ontological distinctions.

For those who embraced evangelical reform, religious identity was no longer held to be a matter cosmologically "given" or assumed as embedded within the hierarchically ordered institutions and elaborate theurgical apparatus of late-medieval sacramental culture which, for more than a millennium, had served to mediate between individual Christians and the divine. In sharp contrast with the traditional hierarchical and sacramental model based upon the ontological assumption of a gradual mediation or *dispositio* of reality whereby the orders of nature and grace, mortal and immortal being, body and spirit were linked together in a continuous and contiguous cosmic whole, the sixteenth-century Protestant reformers insisted rather on a sharply defined hypostatic demarcation between the inner, subjective space of the individual believer and the external, public space of Christian institutional life, whether ecclesiastical, sacramental, or political.[3] One of the momentous consequences of this revolution in "moral ontology" was the abrupt displacement of the hierarchical mediation offered by the intricate structures of late-medieval sacramental culture. This was achieved largely through the instruments of *persuasion*—that is, by means of argument, textual interpretation, exhortation, reasoned opinion, and moral advice—disseminated through both pulpit and press.[4] This alternative culture of persuasion, together with the secularizing process of "disenchantment" that it came to embody, presupposes a radically different conception of ontological mediation between the primary orders of reality.[5] This Weberian theme thus underpins the gradual transforma-

3. A classical formulation of the ontology of hierarchical "dispositio" is found in Augustine's *de civitate Dei*. See Augustine, *The City of God against the pagans*, translated and edited by R.W. Dyson, XIX.13: "The peace of the whole universe is the tranquillity of order—and order is the arrangement of things equal and unequal in a pattern which assigns to each is proper position." For further discussion of the ontology of hierarchy see Kirby, *Richard Hooker, Reformer and Platonist*, 29–44.

4. See Pettegree, *Reformation and the Culture of Persuasion*.

5. On Max Weber's concept of the secularizing process of "disenchantment," see

tion from a ritually grounded "representative" publicity in the direction of what eventually takes shape as a recognizably modern, secular public sphere.

In his *Institutio*, John Calvin formulates with unmatched clarity the theological first principles which underlie the inception and development of the early-modern culture of persuasion.[6] In his rightly famous definition of Christian liberty in Book III, chapter 19, Calvin articulates the principle of this new moral ontology—what one might even risk identifying as the ontology of classical modernity—with his careful (one is tempted to say "Cartesian") distinction between the "spiritual" government of the forum of the conscience (*forum conscientiæ*) and the "civil" government of the external, political forum (*forum externum*).[7] This distinction is the foundation of Calvin's account of the so-called *duplex gubernatio*: "in man government is twofold." That government "by which the conscience is trained to piety and divine worship" he calls a "spiritual kingdom" (*regnum spirituale*), while in sharp contradistinction, he defines the "political kingdom" (*regnum politicum*) as that "by which the individual is instructed in those duties which, as men and citizens, we are bold to perform."[8] A forensic distinction between the realm of the conscience and an external, political realm is traceable back several centuries before Calvin. In Dante's *Paradiso*, Thomas Aquinas introduces the Florentine to one of the shining lights in the heaven of the Sun, the great twelfth-century canon lawyer of Bologna: "Next flames the light of Gratian's smile, who taught / In either forum, and in both gives pleasure / To Paradise, by the good work he wrought."[9] While this allusion to the two *fora* might have puzzled the author of the *Decretum*, by the late thirteenth and fourteenth centuries it had become a commonplace of the Canon Law to distinguish between the outward forum of an external

---

Charles Taylor's introduction to Gauchet, *The Disenchantment of the World*, ix ff. See also Taylor's *A Secular Age*. See also Lassman and Velody, "Max Weber on Science"; Lassman and Velody, *Max Weber's 'Science as a Vocation'*, 3–31, 159 ff.

6. Calvin, *Institutes of the Christian Religion* (Henry Beveridge), III.19. This edition is cited throughout unless otherwise indicated.

7. See also Calvin, *Institutes*, IV.10.3. Descartes distinction between "*res cogitans*" and "*res extensa*" in the *Meditations* displays an interesting parallel with Calvin's account of the twofold government. Descartes, *Meditations*, 55, 128, 188.

8. Calvin, *Institutes*, III.19.15. See van Drunen, "The Two Kingdoms," 248–66; Edgar, "Ethics."

9. Dante, *Paradiso*, X.103–5 ("che l'uno e l'altro foro / aiutò sì che piace paradiso").

KIRBY—A Reformed Culture of Persuasion

jurisdiction exercised in the ecclesiastical courts and the internal forum of spiritual jurisdiction in the practice of penance. The terms *forum poenitentiae* and *forum conscientiae* were virtually synonymous.[10] Thomas Aquinas himself distinguishes between the external forum and the forum of the conscience in his *Commentary on the Sentences*.[11]

According to the systematic structure of the argument of Calvin's *Institute*, the precise character and full significance of the vast gap which distinguishes the two ontological realms associated with the *duplex gubernatio* only becomes fully apparent through a reflection upon the reformer's pivotal soteriological claim concerning "justification by faith alone" in the series of chapters immediately preceding the discussion of liberty, namely in Book III, chapters 1 through 18.[12] On the intimate connection of the first principles of reformed soteriology with this new moral ontology Calvin is categorical; he describes his exposition of the logic of the liberty of conscience in the terms of the *duplex gubernatio* as nothing less than "an appendage of justification."[13] Moreover, Calvin's distinction of this "twofold government" provides the critical groundwork for his later discussion in Book IV of what he terms the chief "external" means of grace comprising three principal components: first the visible church, its jurisdiction, laws, and powers; secondly, the sacraments of baptism and the Eucharist; and thirdly, civil government, a political theology which addresses the duties and authority of magistrates, the external necessity and moral utility of civil laws, and the obligations of citizens to observe both. On two altogether decisive points Calvin is emphatically clear: first, the clear exposition of the nature of Christian liberty is "a thing of prime necessity, and apart from knowledge of it

---

10. Goering, "The Internal Forum," 379–425. See also Mostaza, "*Forum internum—forum externum* (En torno a la naturaleza juridica del fuero interno)," 253–331, at 258 n. 15; 24 (1968): 339–64.

11. "Ad secundum dicendum, quod sacerdotes parochiales habent quidem jurisdictionem in subditos suos quantum ad forum conscientiae, sed non quantum ad forum judiciale; quia non possunt coram eis conveniri in causis contentiosis; et ideo excommunicare non possunt, sed absolvere possunt in foro poenitentiali; et quamvis forum poenitentiale sit dignius, tamen in foro judiciali major solemnitas requiritur; quia in eo oportet quod non solum Deo, sed etiam homini satisfiat." *Scriptum super Sententiis* 4.18.2.2.1 ad 2. Cited by Goering, "The Internal Forum," 380.

12. Calvin, *Institutes*, III.11.1—18.10

13. Ibid., III.19.1

consciences dare undertake almost nothing without doubting;"[14] and secondly, the soteriological principle upon which this liberty depends, namely justification by faith only, is itself by Calvin's own account nothing less than "the main hinge on which religion turns."[15] For these two reasons, Calvin's new moral ontology of the *duplex gubernatio*, and consequently his entire political theology, are anchored at the very core of his theological position.

While Calvin's contribution to the foundations of modern politics has been the subject of extensive critical discussion for many years as evidenced by an enormous and continually growing body of commentary,[16] there are two particular aspects of his radical re-formulation of moral ontology that stand in need of closer attention. First, Calvin's treatment of the "twofold government" may help to elucidate the neglected but vitally important question of the religious and theological underpinnings of the emerging secular public sphere—a sphere marked above all else by its manifestation of what Andrew Pettegree has very helpfully designated the early-modern "culture of persuasion."[17] Diversely manifest in print (e.g., sermons, pamphlets and tracts, printed proclamations, parliamentary statutes) as well as in various other publicly "staged" productions (e.g., the preaching of sermons, performance of plays, public trials and executions, and formal disputations) all of which effectively combined in the middle years of the sixteenth century to fill an increasingly conspicuous void left by a progressive dismantling of the traditional, late-medieval "sacramental culture," the growth of this culture of persuasion finds its focused theological articulation in Calvin's definition of Christian liberty. This definition provides an apt model for the interpretation of the moral ontology of the emerging redefinition of the public sphere. Briefly stated, for Calvin the public sphere is nothing less than the newfound and necessary means of mediating across the immense gulf that reformed soteriology was responsible for opening up between the "two kingdoms" in the first place, namely between the private, inward realm of the individual self—Calvin's *forum conscientiæ*—and the public, outward realm of the common institutional order—Calvin's *forum externum et*

14. Ibid.

15. Ibid., III.11.1, 7.

16. For a helpful critical overview of this extensive literature see Hancock, *Calvin and the Foundations of Modern Politics*, 1–22. See also Kelly, *The Emergence of Liberty*.

17. See Pettegree's Introduction to *Reformation and the Culture of Persuasion*.

politicum. On this view, the public religious discourse of the Protestant Reformers—specifically religious persuasion through translation of the scriptures into the vernacular, biblical exegesis, preaching, and moral exhortation, in short the promotion of *"fides ex auditu"*—presents an early exemplar, indeed arguably the archetype, of a uniquely early-modern approach to negotiating the interaction between the inward spiritual life of the discreet and autonomous individual self, and the outward collective requirements of the wider political community.[18] In this respect, Calvin's treatment of Christian liberty contributes to a radical rethinking of the relationship between private and public space and thus to a substantive reformulation of moral ontology which would in turn give rise to the institutions of modern civil society.[19]

The second major point to be addressed in connection with Calvin's theme of the *duplex gubernatio* concerns the useful light it sheds upon the sources of modern secularity. The secular as we have come to know it presents itself most frequently in opposition to religious concerns. By proposing a consideration of Calvin's theology as counting among the significant sources of the political culture of modernity, it is clear that any simple dichotomy between the secular and the religious is bound to be highly suspect from the outset. On the contrary, it would appear to be self-evident on an attentive reading of Calvin that some of the significant sources of modern secularity derive primary meaning from a profoundly religious discourse. The secondary claim, then, is that this modern secularity is at root a theological orientation, whether or not it knows itself to be so. This is in part a reiteration of Charles Taylor's thesis in the opening chapters of *A Secular Age.*[20]

It must be said, of course, that the general assertion of a close connection of modernity with Protestantism in general and with Calvin in particular is a commonplace, indeed "old hat," so much so as to have become thoroughly unfashionable. The Whig historians, for example, who have been the target of relentless revisionist critique for more than a generation, were apt to point to Calvinism's formative contribution to

---

18. De Koster, *Light for the City*, 63–88. On the individual "irreducible self," see Stevenson, *Sovereign Grace*, 11–58.

19. See the first chapter titled "The Bulwarks of Belief" in Taylor *A Secular Age*, 25–42.

20. See Taylor, *A Secular Age*, chapter 1, sections 6 and 7, 54–75.

modernity, and especially to modern conceptions of political liberty.[21] From the somewhat different perspective of German Idealism, G. W. F. Hegel famously observed in his *Philosophy of History* that it was the Protestant world that had advanced to such a degree in its thinking as "to realize the absolute culmination of self-consciousness" and that this *was* the birth of modernity.[22] Max Weber's thesis of "disenchantment," and the links between the Protestant ethic and modern capitalism to which he drew attention, tends in a similar direction.[23] None of these accounts, however, probe the depths of the deep theological groundwork implicit in their claim. John Witte, Sheldon Wolin, and Quentin Skinner, to name some more recent critics, have addressed this question from diverse angles.[24] Skinner understands modernity as the emergence of a purely secular politics liberated from what he plainly regards as the impediment of religion.[25] Charles Taylor, however, puts his finger on the critical problem when he pointedly remarks at the outset of *Sources of the Self* that the "moral sources of emerging modern identity are far richer than the impoverished language of modernity's most zealous defenders," and he goes on to add that the moral ontology behind any given set of views is more likely than not to remain largely implicit.[26] A critical element of this impoverishment of language is a neglect of the ontological, theological, and metaphysical categories which, in Taylor's view, constitute the groundwork for these sources of modern secular identity. Such has certainly been the case with Calvin's contribution to the formulation of these questions surrounding the emergent culture of persuasion and the sources of an early-modern conception of the secular. We propose that a prime focus for both of these questions ought to include a probing of

---

21. See, e.g., Babington Macaulay, *The History of England*; Gardiner, *History of the Commonwealth and Protectorate*; Jordan, *The Development of Religious Toleration in England*.

22. Hegel, *Lectures on the Philosophy of History*, 463.

23. See the new translation by Stephen Kalberg of Weber's *The Protestant Ethic*. See also Graf, "Calvin im Plural," plenary paper presented at the conference "Calvin et son Influence, 1509–2009," held in Geneva on 24–27 May, 2009.

24. Wolin, "Calvin and the Political Education of Protestantism," chap. 6; Witte, *The Reformation of Rights*.

25. Skinner, *The Foundations of Modern Political Thought*, vol. 2.

26. Taylor, *Sources of the Self*, 3, 7. Taylor argues that modernity "isn't just a story of loss, of subtraction." See ibid., 26–29.

the depth of their common theological foundations in Calvin's discourse on Christian liberty.

CALVIN'S "TWO GOVERNMENTS"

To this end let us examine more closely the hinge which not only links the two orders of being but also ties together the theological and political dimensions of Calvin's thought. Calvin is well aware of the potential for confusion in this delicate negotiation. The pivotal passage in the *Institutio* reads thus:

> in order that none of us may stumble on that stone [i.e. the relation of Christian freedom to the law] let us first consider that there is a twofold government (*duplex esse in homine regimen*) in man: one aspect is spiritual, whereby the conscience is instructed in piety and in reverencing God; the second is political, whereby man is educated for the duties of humanity and citizenship that must be maintained among men. These are usually called the "spiritual" and the "temporal" jurisdiction (not improper terms) by which is meant that the former sort of government pertains to the life of the soul, while the latter has to do with the concerns of the present life—not only with food and clothing but with laying down laws whereby a man may live his life among other men holily, honorably, and temperately. For the former resides in the inner mind, while the latter regulates only outward behavior. The one we may call the spiritual kingdom (*regnum spirituale*), the other, the political kingdom (*regnum politicum*). Now these two, as we have divided them, must always be examined separately; and while one is being considered, we must call away and turn aside the mind from thinking about the other. There are in man, so to speak, two worlds, over which different kings and different laws have authority.[27]

It should be observed that Calvin's thinking on the question of the twofold government has a significant development in terms of its systematic placement over the course of his multiple revisions of the *Institutio*.[28] In the original edition of 1536, this description of the dis-

27. Calvin, *Institutes*, III.19.15; translated by Battles, 847.

28. Five Latin editions of the *Institutio Christianæ Religionis* were published in Calvin's lifetime (1536, 1539, 1543, 1550, and 1559). The first French edition appeared in 1541, corresponding to his 1539 Latin edition. Jean Calvin, *Institution de la religion chrétienne* (1541), edition critique par Olivier Mille. Much like the influence of the Authorized Version of the Bible on standard English, Calvin's French translations of

tinction between two orders of governance is presented as an introduction to his discussion of civil and ecclesiastical government in the final chapter, the chief subject matter of what became part IV on the "external means of grace" in the much expanded definitive version of the work published in 1559.[29] In this final edition there are a number of important invocations of the *duplex gubernatio* in Book IV, e.g., in the discussion of the legislative power and on the necessity of coercive civil government as one of the external means of grace.[30] In IV.10 of the 1559 edition he identifies the two governments as belonging respectively to the forum of the conscience (*forum conscientiæ*) and the external, political forum (*forum externum*).[31] Nonetheless, Calvin places the principal definition of Christian freedom and the twofold government in the third book of the final edition where the primary concern is psychological and soteriological, i.e., focus on the inner, subjective mode of obtaining the gifts of grace, rather than on the political and institutional forms *per se*.

It is clear from the 1559 edition that for Calvin it is insufficient simply to describe secular government as a negative consequence of human depravity. It is not only "owing to human perverseness that supreme power on earth is lodged in kings and other governors, but by Divine Providence, and the holy decree of Him to whom it has seemed good so to govern the affairs of men, since he is present, and also presides in enacting laws and exercising judicial equity."[32] That Calvin regards secular government in a substantially more positive light than Augustine's "penalty and remedy for sin" (*pœna et remedium peccati*)[33] ultimately derives theological justification from the deliberate systematic transposition of the principal exposition of Christian liberty and the *duplex gubernatio*

these Latin editions helped to shape the French language for generations. The final edition of the *Institutes* is about five times the length of the first edition.

29. *Christianæ religionis institutio: totam ferè pietatis summa[m], & quicquid est in doctrina salutis cognitu necessarium, complectens: omnibus pietatis studiosis lectu dignissimum opus, ac recens editum. Præfatio ad Christianissimum Regem Franciæ, qua hic ei liber pro confessione fidei offertur* (Basle: Thomas Platteru[m] & Balthasar Lasium, 1536), chap. 6. For an English translation, see *Institutes of the Christian Religion: 1536 Edition*, translated by Ford Lewis Battles, 178. For the second edition, see *Institutes of the Christian Religion of John Calvin, 1539: Text and Concordance*. Edited by Richard F. Wevers. Grand Rapids, MI: Meeter Center for Calvin Studies, 1988.

30. See, e.g., Calvin, *Institutes*, III.19.15, IV.10.3–6, and IV.20.1.

31. Ibid., IV.10.3.

32. Ibid., IV.20.4.

33. Augustine, *de civitate Dei*, xix.

into the midst of the discourse on soteriology in the earlier third part of the *Institutio*. In terms of this new placement, the distinction between the two modes of governance is given considerably deeper theological significance than the mere distinction between ecclesiastical and civil rule. In this fashion, Calvin transposes the customary institutional sense of the distinction between "spiritual" and "temporal" jurisdiction to the moral ontological plain. Whereas the forum of spiritual jurisdiction under the auspices of medieval canon law referred to the external ritualized procedure associated with the sacrament of penance, for Calvin penitence is radically internalized within the forum or realm of the individual Christian conscience. Conversely, both the spiritual and the temporal jurisdictions are construed as "the external means or aids by which god invites us into the society of Christ and holds us therein," that is to say through the government of the visible church and the commonwealth which together constitute the *forum politicum*.[34] The radical internalizing of the "forum" of penitence in the conscience carries with it the corollary of the profanizing disenchantment of ecclesiastical functions. Moreover, the primary means of mediation between the inward "space" of individual conscience and the outward "space" of the communal, institutional life of the church are "moral instruments" of persuasion. In effect the secular public sphere appears in Calvin's theology as none other than the condition of mediation between the two *fora*.

Calvin's key claim in III.19 that his consideration of freedom and the conscience is "an appendage of justification" alters dramatically the theological register of his account of the *duplex gubernatio*. According to his formulation of justification, the communication of grace to fallen humanity is interpreted as a twofold process:

> We receive and possess by faith, Jesus Christ, as he is given to us by the goodness of God, and by participation in him we have a *double* grace (*duplex gratia*). The first is, that being reconciled to God by his innocence, instead of having a judge in heaven to condemn us, we very clearly have a Father there. The second is, that we are sanctified by his Spirit, to think upon holiness and innocence of life.[35]

On this summary account of Reformation soteriology, the individual believer participates in two sharply distinguished kinds of righ-

---

34. See Calvin, *Institutes*, book IV.1–4.

35. Ibid., III.11.1.

teousness, the primary mode "passive" and the derivative, secondary mode "active"—namely, faith and works.[36] According to this account of grace, the believer dwells mystically "in Christ" by faith and is thus made completely righteous in the presence of God, "*coram Deo.*" At the same time, Christ dwells in the believer, who is dynamically and progressively sanctified by degrees in the world, in the presence of others, that is to say "*coram hominibus.*"[37] In his discussion of liberty and the conscience Calvin makes it clear that the twofold government derives from these two distinct "places" in the reformed account of the operation of grace through these two distinct modes and in keeping with their respective, radically distinct ontological frames of reference—a *duplex gubernatio* proceeding from a *duplex gratia.*[38] In the series of chapters immediately preceding his account of the *duplex gubernatio*, Calvin formally distinguishes these two soteriological modes as the perfect, passive, alien, and consequently "imputed" grace of justification, on the one hand, and the gradual, dynamic, proper, and therefore "acquired" grace of sanctification, on the other. These two modes of grace, while very intimately yoked together, both in their source and in their reception, must nonetheless be kept wholly and clearly distinct.[39] Failure to maintain the distinction between justification and sanctification is, for Calvin, tantamount to the complete overthrow of the foundation of religion, yet the ultimate unity of their source must nonetheless be upheld.

A critical consequence of this dialectical soteriology of the *duplex gratia* is the seeming paradox of the definition of Christian liberty as simultaneously "freedom from" and "subjection to" the requirements of the law. In turn, this dialectical emphasis leads Calvin to assert simultaneously the most radical distinction between the temporal and spiritual orders, *and* their intimate union—the paradox, in fact, which is the "potential stone of stumbling" to which he refers at the beginning of the

36. In all essentials Calvin's position on justification is in agreement with Luther's formulation of the doctrine in his famous sermon *Two Kinds of Righteousness* (1520). See Luther, *Two Kinds of Righteousness*, *Luther's Works*, vol. 31, 293ff. See Kolb, *Martin Luther*, 64–68.

37. See McGrath, *Iustitia Dei*, 199. For a lucid explanation of Calvin's appropriation of this soteriological "dialectic," see Wendel, *Calvin: The Origins and Development*, 237–42.

38. On the soteriological implications for Calvin's treatment of conscience, see Zachman, *The Assurance of Faith*, 224–43, esp. 225–28.

39. Calvin, *Institutes*, III.11.11.

critical passage.[40] As Ralph Hancock expresses this remarkable tension, "Calvin explodes any simple dichotomy between secular and religious concerns; he distinguishes radically between them, but precisely in order to join them fast together."[41] There is a twofold danger in this tension, namely the possibility of confusing the two orders by joining them too closely with one another, or alternatively, of supposing that the two orders are antithetical. Thus for Calvin the moral ontological problem was how simultaneously to unite and yet maintain the distinction between the two forms of governance. It is in this distinctly *dialectical* sense, therefore, that the discourse of the twofold government is, as Calvin states, an "appendage of the discourse on justification." And it is precisely on this link that the new moral ontology of a modern secularity depends.

Calvin's dialectical treatment of the twofold government is thus very carefully constructed on the foundation of the principal modes of the "double grace." Moreover, his approach to the simultaneous union and distinction of the active and passive modes of grace, of faith and works, and his consequent formulation of the relation between the *forum conscientiæ* and the *forum externum* both adhere to a normative dialectical paradigm of orthodox patristic Christology, one of the chief distinctive marks of Calvin's theological method according to some scholars.[42] According to this model, the conscience of the believer corresponds to the principle of hypostatic unity and identity while, at the same time, in this hypostatic unity of conscience the individual is bound to the heterogeneous obligations of two distinct "jurisdictions," namely the "spiritual" and the "temporal." "The former," as he states, "has its seat within the soul," while "the latter only regulates the external conduct." As the passage continues, "when the one is considered, we should call off our minds, and not allow them to think of the other" lest they be confused.

Calvin defines conscience as "a certain mean between God and man because it does not allow man to suppress within himself what he knows, but pursues him to the point of convicting him."[43] Conscience

---

40. Ibid., III.19.15; translated by Battles, 847.

41. Hancock, *Calvin and the Foundations of Modern Politics*, xii.

42. Christocentrism is judged by François Wendel to be the very hallmark of Calvin's theology. See Wendel, *Calvin*, 215–25. See also Helm, *John Calvin's Ideas*, 58–92 and Willis, *Calvin's Catholic Christology*.

43. Calvin, *Institutes*, III.19.15.

64 CALVIN@500

both knows the demands of the law and recognizes the promise of liberty hidden behind those demands. According to Calvin's moral ontology, to confuse the spiritual forum of the conscience with the external political forum has its soteriological analogue in the confusion of faith and works: cosmologically considered, such a confusion is to neglect to distinguish between this present fleeting mortal existence and the immortal condition of eternity, between body and soul; doctrinally it is to imply by consequent a confusion of the divine and the human natures, and thus to overturn the cornerstone of patristic orthodoxy. The question of conscience, of liberty, and of the *duplex gubernatio* is thus elevated to the level of the most fundamental doctrine. The logic of the moral ontology of the *duplex gubernatio* can thus be clearly discerned in Calvin's paraphrase of the christological formula of the Council of Chalcedon in 451:

> When it is said that the Word was made flesh, we must not understand it as if he were either changed into flesh, or confusedly intermingled with flesh, but that he made choice of the Virgin's womb as a temple in which he might dwell. He who was the Son of God became the Son of man, not by confusion of substance, but by unity of person. For we maintain, that the divinity was so conjoined and united with the humanity, that the entire properties of each nature remain entire, and yet the two natures constitute only one Christ . . . Thus the Scriptures speak of Christ. They sometimes attribute to him qualities which should be referred specially to his humanity and sometimes qualities applicable peculiarly to his divinity, and sometimes qualities which embrace both natures, and do not apply specially to either. This combination of a twofold nature in Christ they express so carefully, that they sometimes communicate them with each other, a figure of speech which the ancients termed "*idiomaton koinonia*" (a communication of properties.)[44]

44. Ibid., II.14.1. The christological definition of Chalcedon reads as follows: "Following then the holy Fathers, we all unanimously teach that our Lord Jesus Christ is to us One and the same Son, the self-same Perfect in Godhead, the self-same Perfect in Manhood; truly God and truly Man; the self-same of a rational soul and body; consubstantial with the Father according to the Godhead, the self-same consubstantial with us according to the Manhood; like us in all things, sin apart; before the ages begotten of the Father as to the Godhead, but in the last days, the self-same, for us and for our salvation, born of Mary the Virgin, *Theotokos* as to the Manhood; acknowledged in Two Natures, unconfusedly, unchangeably, indivisibly, inseparably; the difference of the Natures being in no way removed because of the Union, but rather the property of each

So, eleven hundred years after this ecumenical council of the ancient church, Calvin invoked this christological model to lend support to the precarious dialectical task of simultaneously uniting and distinguishing the spiritual and the external orders of reality—the *forum conscientiæ* and the *forum externum*—with their respective modes of governance: "these two [the spiritual and the civil kingdom] as we have divided them, are always to be viewed apart from each other. When the one is considered, we should call off our minds, and not allow them to think of the other. For there exists in man a kind of two worlds over which different kings and different laws can preside."[45]

Yet—this qualifying conjunction is somehow characteristically Calvin's—while there are two distinct orders of reality (or "natures") they are nonetheless hypostatically united within each individual conscience; while the two modes of governance must be kept distinct, Calvin insists that they are by no means antithetical. Indeed Calvin insists that "we must know that they are not at variance."[46]

Calvin reveals the "public sphere" as ultimately an instrument for a public "communication of idioms" between the two realms without which the life of liberty would relapse into complete paralysis. Consequently, the distinction between the spiritual and the civil kingdoms "does not go so far as to justify us in supposing that the whole scheme of civil government is matter of pollution, with which Christian men have nothing to do."[47] On the contrary, civil government is much more than a *remedium peccati*: "magistrates are occupied not with profane affairs or those alien to a servant of God, but with a most holy office, since they are serving as God's deputies."[48] To deprive man of government is to deprive him of his very humanity. Civil government not only promotes peace and tranquillity, it protects "the outward worship of God," the defense of sound doctrine, and the promotion of civil righteousness. Moreover, as the structure of the argument of Book IV of the *Institutio* shows, the external governance of the civil realm is understood by Calvin as yoked

---

nature being preserved and both concurring into One *Prosopon* and One *Hypostasis* . . . one and the self-same Son and only begotten Word, Lord, Jesus Christ." Labbe and Cossart, *Sacrorum conciliorum*, tom. IV, col. 562.

45. Calvin, *Institutes*, III.19.15

46. Ibid., IV.20.2.

47. Ibid.

48. Ibid., IV.20.6

together with jurisdiction over the visible Church and the administration of the sacraments as one of three primary external instruments of the divine governance.

In summary, to return to our original question, does Calvin contribute substantively to the definition of a modern secular identity manifested in an emergent public sphere? It would seem that his sustained theological treatment of liberty and the conscience according to the model of the *duplex gubernatio* plays a highly significant, perhaps even decisive role in redefining the relation between the individual conscience and the external communal order. By this means Calvin effectively dismantles the traditional hierarchical model of a gradual mediation between the temporal and spiritual orders and their respective modes of governance as presupposed by the moral ontology of sacramental culture. Through his dismissal of the primacy of a sacramental mediation by means of a cosmic *dispositio* in favor of distinguishing hypostatically between the orders of reality, Calvin pushes these orders into a radical distinction, yet he does so only to bind them ever more tightly together according to the soteriological and christological models we have considered. Calvin's contribution to the definition of the moral ontology of an emerging secular modernity thus turns on the profundity of his theological analysis of the *duplex gubernatio*.

In sum, the displacement of sacramental culture with its moral ontology of hierarchical mediation, by a culture of persuasion with its alternative ontology sharply demarcating the inner subjective "forum of the conscience" and the "external political forum" of common, institutional life (both religious and civil), calls forth the public sphere as the new and necessary means of mediation, of bridging the distance between the two *fora*. Calvin's account of the *duplex gubernatio* helps to elucidate the vital role played by a public religious discourse in defining the new "moral ontology" of an emerging early-modern civil society, and thus also serves to establish the terms of a uniquely early-modern approach to negotiating the interaction between the conscience of the individual and the wider political community through the instrumentality of a *theologically* and structurally transformed "public sphere."

5

Calvin as Apologist

JASON N. ZUIDEMA

INTRODUCTION

MOST OF US IN Protestant traditions who study the Reformation find little difficulty in exalting the first generation of reformers. Luther, Zwingli, Bucer, and Calvin were the "dynamic" and "visionary" prophets who called the people of Europe back to the basis of faithfulness in Scripture. However, the second generation is another story. Often seen as "scholastic," they were petty and rancorous. Many of them seemed to prefer their denominational differences to the unity that could have been had had they overlooked their own private opinions. Worse, many seem simply to be either hopelessly contrarian or focused only on the details of theological examination. The first generation led the troops forward and the second allowed the troops to fight among themselves.

Maybe this caricature means something to you as well. In our generation we might look at church movements and see the same problematic—the church planters were the visionaries leading forward and those that remained often became "ingrown" and turned on each other. Does this sound familiar?

We can save the study of our contemporary ecclesiastical situation for another conference but I want to speak about the sixteenth-century origins of this problem in Protestantism (actually the problem goes back much further). The problem, in fact, is that this is but a caricature of the situation. Today we are speaking about Calvin. It is true that Calvin

68   CALVIN@500

was a relatively early leader of the reform movement in French-speaking Europe, but he does not quite fit the caricature that we have developed. To put it bluntly, Calvin was involved in polemics throughout his professional life. From the early 1530s to his death in 1564 there is almost never a year that goes by in which Calvin is not writing something serious against those who are attacking him specifically, or the reformed movement he was helping lead more generally.

The problem for those who work in communities which appreciate this reform movement is quite important. If Calvin is supposedly this great model pastor and dynamic leader, what do we do with this constant rancor and critical attitude? As we set this up let me give you an example. In 1544 Calvin critiques the theologians of the Sorbonne for their role in the prohibition of the reading of Reformed books. At the beginning of the document he asks himself the question—what kind of beasts would do this? How could they prohibit the reading of these books without having read them? We will get back to the contents of this document in a moment, but the conclusion is interesting. "What can we call these beasts?" says Calvin:

> We see the great drunkards, who like pigs with their snout flip over all the holy doctrine of our Lord. We see them as horrible dogs who bark at the servants of God. We see beasts as dumb as calves and as slow as oxen. We see them as savage bulls that beat their horns furiously on the Word of God and its ministers. We see lions that are used to devouring that which they find. We find wolves who ask only to invade the flock in order to strangle and kill the poor sheep. We see donkeys whose ears are always shut. By this we can know what they are. Yet, for myself, I could not really find a suitable enough name to describe all their qualities.[1]

---

1. "On voit de gros ivrognes, qui renversent comme pourceaux avec le groin toute la sainte doctrine de notre Seigneur. on voit comme de chiens mâtins, qui abbayent après les serviteurs de Dieu. On voit des bêtes aussi sottes que veaux, et aussi lourdes que bœufs. On voit comme des taureaux sauvages, qui heurtent furieusement des cornes, tant contre la parole de Dieu que les ministres d'icelle. On voit des lions accoutumés à dévorer ce qu'ils rencontrent. On voit des loups qui ne demandent qu'à envahir les troupeaux, et étrangler et meurtrir les pauvres brebis. On voit des ânes qui ont seulement les oreilles cachées. Ainsi on peut savoir quels ils sont. Mais quant à moi, je ne leur saurais trouver nom assez propre pour exprimer toutes leurs qualités." Jean Calvin "Avertissement contre la censure," in *Oeuvres*, 444.

This kind of writing is obviously not "politically correct." So what do we do with it? How does a pastor in the twenty-first century model his ministry after this kind of quotation?

I think there is something to learn, but I do not argue for a simple repristination of the style and content of Calvin. Another example is helpful here: Recently a colleague and I completed a book on the French-speaking reformer Guillaume Farel.[2] I had both professional and personal reasons for studying this figure. On the one hand, I admire his forthrightness and passion for what he considered the truth in situations where the deck was stacked against him. However, I thank the Lord that I do not have to work with him as a colleague. I have read fairly closely all his published works and know that he could be very long-winded. Further, prophetic types can often be difficult to work with in committees!

Maybe I am wrong in my example (I imagine some might disagree), but it is fairly plain that the situation and needs of the sixteenth century are significantly different than our time. More, there was a great urgency to debate and decide the topics Calvin and Farel were treating. In twenty-first-century Quebec these issues are not life-and-death matters—they were for many in French-speaking territories in the sixteenth to eighteenth centuries (and sporadically in the nineteenth and twentieth centuries as well). I know that some missionaries were mistreated in Quebec several generations ago, but no longer. There are very few cases in the last several generations where an evangelical's life or liberty was threatened specifically for publicly advocating what he or she believed was biblical doctrine.

So, what place do the polemics of Calvin, not to mention those of Farel, have in contemporary theological formulation? Other possible methods of answering this question could be proposed, but I propose to look more closely at what Calvin actually says in these polemical writings. In looking not only at Calvin's apologetic method and the content we can be better placed in a concluding section to judge their potential usefulness in contemporary ecclesiastical discussions.

---

2. Zuidema and van Raalte, *Early French Reform.*

CALVIN@500

CALVIN—THE APOLOGIST IN CONTEXT

Several important notes should be made in relation to the context in which Calvin wrote his apologetic writings. First, Calvin was born into a context in which the printed book had taken on and was taking on new forms and importance. It was only in the previous century that the printing press had been in use in Europe by Johannes Gutenberg and its usefulness for reproducing books of all kinds was being continually explored. Obviously, books had been present before this time, but now small books could be produced very rapidly compared to copying them by hand. Although Roman Catholics printed many important books and pamphlets, most historians agree that one of the most important exploiters of this "new" technology was Martin Luther.[3] Luther published a great amount in Latin, but also in German. The figures are striking—in the years preceding 1517 less than 100 printed documents per year were printed in German on average. Hover, that total jumped to almost 600 in 1520 and almost a 1,000 in 1523. Between 1518 and 1523 approximately 600 were published in Wittenberg alone. The numbers remained relatively high because of the threat of war and promise of peace. Most important among all these German books was Luther's translation of the Bible.[4]

Second, Calvin fully embraced this literary culture. Not content to simply preach and pray, he realized that he could have an even greater impact should he write. Others even helped him by copying out certain sermons and speeches and transforming them into the sermon collections that we know today. Like many of the other major reformers we know, Luther, Melancthon, Bullinger, Vermigli, etc. Calvin's literary output is amazing. Wulfert de Greef, a specialist on the literary footprint of Calvin, helps us get a handle on Calvin's writings: "The Reformer of Geneva wrote more in a space of thirty years than one person can adequately study and digest in an entire lifetime. Moreover, the time in which he lived is so far removed from ours, and life in our century is so totally different from his, that it is not easy to bridge the gulf between them. Calvin's use of so many literary genres is yet another reason why

---

3. Consider that both the indulgences that Luther countered and his ninety-five theses against indulgences were both printed documents.

4. Flood, "The Book in Reformation Germany," 43.

an overall picture of the factors that motivated his writing and speaking is most welcome."[5]

Often those looking to Calvin will immediately go to the *Institutes of the Christian Religion*. This might be one of the only books people of our generation know, but it was not the case in the sixteenth century. Rather, Calvin communicated through sermons, commentaries, and, very often, small printed pamphlets and letters. A good deal of it was printed in Geneva—even before Calvin's time a centre of printing in the French-reformed world. Indeed, Calvin's epistolary output was significant in an age before emails and Microsoft Word. An estimate by the group of scholars editing the correspondence of Calvin puts the total at something like 8,200.[6] Many letters are significant theological treatises by themselves.

Third, Calvin also embraced literature in the vernacular. It is not realized in our time, but Calvin, like Luther, was a significant pioneer in the world of printed manuscripts in French—particularly those dealing with theological topics. Although it is beyond my meager abilities to prove this to you, I refer you to the many studies of such important scholars as Francis Higman and Olivier Millet. Both can prove, in ways I cannot, that Calvin's place in vernacular theological literature is major (i.e., in grammatical forms and accents). I can, however, give anecdotal testimony: to study the issue of the Reformed and the Anabaptists I first read Farel's *Glaive de la parole veritable*.[7] It is a long and complicated book to say the least. What a shock or surprise when I read Calvin's essay on the same topic. Clear, short, lucid—in a French I could readily understand.

Indeed, the fourth note I make is that it was not so much that Calvin was first to write theology in French (unlike Luther in German), but that he knew better than his contemporaries—like Marcourt, Farel, Viret, Froment, etc.—how to write clearly, with well-formed arguments. He was a master of writing well and fighting well—constructive and criti-

---

5. De Greef, *The Writings of John Calvin*, 7.

6. Augustijn and van Stam, eds, *I. Calvin, Epistolae*, vol. 1, 27. About 3,000 letters are extant.

7. *Le glaive de la parole véritable, tiré contre le Bouclier de defense: duquel un Cordelier Libertin s'est voulu servir, pour approuver ses fausses et damnables opinions.* Geneva: Jean Girard, 1550.

cal. These were two unified strengths throughout his career.[8] Especially, Calvin knew how to control his verbosity—very rarely does one get the impression that he is just taking up space or repeating himself without reason (an impression I often got in reading certain books of Farel or Marcourt). I am not here engaging in hagiography—even his Roman Catholic critics recognized his eloquence.

CALVIN'S APOLOGETIC LITERATURE

So, what apologetic literature did he write? Probably the most well-known of his works in French was the *Institution chrétienne* (which he translated himself), but there were many other vernacular works besides. I will break them down into two categories—debates with Roman Catholics and debates with others. I could have chosen more, but for the sake of brevity I will speak about the following:

Debates with Roman Catholics

1. The "Preface to King Francis I" in all the editions of the *Institutes*

2. *The Traité des reliques*

3. The debates with Catholic theologians

4. Debates concerning issues treated at the Council of Trent

Debates with Others

1. The "Nicodemites"

2. The "Anabaptists"

3. The "Libertines"

4. The Anti-trinitarians

5. Astrologists

For most of these I used editions of the French original and not various copies in English or modern French. These certainly have their place, but some of the nuance and linguistic punch is lost. In fact, we are

---

8. F. Higman and B. Roussell, "Les deux lignes de force de toute la carrière de Calvin—*enseigner* et *lutter*—sont déjà présentes dans cette première *Institutio.*" in the introduction to Calvin, *Oeuvres*, xvi.

a privileged generation in that great editions are coming regularly from European and North American publishers.[9]

A. Debates with Roman Catholics

1. "Epistle Dedicatory to King Francis I"

I must confess that I consider this short introduction[10] to be one of Calvin's most eloquent single essays on the nature and necessity of reform. It is one of the few parts of the *Institutes* that never changed throughout all of its updates and editions. Although the Institutes itself was meant as a sort of catechism in 1536 and a theology text book in its subsequent incarnations, it never lost this apologetic introduction and tone. Indeed, many have read Calvin's *Institutes* as his chief apologetic work. I would spend more time on it here, but many other fine studies are available so I will focus just on this introduction.

Calvin's goal is to convince the King of France (who probably never read this document) that the French reformed were not only no threat to his kingship, but that they were probably better citizens than the Roman Catholic population. This was a tall order for in the years previous the French reformed had shocked the King by posting the bombastic *Placards* around the city.[11] At the end of 1534 and beginning of 1535, Pierre de Vingle (an exiled French printer living in Switzerland) printed on a large sheet of paper an anonymous four-part attack on the mass. The presence of Christ in the Catholic mass was, for many, linked directly to the King's power, so this was seen as a form of treason.[12]

In this context Calvin came out with his *Institutes* with the preface to that King. Three ideas in this preface ought to be highlighted for our purposes here: first, Calvin wants to defend the cause of all those "hungering and thirsting for Christ" from the "fury of certain wicked persons"

---

9. Besides the numerous recent digital copies of Calvin volumes from the sixteenth to early twentieth centuries, one specially notes the various volumes published by Droz and Neukirchener Verlag and the recent volume of Calvin's *Oeuvres* included in the prestigious *Bibliothèque de la Pléiade* series (published by Gallimard).

10. A critical edition of the first edition of this introduction in French is found in Jean Calvin, *Institution de la religion chrétienne (1541)*, vol. 1, 140–80.

11. An English translation of the *Placards* is included as an appendix in John Calvin, *Institutes of the Christian Religion* (1536), 339–42.

12. See the fascinating discussion in Elwood, *The Body Broken*, ch. 2.

in France.[13] Calvin, one whose only real formal studies were in Law, sets himself up as the lawyer for the evangelical cause. He wants the King to make real study of the evangelical arguments rather than simply dismiss them outright. Second, the specific arguments he takes up are that the evangelical movement is "new," "uncertain," and has no miraculous power on its side.[14] Calvin uses both the Bible and the Church Fathers as his witnesses—he argues that the Roman Catholic Church might have a good deal of medieval teaching on their side, but not the Fathers or the Bible. Hence, if anyone has "novel" teaching it is the Catholics. Finally, his argument on the church merits consideration. Calvin argues that the church ought not to be first considered institutionally, then spiritually, but the inverse: "By their [our Roman Catholic adversaries'] double-horned argument they do not press us so hard that we are forced to admit either that the church has been lifeless for some time or that we are now in conflict with it. Surely the church of Christ has lived and will live so long as Christ reigns at the right hand of his Father."[15] The Roman Catholics want to paint the evangelicals into a corner, but Calvin argues that the church is about much more than physical institutions. Hence, that the evangelicals left (or, were forced to leave) these buildings is not such a death-blow to their cause. Being part of the spiritual church in Christ is the primary concern. The King need not wait only upon the Roman Catholic Church for power, but seek it first in God's truth.[16]

2. *Traité des reliques* (1543)

In the 1530s and early 1540s Calvin was almost continually involved in a defense of the evangelical movement against Roman Catholic critics. I could mention Calvin's participation in the Colloquy of Lausanne (1536) or those in Hagenau, Worms and Regensburg during his stay in Strasbourg, his letters to Louis du Tillet and Cardianal Sadoleto, or the *Epistolae duae* (1537).[17] For the sake of brevity we skip ahead to the *Avertissement sur les reliques* published in 1543.[18]

---

13. Calvin, *Institutes* 1536, 1.

14. Ibid., 5ff.

15. Ibid., 9.

16. Ibid., 13–14.

17. See de Greef, *Writings of John Calvin* 149–50.

18. Calvin, *Oeuvres*, 389–434.

Although I find the preface to Francis I the most eloquent single document, the most entertaining is no doubt the treatise on relics. This is a real gem of a document which evidences the rhetorical power and wit of the leaders of the Reformation. No doubt the Roman Catholic hierarchy did not like Calvin's document (if they read it), but it certainly helps us get a handle on Calvin's apologetic.

Several important points: (1) Calvin begins again by citing the authority of Scripture and Augustine. He notes that already in Augustine's time the abuses were known and condemned.[19] (2) Like many a professor he wants to show the ambiguities and contradictions in the situation. Hence, he notes the multiplicity and silliness of relics coming from the life of Jesus, Mary, the Apostles, and other important church figures. For him it ought to seem like common sense that Catholics should realize that Jesus' cross would have been mammoth had it been made up of all the parts of the "true" cross that were scattered around Europe (not to mention the oriental churches). A famous quote: "Therefore, if we would collect all that is found in them, we could load up a good-sized boat."[20] Further, how did the church even get things like Jesus' foreskin, milk from Mary's breasts, or other sundry objects? Only completely ignorant people would believe this, thinks Calvin. Which leads Calvin to his final observation. (3) Even if these things were the real thing (i.e., if it could be proven that one of the three foreskins that was known to exist in Europe was actually Jesus'), it would still be unwise to make much of it. In fact, it is clear to Calvin that the Catholic hierarchy was promoting relics for power and profit[21] and, as such, this promotion led people to devote themselves to objects not worthy of real devotion. Because those who allow relics as part of devotion are mixed up between the worship of creature and creator, they have fallen into idolatry.[22] What seems so pious[23] is actually leading to spiritual shipwreck, thinks Calvin.

---

19. Ibid., 389.

20. "Bref, si on voulait ramasser tout ce que s'en est trouvé, il y en aurait la charge d'un bon grand bateau." Ibid., 401.

21. "par cette opinion il se fait craindre et redouter. La crainte a engendré dévotion, laquelle a aiguisé l'appétit pour faire désirer d'avoir son corps, à cause du profit." Ibid., 429.

22. "c'est l'idolâtrie exécrable d'adorer relique aucune, quelle qu'elle soit, vraie ou fausse." Ibid., 432

23. "les reliques ont une 'espece et couleur de bonne dévotion." Ibid., 390.

3. Debates with Catholic Theologians

Here again we could mention a number of debates with various Catholic theologians, like Albert Pighius, but I choose to focus on the *Avertissement sur la censure qu'ont faite les Bêtes de la Sorbonne, touchant les livres qu'ils appellent hérétiques* written in 1544. For about twenty years the theologians of the Faculty of Theology of the University of Paris would give judgment on books on a case by case basis, but beginning in about 1540 the rhythm of censure began to change radically. In these years the theologians brought their critique together to make a list of proper theological positions and a list of books which did not measure up (these are part of what would be called the *Index*). Many of the newly banned books came from publishers in Geneva, so it was natural that a defense of their contents would come from there.[24] The work is actually anonymous, but there is little doubt that Calvin was its author.[25]

We have already noted above the main question for which Calvin wanted an answer—what kind of "animals" are these theologians? By this rhetoric we see his implicit criticism. Much of his concern was (like in his preface to Francis I) that these books not be judged without proper trial. Indeed, Calvin argues that in life in general "foolishness is principally shown when a judge gives sentence without having seen anything."[26] The theologians of the Sorbonne can tolerate many other books which are inimical to the faith (i.e., romance novels), but not those which seek honest and open discussion of important subjects. Actually, Calvin writes, it seems that these theologians would prefer that everyone stop reading—this is what seems to be happening in the case of the Bible. They would rather make the Bible into another kind of relic (i.e., idol) than have it read by the faithful.[27] Calvin says that his overriding concern is that the common people ("les simples gens") could have access to this good literature and be defended against ravaging wolves.[28]

---

24. See editor's notes in ibid., 1243.

25. See editor's notes in ibid., 1242.

26. "La folie se montre principalemnt quand un juge prononce devant qu'avoir rien vu." Ibid, 436.

27. Ibid., 440.

28. The "simple people" defence is common in most Protestant writings (and Catholic responses, to be sure). "mais ils ne veulent nullement permettre que l'écriture soit lue en langue française, pour ce que la lecture en est dangereuse, ce leur semble.' Ibid., 439.

4. The Council of Trent

A fourth example of a kind of writing against Roman Catholicism is that in later life in the context of the build-up to the Council of Trent. Although Trent was first hoped to be a meeting open to Protestant theologians, these theologians soon realized that its outworking was rather for their condemnation. The council did deal with internal Catholic reform, but its major preoccupation was to affirm and reaffirm positions on scripture and tradition, salvation by faith and works, the sacrifice of the mass and transubstantiation.[29] In fact, Trent was not the only meeting where these issues were being disputed. In 1561 at the same time as the Estates General of France, there was a meeting of theologians before the queen Mother, Catherine de Medicis, at Poissy (just West of Paris). Even though Calvin did not represent the Protestant group (this task was taken up by Thèodore de Bèze) he did have a formative impact on it. For example, in the context of this Colloquy Calvin wrote a small document (anonymously) against Gabriel de Saconay who had recently republished works in favour of the Roman Catholic understanding of the Mass.[30]

Calvin picks up themes seen elsewhere, especially the sovereignty of God in forms of worship and our service of him. Transubstantiation and a kind of "free" will are categories which sound pious, but really downplay the glory of God. Calvin thinks the Holy Spirit ought not just be the "chambrière" (maid) of a "free" will, but that the Spirit actually has the power to bend it.[31] Further, Calvin thinks that transubstantiation is a "special treasure of Satan."[32] These statements are very categorical. Yet, Calvin is clear in this document to note that his critique of the Roman Catholic Church is not a critique of the *church*, but of the *Roman* traditions he thinks have crept into and perverted its teaching and practice. Calvin writes that de Saconay's criticism of him as the new "Genevan idol" is totally out of order—it is like the pot calling the kettle black. If any are idolaters it is de Saconay and the hierarchy of the Roman Catholic

---

29. See the documents of the Council in Pelikan and Hotchkiss, eds. *Creeds and Confessions of Faith in the Christian Tradition*, Vol. 2, 813–74.

30. Calvin, *Oeuvres*, 470ff.

31. Ibid., 471.

32. Ibid., 476.

CALVIN@500

Church whom Calvin sees as bent on the destruction of the evangelical movement and biblical teaching.[33]

B. Debates with Other Movements and Individuals

These remarks give us at least the flavor of Calvin's apologetic against Roman Catholic thinkers. However, we must recognize that Calvin was also dealing with others who equally challenged the evangelical reform he wanted to lead. It is important to remember that these "others" often presented greater challenges to the leaders of the reform movements than did the Roman Catholic hierarchy. For example, it is possible to argue that Luther was troubled more by the revolting peasants and other radical reformers than he was by the Roman Catholic theologians. No doubt Luther bemoaned the fact that from his perspective these supposed "brothers" were giving him a very bad reputation. For Calvin the situation was much the same.

1. "Nicodemites"

A first group of texts dealing with another movement comprise those written against the problem of those whom Calvin named the "Nicodemites." This is a term used by Calvin to talk about those who believe evangelical doctrine inwardly, but live Roman Catholic practice outwardly. The analogy is that of Nicodemus, a Jewish leader, who, as it is written in John 2:3, came to Jesus "at night" (i.e., so that others among his peers would not see him). Calvin sees this problem most particularly in France. He admits that there are some in France who do not yet understand evangelical doctrine well enough to know the perilous situation they are in. Yet, for those who know, the choices are clear. If they can leave to a place where they can worship purely, they must. If they cannot leave, then they should try to not take part in any idolatry. If they cannot even do this, then they need to do what they can and long for the swift coming of the next life. What they cannot do is continue to participate in Roman Catholic worship, for it is no worship at all in Calvin's judgment—it is pure idolatry.

In the 1540s and 50s Calvin wrote a number of public letters and tracts concerning this problem. Calvin had heard of arguments from figures such as Naaman in the Old Testament who was allowed to go back

---

33. Ibid., 495.

ZUIDEMA—*Calvin as Apologist* 79

to Syria or the apostle Paul who cut his hair even though he knew it was only to please the Jews. Yet, Calvin was not persuaded. These texts were being mishandled and did not apply in this situation. In both situations the characters were not being asked to participate in idolatry like that of the mass. Importantly, the mass is not just a lesser good, but, says Calvin, "I think that the papal mass is pure abomination, which might only bear the title of the Lord's Supper in the same way as the Devil can transform himself into an angel of light."[34]

Very soon Calvin began to hear the critique of some in France who argued that it was easy for Calvin to have such a strong opinion as he sat safely in Geneva, but that he did not know what the real pressures of life in France were like.[35] Calvin, as is typical, spins this argument on its head. What is at stake here he says is not the comfort of Calvin, but the honor of God. It is a matter of *principle*, not just convenience or ease. Calvin writes: "Since God created both our bodies and souls, and feeds us and takes care of us, it is good that he is served and honored."[36] From Calvin's perspective these "Nicodemites" are quite concerned about their bodily health, but should be equally, if not more so concerned about their spiritual health. It is impossible to be spiritually healthy while partaking of the mass.

2. "ANABAPTISTS"

In the introduction to the second volume in the series of Calvin's doctrinal and polemical works in the new Calvin *Opera Omnia*, Mirjam Van Veen, the editor, notes that Calvin wrote this work at the request of Farel, who was dealing with a surge of Anabaptist teaching in Neuchâtel.[37] Farel wrote to Calvin asking him to respond to this teaching.[38] Van Veen claims that Farel was awkwardly positioned in the debate on Anabaptism

---

34. "Quant à moi, j'y vois bien une perplexité. Car j'estime que la messe papistique est une pure abomination, laquelle n'est autrement colorée que de titre de la Cène, sinon comme le Diable se transfigure en Ange de lumière." Ibid., 547.

35. Ibid., 541.

36. "Car puis que Dieu a créé nos corps comme nos âmes, et qu'il les nourrit et entretient, c'est bien raison qu'il en soit servi et honoré." Ibid., 551.

37. Jean Calvin, *Brième instruction . . . contre les erreurs de la secte commune des anabaptistes. Series IV. Ioannis Calvini Scripta didactica et polemica*, Vol. II, 14ff.

38. Calvin, *Brève instruction*, 16 n. 25.

and had taken a rather irenic position on Anabaptism until this point.[39] Therefore, Calvin was better placed to write.

Calvin's response is largely a point-by-point refutation of the doctrine of Michael Sattler's *Schleitheim Articles*, of a docetist Christology, and of a doctrine of soul-sleep. Calvin's rhetoric has been often studied in secondary literature.[40] This treatise provides a good case-study to see this rhetoric at work again. Calvin's most useful tactic is turning the argument of his opponents back on itself. Hence, when his opponent says, "we are biblical," Calvin will say, "not only are you not biblical, but, in fact, you are directly and fundamentally *anti*-biblical." A few examples to see this rhetoric at work:

Calvin writes that the Anabaptists argue for believers' baptism based on several New Testament texts. Calvin argues that this is true in so far as new believers must be instructed in the faith and believe before being baptized. But, says Calvin, the children of believers, as was the case in the Old Testament, are included in God's promise. Calvin argues that if we say the children of believers are not to be recognized as belonging to God's promise, then the Jews of the Old Testament would have more grace than the believers of the New. Calvin thinks this takes away from the importance of Christ and the power of God's promise.[41]

As a second example, note that Calvin argues that the Anabaptist position on the magistrate is based on what he claims is faulty biblical rationale. To say that the sword and the magistrate do not belong in the perfection of Christ might *seem* to be based on certain New Testament texts, but when compared to the rest of Scripture, says Calvin, it makes little sense. In holding dearly to their interpretation of these few New Testament texts, the Anabaptists take the sense out of the rest of Scripture.[42]

---

39. Curiously, Van Veen does not mention Farel's 1533 edition of the *Manière et Fasson* or the 1536 *Genevan Confession* which Farel helped to write. Farel's paedobaptist position seems fairly clear in these two writings. Nevertheless, it is true that neither of these documents has a clear argument against the Anabaptist position. In any case, it is known that Farel admired Calvin's gifts as an author (see appendix to the 1542 *Summaire*) and wanted him to take up his pen against the Anabaptists.

40. See, for example, Olivier Millet's *Calvin et la dynamique de la parole: étude de rhétorique réformée*.

41. Calvin, *Brève instruction*, 47.

42. Ibid., 65, 74, 80.

These two examples stand for many others in Calvin's little work. Both examples show that Calvin wants to pay close attention to the logic of the texts that are cited by the Anabaptists. Often he will want to confront what he sees as faulty logic with other passages from Scripture or connect it to what he considers other early church heresies.[43] He pleads that his mission is not sophistry or mind games, but more clarity in the debate.[44]

3. "LIBERTINES"

In another new volume of the series *Scripta didactica et polemica* in the *Ioannis Calvini Opera Omnia*, Mirjam Van Veen groups together three short treatises of Calvin against several "spiritualists" affecting the church in France and the Low Countries.[45]

In the first two texts, *Contre la secte phantasque et furieuse des libertines qui se nomment spirituelz* (1545) bound with the second, a letter against a "Cordelier" (the name taken by a certain group of Franciscans in France), Calvin lays out a very clear (compared to the convoluted *Glaive de la parolle veritable* of Guillaume Farel written against the same person) case against those whom he considers to be trapped in the "chasm of this bestial sect of the libertines."[46] Typical of the magisterial reformers reaction against the Anabaptists and radicals, Calvin views this sect as more pernicious than all others. He so forcefully confronted their doctrine because from his perspective they pretended to base it on Scripture, but came up with radically different conclusions. In fact, it is this *hermeneutical* problem which characterizes Calvin's argument throughout. The problem in Calvin's eyes is that they read their own opinions into that which Scripture teaches—rather than letting Scripture form their doctrine as Calvin claims he has done. The result, argues Calvin, is that they have doctrine which is both new (in the negative sense of the term—invented after Scripture) and old (in the negative sense of the term—in a league with Valentinus, Donatus, and the Manicheans). Calvin's goal, then, is to keep the church on the proper, biblical path. Calvin continually brings the debate back to his understanding of scriptural norms—especially testing the logic of the

43. Ibid., 95.

44. Ibid., 141.

45. Calvin, *Contre les libertines spirituelz*.

46. Ibid., 67.

spiritualist position by it. Calvin argues that the spiritualists can pretend that the ideas of sin, the devil, hell, the world, the mortal soul, etc. are all figments of the imagination (from the "cuider"—a key word in the spiritualist argument), but Scripture says they are still a reality. They think their arguments are based on Scripture, says Calvin, but really they have twisted Scripture for their own goals. Herein lies the big problem for Calvin; one might pretend sin is no longer real, but this simply gives more room for sin to exist. As such, this doctrine might *look* attractive (who would not want a world free from sin and the Devil?), but it actually destroys the person by letting sin run free.

A problem with evaluating these texts of Calvin is that we do not have the original texts against which he was writing. As such, it is harder to be "objective" in our assessment of his opponent's texts—all we have is the very negative portrait by Calvin. Thankfully, Van Veen has found the text against which Calvin wrote the third text, the *Response à un certain Holandois*. Throughout the text she cites the original in the notes—most of the time Calvin's quote is faithful to the original.

Although the subject of this third text seems to deal more with a question of Nicodemism, whether a Christian can attend the Mass, the arguments, as Van Veen notes, are clearly of the same nature as those found in the previous two texts. Calvin attacks this "certain Dutch man," Dirck Volckertsz Coornhert (1522–1590), by divorcing religion from outward action. Religion needs to be of the heart, says Calvin, but it is accompanied by exterior actions commanded by God. Like the Libertine's, Coornhert's problem is a poor interpretation of the Bible and the outward practice of religion. Calvin argues that while Coornhert pretends to lighten their load, he is actually making it infinitely heavier.

4. THE ANTI-TRINITARIANS

Calvin is probably most well-known for his critique of the anti-trinitarians—i.e., in that he has often been said to be ultimately responsible for the execution of the Spanish anti-trinitarian Michael Servetus. We need not enter this debate too deeply, but suffice it to say that Servetus was not the only theologian who challenged certain settled points of trinitarian understanding. Calvin had once been criticized for being ambiguous on his adherence to traditional trinitarian language (he was not against it, but did not want to answer loaded questions of an opponent at one debate). For example, Calvin needed to respond to the theological positions of Francesco Stancaro, an Italian theologian who had moved on to Poland. Calvin had to write several public letters to disassociate himself from Stancaro's theology and show that Stancaro's ideas were unorthodox. Particularly, he wanted to show that although Stancaro's position on the mediatorship of Jesus Christ *seemed* to be a better fit for evangelical theology, it was really faulty at its core. Rather than make a more helpful Christ, it made Christ impotent since he was no longer truly God and truly man (Calvin basically says Stancaro was an Arian).[47] This little controversy takes us out of French language publications, but it is an example of something more generally seen in the *Institutes* and other places in French.

5. AGAINST ASTROLOGY

A final example of the type of idea critiqued by Calvin is that of astrology. In his 1549 treatise *Advertissement contre l'Astrologie judiciaire*, Calvin shows the dangers of this type of pseudo-science which seeks to explain our past and predict our future.[48] The stars are good, says Calvin, but not for this kind of prediction. They help us tell time and plan growing seasons, but they do not speak to us about our lives. Yet, astrology seems to have a strong hold on people's minds: "This is why it has been said for a long time that these so-called mathematicians were good at emptying wallets and filling ears, especially because in telling a good fortune they calm the hearts of the curious and take from them all they want after they have deceived them."[49] It has the appearance of truth and grabs the interest of the hearer, but it is, like so many other things for Calvin, "a horrible labyrinth" which leads to all other tricks of the Devil.[50] More importantly, and, again, just like many other ideas, astrology steals

47. See Williams. *Radical Reformation*, 934ff. and ch. 25; Tylenda, "Christ the Mediator," 5–10; Edmondson, *Calvin's Christology*, 36.

48. Calvin, *Advertissement contre l'astrologie judiciaire.*

49. "Voyla pourquoi il a esté dit de long temps que ces mathematiciens masquez estoyent bons pour vuider les bources et remplir les aureilles, d'autant qu'en disant la bonne fortune ilz paissent de vent les curieux et tirent d'eux tout ce que ilz veulent apres qu'une foiz ilz les ont ensorcelez." Ibid., 63.

50. "Or, comme c'est un horrible labyrinthe et sans yssue que des folies et superstitions, desquelles les hommes s'enveloppent depuis que ilz ont une fois lasché la bride à leur curiosité, beaucoup d'esprytz volages, apres s'estre amusez à la divination des astres, se fourrent encore plus avant, assavoir en toutes especes de divinations, car il n'a nulle tromperie du Diable où ilz ne prennent goust, depuis qu'ilz ont esté affriandez à une." Ibid., 94.

CALVIN@500

the honor that is due to God alone. Only God, by his Spirit, can give meaning and lead the lives of his creatures.[51]

CONCLUSIONS

This rough survey of Calvin's apologetic remarks which would have reached the ears of a French-speaking audience can lead us to several concluding remarks:

1. Due to the continual and diverse nature of his apologetic writings, Calvin clearly saw this task as central to his pastoral duties. First, he saw the "little people" of France, especially the Reformed, as an extension of his parish. He often presented himself as their representative, since they could not speak for themselves. A recurring theme in all these various documents is that something might look quite good, but actually rots the soul. I suppose this was a particular strength of Calvin's critical abilities— to find what was the greatest strength and weakness. Very often, Calvin's argument ran something like, "you think this is your strongest argument, but I will show you that it is in fact your Achilles heel." This is, I think, a key to much of the argument of the *Institutes* as well: "You think your self-knowledge makes you so great, but your knowledge is actually what puffs you up and drags you down to damnation." As in the *Institutes,* all the issues occasioned by these smaller vernacular tracts need to be reviewed according to the knowledge of God in Scripture. If not, one inevitably falls into what Calvin thinks is the pit of Popery, the lie of Libertinism, the night of Nicodemism, the anarchy of Anabaptism, or the idiocy of Astrology, to name a few. All of these are "labyrinths" from which it is impossible to escape without God's revelation and power.[52]

2. Although it is impossible to delve into another subject in depth, it is important to say that Calvin was not simply a controversialist. For example, the 1549 *Consensus Tigurinus* is one of several examples of creative and diplomatic efforts for unity in the Reformed movement. This could be more generally said—we might look at this and other confessional

---

51. Ibid., 100–101.

52. William Bouwsma might not be right in his claim that Calvin is one stuck in "labyrinths." In my study of Calvin, I come across the term quite often and it is almost always applied to what he considers false teaching. Bouwsma, *John Calvin*, 45–48.

documents as a source of division, but these documents were originally attempts at gathering diverse groups together.[53]

Yet, he was a controversialist. So what to do? Often readers in our generation look to Calvin's theology (especially the supposed "five points of Calvinism") as his contribution to the church. I would imagine that this is the general tendency in both mainline and evangelical churches. There is a tendency to separate *what* he said from *how* and when he said it. Is this proper? Can Calvin really be understood without encountering his deep displeasure with all "labyrinthine" (i.e., sinful) thinking without feeling his passion (misguided or not) for God's glory?

I would submit that Calvin's apologetic content and style are as important as his biblical exegesis or systematic elegance. In fact, I think Calvin thought it particularly important to model an apology for his parishioners so that they could give form to their own ideas about reform and the church. I would underline one idea in specific—that an idea or practice might *seem* to be something far other than it actually *is*. The distinction between what *seems* to be and what *is* seems to me to be a particularly important quality in pastoral ministry which so often has to judge between appearance and reality.

---

53. This is seen, for example, in the writing of the *Heidelberg Catechism* in the early 1560s.

6

John Calvin and the "Still-born" Third Option in the French Reformation

AXEL SCHOEBER

TIMOTHY GEORGE HAS RECENTLY written an article he entitled "Calvin's Biggest Mistake." It follows a fairly typical historiographical perspective and refers to Calvin's consent to the execution of Michael Servetus for heresy.[1] Servetus had written openly against the doctrine of the Trinity and lived constantly under the shadow of impending imprisonment or execution. Even Martin Bucer in Strasbourg—who was persistent in shielding dissenters like Anabaptists who were treated harshly in most other locales— was not able to prevent Servetus from being forced out of his city. Servetus was passing through Geneva in disguise, though we are not sure of his destination. (In 1536, of course, William Farel had called down the wrath of God upon the unfortunate traveler, Calvin—who was only intending to sojourn one night on his way to Strasbourg—if he did not stay and provide leadership for the Protestant Reformation that was coming to birth in the city of Geneva.) You would think that Calvin might have had more sympathy for one who was travelling through town and then was surprised by the agenda of another! Calvin's former collaborator, Sebastian Castellio, wrote firmly against the execution, summarizing his case straightforwardly: "To kill a man is not to defend a doctrine, but to kill a man."[2] The passionate longing for participation in a "pure" Christian society that dominated almost all

---

1. George, "Calvin's Biggest Mistake," 32.
2. Cited in Kaplan, *Divided by Faith*, 21.

Europeans of the era will help us understand Calvin's choice, and soften our condemnation of him. Still, we can agree that his assent to Servetus' death was a big mistake.

My question, however, concerns whether it was his *biggest* mistake. The controversy over Servetus was sharply defined and very visible. Yet I want to suggest in this paper that a bigger mistake can be identified. Calvin's campaign against Nicodemism ultimately affected the lives of countless folk over centuries, with results that many of us would describe as unfortunate. Nicodemism was the label Calvin applied to those whom he thought were afraid to embrace the "true faith" openly: *messieurs les Nicodemites*.[3] The slur derived from Nicodemus in John 3—a Jewish leader intrigued by Jesus, who nonetheless visited the latter at night to avoid detection by other Jewish leaders. (The slur involved turning the tables on those whose behavior Calvin was challenging: they had referred to Nicodemus as an example to be imitated![4]) In concert (not cooperation!) with his archenemies at the Faculty of Theology at the University of Paris (commonly, but somewhat inaccurately called the Sorbonne, an error prevalent already in Calvin's time[5]), he succeeded in eliminating a significant movement within the church in France that was warm, vigorous, non-schismatic, and peaceable. Had this movement prevailed it could well have mitigated much of the religious aggression that followed, not only in France, but in much of Europe as well. Let me explain my suggestion, by telling two stories, the first one more briefly.

Princess Renée of Ferrara hated the Salic Law.[6] Established by the Merovingian Franks a millennium earlier, it controlled the succession to the French monarchy. One of its stipulations required the heir to be male. As the daughter of the warmly regarded King Louis XII, she would have ruled France, since she had no brothers. As she put it herself, "Had I had a beard I would have been the king of France. I have been defrauded by that confounded Salic Law." Instead, her cousin became the famous Francis I. Yet Renée's impact was nonetheless significant.

3. Calvin, *L'Excuse de Jehan Calvin à Messieurs les Nicodemites* (1544).

4. In response to an earlier tract of Calvin's, *Petit traicte monstrant que c'est que doit faire un homme fidèle, cognoisant la verité de l'Evangile quand il est entre les papists* (1543). See the insightful discussion in Farris, "Calvin's Letter to Luther," 61–73.

5. Farge, *Orthodoxy and Reform in Early Reformation France*, 3–4, 38.

6. The story is told by Ruth A. Tucker, "John Calvin and the Princess," *Christian History and Biography*, found at http://www.christianitytoday.com/ch/bytopic/women/johncalvinandtheprincess.html.

Born a year after Calvin (1510), she was a valuable asset to her father in the dynastic matchmaking that was a key part of foreign policy in this period. She was married, at seventeen, to Ercole II of Ferrara, which gave her influence in both Italian and French societies. Ercole happened to be the son of the scandalous Lucrezia Borgia and the nephew of the murderous and ambitious Cesare. His grandfather Rodrigo had been the immoral, self-indulgent and violent Pope Alexander VI—whose escapades prepared many Europeans for the thought that the welfare of the church of Christ could perhaps be entrusted to better hands than the papacy. In this environment, her reputed "strong will" could have been a means of survival. It also provided important protection for the early Protestant movement in southern Europe. After the *Affaire des Placards* in October, 1534, many Protestants—including Calvin himself—fled France, fearing for their lives. Francis I had often, though not always consistently, protected Protestants from prosecution by the Faculty of Theology and its many allies in the *Parlements* (more courts than legislative bodies). The *placards* presented a hard-line Zwinglian theology not reflective of the spirit and attitude of the French *évangéliques*—a large number of people who longed for church renewal. These public denunciations of the Mass as an "execrable blasphemy" permanently turned Francis against Protestantism. He now allowed traditionalists the freedom to initiate the pincer movement that destroyed the viability of this evangelical "Third Option" in the French Reformation era. One of the posters even raised questions of national security: it was nailed overnight to the door of the king's bedchamber![7]

Renée's cousin, Marguerite of Navarre, was Francis' sister and a noted Protestant sympathizer and protector—who nonetheless (like many in the "Third Option") never abandoned the Catholic Church. Renée also began to welcome Protestant refugees to her court in Ferrara, including a man in disguise known as Charles d'Espeville. It was none other than Calvin himself, who stayed for a month in the spring of 1536—just before he encountered Farel in Geneva. During this time, Renée became convinced of Reformed teaching, so much so that Calvin praised her "fear of God" and her "real desire to obey Him." Yet she remained a

---

7. See Monter, *Judging the French Reformation*, 69–74, for a useful summary of the Affair of the Placards. The fact that many Protestants disagreed with the teaching on the Lord's Supper expressed in the placards was a "fine point" understandably lost on many Catholics of the day. See Higman, *Censorship and the Sorbonne*, 44.

faithful Catholic in public practice. Many assume that such an approach represented a form of dissimulation for the purpose of maintaining personal safety.[8] I want to suggest an alternative perspective: the Third Option consisted of many, including Renée, who were sympathetic to Protestant teaching but refused to enter into schism—*out of conviction*. Ercole would have none of it, however, placing her under house arrest for her beliefs and confining her daughters to a convent. After a week she called a priest for confession and communion, and her daughters were then able to join her in house arrest.

Calvin's response was strong: "I fear you have left the straight road to please the world. And indeed the devil has so entirely triumphed that we have been constrained to groan, and bow our heads in sorrow." As was his consistent response to Nicodemism, he urged her to return to the Protestant faith.[9] When she returned to France—forced out of Ferrara by her son when he became duke—Renée and Calvin continued to correspond and to work cooperatively on behalf of Protestants. She was adamant, however—not unlike others who had embraced the Third Option—in her rejection of acts of violence perpetrated by the Protestants and did not accept the notion that Catholics were destined to hell.[10] For his part, Calvin remained opposed to her attempts at confessional bridge-building, viewing them as a sign of weakness in faith. When Renée died several years after the St. Bartholomew's Day Massacre in 1572, the Third Option had proven "still-born." Neither her fellow French nationals (over whom she nearly ruled as queen), nor even her own family, affirmed her understanding of the Christian faith—warm, committed, biblical, yet peace-loving.

Yet it was not always so. Church reform had been an important thrust in France for decades already when the sixteenth century began. I will seek to convey a sense of its character by looking at the differing ways scholars of the period use a significant term, *pré-réforme*. It has been very difficult for scholars to agree on the time period it covers, and on those who belonged to the movement. Larissa Taylor uses the term to

8. Tucker herself does, "The Princess," 3, calling Renée's behavior a "public pretense."

9. Calvin did, however, seek the opinions of both Melanchthon and Luther on the topic—at the request of French Protestants, who apparently sought some softening of his rigor. See Farris, "Calvin's Letter to Luther." It seems that Calvin was open to some modification of his stance, if he could be persuaded.

10. She grieved when her son-in-law, a Catholic, was assassinated and accused Calvin of consigning him to hell. Tucker, "The Princess," 4.

refer to the longing for church reform that marked the late fifteenth and early sixteenth centuries among French *Catholics*. Religious reformation was an ongoing process that began not with Luther's published attack on indulgences, but early in the fifteenth century in response to a church wracked by schism, a church that many thought had lost sight of its original mission. The problems of bureaucracy, venality, anticlericalism, and related issues so preoccupied later fifteenth-century preachers that they began to make an attempt from within to correct the faults of the church and its priesthood.[11]

To urge on such reform the preachers of the period were warm-hearted, for the most part, and practical. Their prescriptions were generally consistent with the Catholic sacramental system. Yet their preaching was Christ-centered, both for salvation and for living. Innovation was encouraged, especially when it could be justified through appeals to the church's original documents, an emphasis of the Renaissance. The Bible, especially the New Testament, and the church fathers were quoted widely. It was only after "it became clear that Luther's beliefs could not be contained within the Catholic Church" that innovation "and heresy became virtually synonymous."[12] Only then did pressure mount to abandon any practice or teaching that hinted at innovation.

Augustin Renaudet in his work, *Préréforme et Humanisme à Paris*, uses the term *pré-réforme* as Taylor does.[13] This renowned book was first published in 1916. It established well that a reforming spirit was active in this period. Yet, what was once part of a single stream later diverged significantly. The reform encompassed monastic houses, particularly through the *devotio moderna* originating in the Netherlands, and the universities, through the impact of humanism on intellectual life. The reforming movement in the monasteries ended up in the service of "l'armée de la Contre-Réforme."[14] On the other hand, some of the university-based humanists would end up Protestants. Still, it was often difficult to distinguish between the latter and other humanists who had no intention of furthering schism.

Why was it hard to discern the difference between schismatics and non-schismatics? One of the surprising and highly fascinating conclu-

---

11. Taylor, *Soldiers of Christ*, 233.

12. Ibid., 208–9. She calls this innovation "heterodoxy."

13. So does Holt, *The French Wars of Religion*, 14–17.

14. Renaudet, *Préréforme et Humanisme*, 703.

sions from investigations into this period is that the piety of this Catholic reform movement was virtually identical to the piety of the emerging Protestants. As Higman puts it:

> We may hope that this presentation has allowed some better grasp of a phenomenon for these years 1525–50 that is both of great importance yet little known, namely a piety in the French church which could be at the same time both "Lutheran" and "orthodox," radical as well as rooted in the traditional church, in a word, *evangelical*.[15]

Emphasizing preaching, Taylor agrees: it "is virtually impossible to differentiate between the evangelical preaching that had been part of the French *préréforme* movement and early 'reformed' preaching, at least in the 1520s and 1530s."[16] Doctrinal differences would soon separate the humanists, who remained loyal to core Catholic teaching, from the Protestants. Yet there was much conscious common ground among these *évangéliques*, and this fact is lamentably "little known."

One important conclusion may be drawn from the work of those who use the term *pré-réforme* to refer to reforming sentiment prior to Luther. Lutheran ideas did not spark the Reformation in France. They made a strong impact[17] on a movement that already existed prior to 1517. The *pré-réforme* was not an import and "Protestant-sounding" ideas had already had a wide currency for decades.

In contrast, J. H. M. Salmon and Nancy Roelker use *pré-réforme* to refer to the earliest Reformation period, prior to the establishment of the Reformed church in France.[18] In 1559 representatives gathered secretly in Paris to form a national synod. In hindsight, we can see this organizational event as marking the end of a transitional period. In the 1520s it was far from clear that Protestant differences would harden into

---

15. Higman, *Lire et Découvrir*, 199–200. "Espérons … que cette présentation … aura permis de saisir un peu les grandes lignes d'un phenomène très important et peu connu des années 1525–50: la piété de l'Église gallicane en même temps 'luthérienne' et 'orthodoxe,' radicale et ancrée dans l'Église traditionelle: somme toute, *évangélique*." Italics his.

16. Taylor, "Dangerous Vocations," 101; see too Taylor, *Soldiers of Christ*, 208.

17. Higman, in "Ideas for Export," demonstrates that Luther was easily the dominant author during the first twenty years of translating Reformation works into French. So, when the *pré-réformistes* were accused of being "Lutherans," the stereotype had some validity.

18. Roelker, *One King, One Faith*, 189–91; Salmon, *Society in Crisis*, 87 and Glossary.

the nearly exclusive streams they later did. So, the period from Luther's Ninety-Five Theses in 1517 to the *Affaire des Placards* in 1534 was very fluid. There was then a quarter-century transition to the highly structured Reformed pattern of ecclesiastical life. Certainly, Protestants were vulnerable prior to 1534.[19] Yet, Francis I was supportive of Renaissance learning and arts, and often shielded the Protestants under this umbrella—an action not inappropriate, since so many Protestants were humanists. Calvin attempted to appeal to this tendency in Francis when he dedicated his *Institutes* to the king in 1536. However, we can see in hindsight that, after the *Affaire des Placards*, Protestants would no longer receive protection from him. From 1534 until 1559, the early, more fluid Reformation is steadily swallowed up by an increasingly organized and defensive Reformed Protestantism. Salmon and Roelker call this time from 1517 to 1559 *préréforme*.

So we have two possible time periods for the *pré-réforme*: a reforming movement predating 1517, and the fluid years of the early Reformation itself. Clearly the choice of time period affects our understanding of who participated in the *pré-réforme*. Yet, crucially for my purpose today, a summary of what *pré-réformistes* considered important would accurately describe participants in either era, a confirmation of Higman's and Taylor's arguments that their piety was more Gallican and *évangélique*, than Catholic or Protestant.

What then is the *pré-réforme*? It is a new way of thinking, tied in with the humanism stemming from the Renaissance and with a fresh reading of the Bible, encouraged by many, but most famously by Martin Luther. (Hence, many *pré-réformistes* in the 1520s were labeled Lutherans. In many cases, however, they were *not* Protestants.[20]) While these early reformers certainly had extensive networks among themselves, there was little about the movement that was organized, systematized or disciplined, as the Protestants later would be. They simply wanted to be "good news" people who sought to recapture what they felt had been lost: the joy of the gospel of Christ. It was this spirit that marked, though imperfectly, the *pré-réforme*. As Higman summarizes: "The Erasmian reform

19. See Monter, *Judging*.

20. See Higman, *Censorship and the Sorbonne*, 39: "in many cases, the French *évangéliques* were saying the same things as Luther; but that does not make them Lutherans." See too ibid., 45. Mack Holt stresses that the earlier (pre-1517) humanists as a group "were clearly not proto-Protestants": Holt, *Wars of Religion*, 15. Emphasis mine.

SCHOEBER—*John Calvin and the "Still-born" Third Option* 93

was concerned much less with creedal statements, intellectual defini-
tions of a truth which, in any case, is beyond human comprehension,
than with a quality of life, an attitude of mind and soul, the imitation of
Christ, the living relationship of man with God."[21] This spirit can be said
generally to mark either era that we can label *pré-réforme*.

So, why this excursus to discuss the concept of *pré-réforme*? Simply,
I wanted to demonstrate the amazing similarity in spirit and in doctrinal emphasis between all reformers—Protestant and Catholic—in this
drawn out period of church reform that considerably predated 1517,
while—of course—continuing after that date as well. I hope its irenic
tendency in bridging certain differences that later became firmly divisive
has also been apparent. In the earlier part of the sixteenth century it
was unclear whether a traditional or more flexible perspective would
become dominant in French Catholicism. In fact, just prior to the *Affaire
des Placards*, optimism seemed to reign that the *évangélique* spirit would
prevail.[22]

Gérard Roussel participated in this evangelical movement. As a
young man, he received a humanistic education and was recruited to
be part of a circle of preachers called together by a reform-minded
bishop, Guillaume Briçonnet, to renew the diocese of Meaux, just east
of Paris. They were joined by the widely regarded humanistic biblical
scholar and translator, Jacques Lefèvre d'Étaples, who functioned as a
"senior statesman." William Farel was another of these preachers until
he was expelled because his preaching was too radical. He quickly declared himself a Protestant, and headed for Switzerland. Roussel almost
certainly was one of Lefèvre d'Étaples' "disciples" that assisted him in
producing a preaching manual, *Épistres et Évangiles pour les cinquante et
deux sepmaines de l'an*.[23] Though the original title page listed no author,
it was widely understood at the time—including by the Sorbonne when
it condemned the work— that it was written by Lefèvre d'Étaples *et ses
disciples*. Published in 1525, it was produced by the Meaux preachers.

21. Higman, *Censorship and the Sorbonne*, 38. See also his "*Premières réponses catholiques*," 513.

22. See Higman, *Censorship and the Sorbonne*, chap. 3, "Religious Policy;" and
Higman, "*De l'affaire des Placards aux nicodémites*," 619–25; and Crouzet, *La genèse de
la Réforme français*, 216–20. Farge, *Faculty*, 161–62, conversely argues that the Sorbonne
largely determined orthodoxy in France already in the 1520s. It is open to question
whether the majority of opinion-shapers in that decade would have agreed.

23. *Fac-similé de la première édition* Simon du Bois.

The preachers did their job well. Meaux had been a neglected and lax diocese.[24] It developed a warm and vibrant spirituality that remained so for decades. The manual is indicative of the approach of the évangéliques. It warmly commends faith in Christ, and contains many variations on the theme of a living confidence in Christ and in the Bible as the Word of God. It also urges appropriate moral choices in response to these spiritual teachings. Notably, however, it stayed clear of attacking two key things: the prerogatives of the Catholic hierarchy and the theology of the Mass. (The preachers did allow themselves critical comment on the *abuses* perpetrated by church leaders.) Despite its restraint, the manual encountered the opposition of the Faculty of Theology who took advantage of the king's preoccupation with his war in Italy against Charles V to press legal charges. By 1525, the Circle of Meaux had been disbanded.

Roussel continued his efforts at church renewal, however.[25] When the Circle was dismantled in 1525, he wrote to Briçonnet with excitement about the reformation preaching he was hearing in Strasbourg.[26] He then became a court preacher under the patronage of Marguerite of Navarre. In 1534 he preached these "new doctrines" during Lent in Paris, at first drawing large crowds.[27] He also drew enormous opposition from the Faculty. Francis I, displeased at the resulting tumults, punished several key traditionalists with banishment from Paris—although the *Affaire des Placards* in October brought them back into favor. In 1536 Roussel accepted Marguerite's nomination to the bishopric of Oléron in the southwest of what we now call France. Roussel would seek to be a faithful bishop, publishing instructions on visitation within the diocese and a series of lectures on the formation of pastors known as the *Familière Exposition*.[28] The Sorbonne again denounced Roussel in 1550, condemning the evangelical nature of these lectures.[29] He even, it seems,

24. See Taylor, *Soldiers of Christ,* 16, 246, n.1; de la Tour, *Les Origines de la Réforme,* t. III, 112–15.

25. Farge, *Faculty,* 173.

26. Taylor, *Le Picart,* 39.

27. For details of the tumultuous events that resulted, see Taylor, *Le Picart,* 46–51.

28. "*Forme de visite de diocèse*" found in Charles Schmidt, *Gérard Roussel,* 226–39; *La Familière Exposition du symbole, de la loi et de l'oraison dominicale* found in Landa, *The Reformed Theology of Gerard Roussel,* 269–610.

29. Higman, *Censorship and the Sorbonne,* 43; text found in Schmidt *Prédicateur,* 240–43.

cooperated with his former colleague, William Farel, in the translation into French of a children's catechism originally produced in German by the Lutheran Johann Brenz.[30] The fact that many are surprised at such cooperation demonstrates how we have conditioned ourselves to read the religious history of the first half of the sixteenth century through the hardened confessional lens of subsequent years. Roussel was willing to be controversial in the eyes of the traditionalists, because he felt that they were getting in the way of desperately needed church renewal. Otherwise, he worked irenically and cooperatively with many—Protestant or Catholic—in the interest of promoting a biblical Gallican spirituality that would renew a church that most people knew needed renovation. Thierry Wanegffelen has argued—in a work whose title is very suggestive, *Ni Rom, Ni Genève*—that the majority of French folk did not want to participate in the battle between the Catholic Church hierarchy and the increasing influence of Geneva as the centre of the international Reformed movement.[31] They simply wanted to be Christian. In the face of an historical narrative that argues that religion is persistently violent, it is a story that needs to be told. This mindset was already clearly present in the 1520s. Roussel remained Bishop of Oléron until he died in 1550. His death reflects the controversies of his life: "an ardent Catholic took a hatchet to his [elevated] pulpit while he was preaching. Pinned under the collapsed structure, Roussel was dragged free by his supporters, but died en route to Oléron."[32] Still, he died a Catholic bishop, a Catholic *évangélique*. His attacker, Arnauld de Maytie, was tried by the *Parlement* in Bordeaux. They acquitted him because of his *"pieuse et belle action."*[33] It is a sign of the way the tide had turned since the *Affaire des Placards*: During Lent in 1534, it seemed that even Paris would be caught up in an evangelical renewal of the Gallican church; by 1550, the murderer of a leading light in that movement would be officially commended for his action with little popular protest. The traditionalist side of the pincer that destroyed the *évangéliques* had become a very powerful force.

---

30. So argued by Marc Venard, *"Un catéchisme offert à Marguerite de Navarre,"* 5–32. The text of the *"Initiatoire instruction en la religion chrestienne pour les enffants"* is found in the *Annexe*.

31. Wanegffelen, *Ni Rome Ni Genève*.

32. Taylor, *Reformations*, 195.

33. Schmidt, *Prédicateur*, 164.

It was when Roussel became a bishop that Calvin turned against him, forming the other side of the pincer. Calvin, during his stay with Renée of Ferrara, wrote to "an old friend, but now a bishop." His letter was called, "*sur le devoir de l'homme chrestien, en l'administration ou rejection des bénéfices de l'Église papale.*"[34] In his contest with the Nicodemites several years later, he seems to refer to Roussel, without naming him, as one type of compromiser: a preacher that will preach the gospel in some fashion, but who will not press on to preach a "pure Evangel."[35] High ecclesiastical officials and philosophers, both of whom happily separate words from action, were two other types. A final type—most interesting in light of Wanegffelen's claim about the spiritual attitudes of most French folk in this era—was common folk "who only want to be left alone to pursue their ordinary occupations."[36] Calvin implies a spiritual indifference motivated them; but what if Wanegffelen is correct and their attitude was more positive: "Leave us out of these political struggles so that we can more effectively engage in lives of Christian neighborliness?"[37]

I have shown that there existed in France in the early sixteenth century an indigenous humanistic reform movement. It sought, in line with Renaissance ideas, a return to ancient sources, particularly the Bible in its original languages. It also sought to make this learning available in the vernacular to produce for many people a faith that was more "learned" and less "material," with a greater sense of "interiority" and a deeper personal morality. It placed much emphasis on the individual and on humanity. It was wide open to Luther, sharing his piety to a great extent and giving considerable approval to his doctrines. Ultimately, many involved in the movement refused to accept Luther's schism. Irenicism was a prominent feature of this widely affirmed spirituality, and, for a time, many were optimistic that this evangelical movement would, in fact, renew the Gallican church. The traditionalists successfully used powerful political and legal tools against this movement. Yet Calvin's attacks from Geneva contributed significantly to their diminished influence and, ul-

---

34. Cited in ibid., 114.

35. Farris, "Calvin's Letter to Luther," 67 n.19, summarizes the four types of Nicodemites, according to Calvin.

36. Ibid.

37. Marsh, *Popular Religion in Sixteenth-Century England*, describes just such an attitude for common folk in England during the Reformation period.

timately, isolation. In light of the Wars of Religion that began in France in 1562 and the subsequent history of aggression launched (usually by the nation state but) in the name of faith during the era of confessionalization, perhaps we can see how valuable an irenic, effective, and non-schismatic church renewal movement could have been. Contributing to its downfall, may have been Calvin's biggest mistake.

7

Pilgrimage

Calvin and the Rehabilitation of a Reformation Renegade

LYNNE MCNAUGHTON

OVER THE LAST DOZEN years of leading pilgrimages to Christian sites in Europe, I have occasionally encountered a slight hesitation from a number of my Protestant colleagues, as if pilgrimages were still somewhat suspect. I have been curious about this. My research has focused on Pilgrimage in its revival as a contemporary spiritual practice among Protestants.[1] I have looked at the meaning of pilgrimage for participants, how movement is crucial to its sense and function, how it is spiritually transformative for people, how the pilgrimage of an individual changes his or her relationship to the institutional church, how a profound experience of "communitas" develops during pilgrimage.[2] In this paper I explore how the meaning and practice of pilgrimage shifted during the Reformation.

Embarking on a pilgrimage, the pilgrim sets out on a journey to a holy place, a location where God has been encountered by others in the past. In the fourth century, when the Emperor Constantine's mother Helena brought back to Rome a piece of the "True Cross" from Jerusalem, the shrine built to house this relic quickly became a lodestone for religious visitation and prayer. Very rapidly, Christians also came to adopt this spiritual practice found in almost all religions. Beginning in

1. McNaughton, *Pilgrimage Leadership.*

2. See the classic anthropology of pilgrimage by Turner and Turner, *Image and Pilgrimage in Christian Culture.*

the fifth century, pilgrimage became highly valued for Irish Christians of the early middle Ages; to be *"peregrini pro Christo,"* "wanderers for Christ" was considered a form of martyrdom, of witness and giving oneself completely to God.[3] Pilgrimages were sometimes undertaken, too, as penance for a crime or sin. The practice grew in importance for all of Western Christianity in the High Middle Ages during and after the Crusades. However, in the fifteenth and sixteenth centuries there were a growing number of calls, from both Catholics and Protestants, for reform of the many abuses that had become associated with the huge numbers of travelers. The practice of pilgrimage abruptly came to an almost complete halt during the Reformation; several hundred significant pilgrimages were stopped within decades. But by the seventeenth century, pilgrimage was again being used as a root metaphor for the Christian life, in the poetry of Edmund Spenser and of George Herbert,[4] and in that best seller for Puritans, John Bunyan's *Pilgrim's Progress.*

What happened to the meaning and practice of Pilgrimage during the Reformation, and where does John Calvin fit into this change? This paper explores the critique of the practice of pilgrimage by several Reformers prior to Calvin, and suggests, surprisingly, that Calvin actually was an important hinge in a re-direction of the practice of pilgrimage, rehabilitating rather than discarding the notion of travel for a holy purpose.

THE REFORMATION CONDEMNATION OF PILGRIMAGE

Critique of the abuses of pilgrimages did not begin, of course, in the sixteenth century. Geoffrey Chaucer has a host of satirical characters and lines in *The Canterbury Tales.* One of the early and best known voices of critique of pilgrimage at the outset of the Reformation was Erasmus (c.1466–1536), the Dutch Renaissance humanist, priest, and theologian, who lived and died a Catholic.

In his exposition of Ps 4, as he examined the phrase "offers sacrifices of righteousness" (Ps 4:5), Erasmus notes, with irony,

> Now let us consider people who, overwhelmed by penitence for their earlier lives, set out for Jerusalem, or sail to Compostella,

---

3. For an excellent discussion of this, see O'Loughlin, *Journeys on the Edges.*

4. For example, Spenser *The Faerie Queene*, Canto X, lxi; Herbert, *The Temple,* "The Pilgrimage."

thinking that they are offering the "sacrifice of righteousness."
I do not intend to condemn such expedition entirely, but I am
afraid those who hope to achieve *righteousness* by them are mis-
taken. If God has promised anyone righteousness as a result of
them, then His promise must be believed; if not, then what is
done is not done out of faith.[5]

He names Compostella, the most widely known pilgrimage route of
the middle ages, the *Camino Santiago,* or "the Way of St. James," with
routes beginning throughout Europe and leading to the cathedral city of
Compostella in north-west Spain. Incidentally, the last few decades have
seen a renewed interest in Compostella; this medieval pilgrimage route
enjoys a huge popularity today.

Here, Erasmus does not condemn pilgrimage as such, but he raises
a serious theological concern—which we will see in a moment echoed by
Luther, Bucer, and other Reformers—that pilgrimage must not be seen
to take the place of grace. This would be, of course, a central concern of
the Protestant Reformers, that no religious practice can gain or merit
our salvation.

Erasmus' *Colloquies* were an immensely popular and widely-read
series of educational dialogues written across a number of years. Their
devastating wit alarmed many church defenders, including Erasmus' own
friend Thomas More. Three of these pertain specifically to pilgrimage.

The first is titled "On Rash Vows."[6] This dialogue is very humorous,
caustically pointing out the moral dangers and temptations encountered
by pilgrims. He also questions whether anyone, having, *in extremis,* made
vows to a saint to go on pilgrimage in exchange for healing, should fulfill
these vows, if in the process they must leave behind day-to-day responsibilities. His tone is such that Thomas Topley, an Augustinian friar, is said
to have remarked that reading this particular colloquy caused his faith to
shrink; "I was almost withdrawn from devotion to saints."[7]

The second colloquy, "The Shipwreck," is a satire on many of the
superstitions found in the various religious practices of the time; it is full
of irony, and his opponents condemned his writing as irreverent. Again

5. Erasmus, *In Psalmum Quartum Concio,* 259.

6. Erasmus, *De votis temere susceptis* (1522) *Colloquies.* In Erasmus, *Collected Works
of Erasmus,* vols. 39/40, 37–43.

7. John Foxe. *Acts and Monuments,* V, 40 quoted by Craig Thompson in Erasmus,
Collected Works of Erasmus, vols. 39/40, 36.

McNaughton—*Pilgrimage*

he is scornful of those who bargain with the saints, in this case for safety in a shipwreck, giving as an example of such deals: "I'll go to Rome if you rescue me."[8]

The third, "A Pilgrimage for Religion's Sake," was probably written after his public battle with Luther over the freedom of the human will. This piece is a dialogue between his character *Menedemus* (meaning "Stay-at-home") and *Ogygius* (meaning in general "primeval.")[9] The latter is back from a pilgrimage to Walsingham, the popular shrine to Mary in Norfolk, England, one of the most notable pilgrimages in England. Ogygius produces a letter sent from the Virgin Mary to *Glaucoplutus*, a thinly disguised naming of Huldreich Zwingli, the Protestant Reformer of Zurich.[10] What makes this humor so mordant is that in his pre-reformer life, Zwingli had been chaplain at the great Marian shrine of Einsiedeln. In a heavily sarcastic tone, Mary writes, "I am deeply grateful to you, a follower of Luther,[11] for busily persuading people that the invocation of saints is useless." She outlines in detail how she is exhausted by the "shameless entreaties of mortals," but complains that she is now poor because no one is going to her shrines.[12] The dialogue goes on between Menedemus and Ogygius in a cutting style, critiquing every abuse that happens on pilgrimages, such as fake miracles and fabricated relics to dupe the pilgrims, as well as immoral behavior on the part of the pilgrims themselves.

In his letter to the English Cardinal Thomas Wolsey defending the Colloquies, Erasmus is very concerned by those who "run off to Compostella, deserting a wife and children left at home ... People say I make fun of Christian fasts, of solemn vows ... and pilgrimages undertaken for the sake of religion. They're simply liars. Superstition of some people in these matters I do mock; *Superstition* richly deserves mockery."[13] For Erasmus, superstition prevails "when everything is

8. Erasmus, *Naufragium* (1523). Erasmus, *Collected Works of Erasmus*, vols. 39/40, 356.

9. Erasmus probably uses this name in the sense of "committed to ancient practices."

10. Craig Thompson in Erasmus, *Collected Works of Erasmus*, vols. 39/40, 653 n. 23.

11. An epithet Zwingli would have resented.

12. Erasmus, *Collected Works of Erasmus*, vols. 39/40, 624–55.

13. Quoted by Craig Thompson, in Erasmus, *Collected Works of Erasmus*, vols. 39/40, xl.

sought from saints as though Christ were dead, or when we beg the help of saints as though they were more compassionate than God."[14]

His tone is so mocking it is hard to imagine that anyone who read them would ever set out on a pilgrimage again. However that may be, consistently Erasmus says in his defense of the Colloquies, that the religious practice of venerating saints, (and by inference pilgrimages), is tolerable if the "superstition is excluded."

As has been said, where Erasmus uses a rapier, Luther wields a broadsword. Martin Luther (1483–1546), German priest and professor of theology, was initially deeply influenced by Erasmus. Luther's emphasis on grace, his theology that salvation is a free gift and therefore not earned from good works, made him suspicious of the practice of pilgrimage. In "An Appeal to the Ruling Class" (1520), his treatise urging the nobility of German nationality to reform the Church since the clergy would or could not, Luther, like Erasmus, attacks the abuses, and advises that pilgrimages "should be disallowed."[15] He spends most of his time denouncing pilgrimages to Rome in particular, (perhaps because he himself took an earlier pilgrimage to Rome and had firsthand experience of the corruption and exploitation involved), although later he will include *all* pilgrimages.

Luther outlines several reasons for not going on Pilgrimages. Among these, in summary:

- There was scandalous behavior. Pilgrimages were "frequent occasion for sin."[16]

- Theologically, "pilgrimages seduce untrained minds" into thinking these are "acts of merit." It is a "satanic delusion" that this is a good work. In this concern he echoes Erasmus.[17]

- Socially, pilgrimages take people away from their responsibilities to family and neighbor. Undertaking a pilgrimage is expensive, which may also mean neglect of the family. Again, this concern that pilgrimage not be an excuse for shirking one's duty reiterates an apprehension of Erasmus.

14. Erasmus, in a letter defending the Colloquies, quoted by Craig Thompson in Erasmus, *Collected Works of Erasmus*, vols. 39/40, 621.

15. Luther, *Selections from his Writings*, 443.

16. *"An Appeal to the Ruling Class"* in Luther, *Selections from his Writings*, 444.

17. Ibid., 443.

- Luther is clear that new pilgrimage sites are unnecessary: "if their faith was as it should be they would find everything necessary in their own churches."[18] (This is an appeal to the traditional monastic call for stability in community, a concern which, we shall later see, is not a concern for Calvin and Knox when they are shaping the Reformed Church.)

- Pilgrimages increase greed; he states baldly that the Pope "fleeces people"! "What you have to buy from the Pope is neither good nor godly."[19]

Luther asserts that if people have made a vow to go on pilgrimage, they should be released from their vows, although he recognizes that pastorally for conscience' sake someone might need to go to fulfill their vow.[20] Luther does say that if they want to travel for curiosity's sake, not for religious reasons, that is fine. Remember he is writing to the nobility; he knows they like to take holidays!

Martin Bucer (1491–1551), Calvin's mentor and friend, also writes directly against the practice of pilgrimage. In his 1527 commentary on the Synoptic Gospels, in his discussion of the story of Herod's foolish vow to Salome which cost John the Baptist his head (Matt 14), after a lengthy condemnation of monastic vows, Bucer denounces vows to go on pilgrimage. These, he asserts, also displease God.

> Let me say accurately of vagrancy[21] unto various shrines of saints that these are similar [to monastic vows]. For they also are taken up as if pleasing to God and out of superstition, as if God were more present in one place than in others, or requires some other worship than godliness, let alone a worship of his saint, all which things grossly offend God. Therefore to fulfill these vows is not only a vain service to God but even sins against faith and love. Against faith, because one seeks more of God's grace in one location than in another. Against love, because works and expense are lost uselessly, with which the neighbor ought to have been served. I won't even mention the pernicious scandal which is associated

---

18. Ibid., 456–57.

19. Ibid., 459–60.

20. Ibid., 444.

21. This is the word he uses for pilgrimage!

with some pilgrimages. So these vows cannot be fulfilled by the
godly, however someone vowed them in a holy manner.[22]

Bucer strongly disapproves of pilgrimage and uses reasons similar
to the other key voices of the early Reformation, Luther and Erasmus,
that pilgrimage treads on the dangerous theological ground of superstition and the worship of saints, and that it is a waste of resources better
spent on neighbor.

CALVIN AND VERMIGLI

How then does Calvin fit with these other Reformers in his treatment of
pilgrimage? A review of his references to pilgrimages will reveal first that
there are far fewer in Calvin's writing than one might expect, and then
that Calvin ultimately becomes a hinge for a change in attitude towards
pilgrimage, eventually arguing that there well may be benefit in travel
undertaken with godly intention.

Did the Catholic Calvin himself ever go on pilgrimage? In preparation for leading a pilgrimage to explore sites of Calvin's ministry, I was
in Noyon, France, where Calvin was born. Right past the door of the
house where he grew up runs the great pilgrim road to Compostella;
one would have to imagine that as a child he saw pilgrims on the road,
as well as praying in the Cathedral of Notre-Dame de Noyon that stands
100 meters from his home. Only once does he mention this, near the end
of his 1543 *Treatise on Relics*, with the delightfully plenteous title, "A very
useful notice on the great benefit which would come to Christendom,
were it to inventory all the holy bodies and relics found in Italy, France,
Germany, Spain and other kingdoms and countries."[23]

With a mocking tone similar to Erasmus, he writes: "Anna, mother
of the Virgin Mary, has one of her bodies at Apte in Provence, and another in the church of Mary Insulan at Lyons. Besides, she has one of
her hands at Treves, another at Turin, and a third in a town of Thuringia
which takes its name from it. I say nothing of the fragments which exist
in more than one hundred places. Among others, I remember having

---

22. Bucer, *Commentary on Matthew*, Vol. 2. Strasbourg, 1527. My thanks to my colleague, R. Gerald Hobbs, who translated this passage from the Latin.

23. CR 6, 405–52.

myself, long ago, kissed a portion of it, at Ourscamp a monastery near Noyon, where it is held in great reverence."[24]

In Calvin's *Institutes* the only negative reference to contemporary pilgrimage is precisely where one would expect it, under the subject of abuses of the Church's authority, in relationship to the issue of works righteousness. Like Erasmus, Luther and Bucer, he is disturbed by the practice of making a vow to go on pilgrimage. In Book Four, chapter thirteen, under the heading "Vows; and How everyone rashly taking them has miserably entangled himself," section 7 "Perverse vows," he notes "for men esteemed it great wisdom to undertake votive pilgrimages to holier places, and sometimes to make their journey either on foot or half naked, in order to obtain more merit through their weariness."[25] The problem, for Calvin, is that anyone might think they would gain righteousness by embarking on a pilgrimage. The spiritual danger was people placing their hope of divine favor in any form of external observance.

Like Erasmus, Luther, and Bucer, Calvin is also concerned with superstition. In 1547, he wrote regulations for the country churches of Geneva, where he simply names pilgrimage in a list of "Faults Contravening the Reformation," but his critique is not of pilgrimage *per se* but of the superstitions one needs to eradicate in one's parish in order to promote a Reformed church. He names as suspect "any who shall have been on pilgrimage or similar journeys."[26] It seems here it is those who go on *repeated* pilgrimages that need to be dealt with pastorally, presumably because repetition indicates they are placing hope in the practice itself.

In his *Tracts and Treatises,* in the *Antidotes,* Calvin's response to the Roman Catholic Faculty of the Sorbonne, after a whole series of articles on the veneration of the Saints, he has a short piece (Article 14) on Pilgrimage. His argument here is that Jesus abolished the idea of the holiness of particular places, quoting from John's gospel the story of Jesus' encounter with the Samaritan woman at the well: "The hour

24. Calvin, *Opera,* CR 6, 442; Calvin, *Tracts and Treatises on the Reformation of the Church,* Vol. 1, 329.

25. Calvin, *Institutes of the Christian Religion.* Vol. 2. Book IV, edited by J. T. McNeill, 1260.

26. Calvin, "Ordinances for the Supervision of the Churches in the Country," in Calvin, *Calvin: Theological Treatises,* 80. Reference also found in Hexham, "Protestant Reformers, Travel, and Pilgrimage." http://www.christian-travelers-guides.com/culture/pilgrimreform.html.

comes, when not at this mountain, or Jerusalem, but everywhere shall the true worshippers worship God in spirit and in truth." (John 6:21, 23) Calvin sees the danger of idolatry of place, and calls it a new Judaism.[27]

In the article on "Human Traditions," Calvin disputes any practice binding on human conscience which is "not commanded by God."[28] He uses strong language here, calling it "perverse doctrines of Satan" that the institutional church requires something that God does not require. He mentions pilgrimage in a list of the Catholic Church's requirement of such things as prohibition of marriage for clergy, confession, and distinction of foods. Any such commandment destroys Christian liberty, negating Paul's resounding proclamation in Gal 5:1 "For freedom Christ has set us free." Calvin's concern here, then, is only when pilgrimage is a *required* act of piety.

The last negative reference is in Calvin's letter written to the Emperor Charles V at Bucer's request. He alludes to pilgrimage when he names his objections to the idolatry of statues and superstitions.

> I have not yet averted to the grosser superstitions, though these cannot be confined to the ignorant, since they are approved by public consent. They adorn their idols now with flowers and chaplets, now with robes, vests, girdles, purses and frivolities of every kind. They light tapers and burn incense before them, and carry them on their shoulders in solemn state. They assemble from long distances to one statue, though they have similar things at home. Likewise, though in one shrine there may be several images of the Virgin Mary, or someone else, they pass these by, and one is frequented as if it were more divine.[29]

What one finds then is that Calvin has objections to pilgrimage similar to those of the earlier Reformers; he mocks the superstition and the worship of saints.

What has just been laid out is not simply a few examples chosen out of extensive critique of pilgrimage in Calvin. On the contrary, the above are the *only* five negative references I could find in all of Calvin's writing. All are the same arguments to be found in Erasmus, Luther, and Bucer. Calvin lists pilgrimage as one example of many instances where his main concern is superstition and idolatry, veneration of relics.

---

27. Calvin, *Tracts and Treatises on the Reformation of the Church*, Vol. 1, 95–96.

28. Calvin, *Theological Treatises*, 31–32.

29. Ibid., 189–90.

Where Calvin differs remarkably from his predecessors, where he becomes a hinge for a new way of viewing pilgrimage, is in his positive images of pilgrimage, his surprising statements that it can be good to travel for religious reasons!

First, appropriately, Calvin discovers affirmation of pilgrimage in Scripture. Luther had said of pilgrimage "God never gave such a commandment."[30] Calvin, in contrast, discovers in the Bible the impetus for pilgrimage as something to which God may call a person of faith. First, in Calvin's commentary on Gen 12, he examines the story of Abraham, the Biblical pilgrim *par excellence*. On the phrase "'Abram moved' (12:8) . . . we ought not to doubt that he was, by some necessity, compelled to do so. But if Abram bore his continual wanderings patiently, our fastidiousness is utterly inexcusable, when we murmur against God, if he does not grant us a quiet nest.[31] Of course, one wonders how autobiographical this is for Calvin, who moved from Noyon, to Paris, Orleans, Bourges, Paris, Basel, Ferrara, Geneva, Strasbourg, Geneva—nine moves before he settled in Geneva at the age of thirty-three! No quiet nest for him! Abram's journey, according to Calvin, is in contrast with that of "fickle persons impelled by levity, by foolish hope or by any allurements . . . Abram did not voluntarily or for his own gratification run hither or thither, as light-minded persons are wont to do."[32]

So Calvin attacks pilgrimage when it is for frivolous purpose, but does not oppose it in and of itself, finding biblical precedent and acknowledging there may be good godly reasons for travel. In the *Institutes,* commending the metaphor in Hebrews, he writes "the Lord teaches us that the present life is for his people as a pilgrimage on which they are hastening toward the heavenly kingdom."[33]

The other positive, if unexpected, contribution Calvin makes to rehabilitating the practice of pilgrimage was his encouragement for people to move about for more frequent communion in the different parish churches of Geneva. He clearly thought the ideal was weekly communion (citing the practice of the first Christians) but, at the insistence of the Magistrates, the churches in Geneva had communion only

30. Luther, "An Appeal to the Ruling Class" 443.

31. Calvin, *Commentaries on the First Book of Moses,* Vol. I, 356.

32. Ibid., 357.

33. Calvin, *Institutes,* III, vii, 3. Edited by Battles Vol. 1, 693. Gerald Hobbs has dealt with this at greater length in his contribution to this volume.

four times a year. Calvin convinced the city authorities to stagger these times, so people could travel to different churches and receive communion once a month.[34] This encouragement of movement, we shall see shortly, will develop into the communion seasons of seventeenth- and eighteenth-century Scotland.

When one traces how pilgrimage practice evolved after Calvin, one can see how he was the hinge between the Reformation first discarding pilgrimage and the later reclaiming of forms of travel for holy purposes.

Peter Martyr Vermigli, (1499–1562) Calvin's immediate successor as theology professor in Strasbourg, likewise had a long career of holy movement, first fleeing the Inquisition in Italy, then moving to Strasbourg, Oxford, Strasbourg, and back to Zurich. By the time of his death he enjoyed a theological stature amongst the Reformed second only to Calvin. Vermigli speaks at length about pilgrimage when he lectures on *The Book of Judges* in Strasbourg between 1553 and 1555. While this may seem at first an unlikely source for widespread influence, Vermigli's question-and-answer style (known as the *loci* method) brought this passage to a broad readership in his posthumous *Commonplaces*. When looking at the Kenites (Judg 1:16), the descendants of Moses' relatives who moved to the land of Canaan, Vermigli asks: "Why leave one's homeland and move to another place?" "What are the best causes of *Peregrinatio*?" (Latin for pilgrimage)

Vermigli acknowledges there can be good reasons to travel for one's faith and that not all good people travel for the same reasons. In the unit "Of Peregrinations" he outlines the following as exemplary:

- People "leave their country because they may not worship God there after the sincere and lawful kind of worshipping";

- Or because of persecution

- Or "to attain more profit and be more instructed in things divine and necessary for salvation." He commends Plato for travelling to Egypt and the Queen of Sheba to meet Solomon. "So the Kenites (back to his Judges text) who already worshiped one God, yet nevertheless they desired to be still more instructed and more absolutely to receive the laws, the ordinances and worship of God."

- Or to help other people.

---

34. Calvin, *Institutes* IV, xiii, 46; *Draft Ecclesiastical Ordinances*, 66–67.

Vermigli concludes that "travels which are willingly taken in hand are honest and praiseworthy," so therefore "let the godly men when they travel have regard for these causes" of spiritual benefit. He counsels laying aside the abuses and "wicked affections" that had plagued the previous practice of pilgrimages.

He summarizes by saying that if one travels "to be bettered in godliness and learning, they shall justly be said to wander (i.e., *peregrinari*) rather than to travel." Spartan law, he notes, forbade travel because some people were affected by wickedness (same argument as Erasmus, Luther, Bucer) but Vermigli counters this, saying pilgrimage is permitted as a way to "improve godliness and learning." [35]

Within a generation of Erasmus and Luther, then, there is a more nuanced opinion of pilgrimage amongst Protestants, that it may be undertaken legitimately for godly reasons. Was it that by then the abuses, such as veneration of the relics of saints and people avoiding family responsibilities, with which the early Reformers were so concerned, had been long subdued and were no longer a problem for Reformed Christians? Was it that a generation now steeped in a theology of grace would not be in danger of thinking any righteousness was to be gained by pilgrimage? Clearly for Vermigli and Calvin, *peregrinari* (travel for Christ) could avoid the abuses and fill a good purpose, and they set the stage for reclaiming godly travel.

RE-EMERGENCE OF THE PRACTICE OF PILGRIMAGE

It lies beyond the scope of this paper to document the full re-emergence of this once maligned religious rite. Two examples from the British Isles will suggest its enduring spiritual power, even in the relatively austere piety of the Reformed tradition. The permission to travel for godly purpose, for spiritual benefit and learning, developed into the practice of Communion Seasons and of Preaching Festivals.

From 1554 through 1559/60, John Knox, William Whittingham, and the other refugees from Queen Mary's restoration of the Roman Catholic Church in England fled to Geneva where they formed an English church. This church was naturally shaped by what they saw in Geneva. They would have taken part in the movement to various churches in the city on different Sundays to receive more frequent communion. They

35. Vermigli, *The Commonplaces*, 191–92.

experienced on a weekly basis the practice of people travelling to hear Calvin's preaching in St. Peter's Cathedral, four times every two weeks and several lectures on Scripture.[36] Calvin's encouragement of travel for educational purposes and spiritual benefit had taken root. Even people from the country were directed to travel frequently to Geneva to hear preaching, on often impassable roads. This practice, known as "prophesying," had come from Zwingli in Zurich, with his understanding that the Holy Spirit operated best when people gathered around the study of Scripture and preaching. Knox and Whittingham encountered this tradition of "prophesying." They then took these practices back with them to England and Scotland, when they were allowed to return under the reign of Elizabeth. Concerned for a more thorough reform of the church, they implemented the same pattern of urging congregants to go to where scholarly preaching could be heard and where communion was held. Given that in some parishes, evangelical preaching was never heard, people began to travel to hear good preachers, sometimes hearing as many as three sermons on a Sunday.

Brian Spinks, in *Sacraments, Ceremonies and the Stuart Divines,* traces this development in Scottish Puritanism. He discusses the formation of the Scottish Covenanters, and the development of "Communion Seasons." These "festal communions" were characterized by "outdoor preaching, great concourses of people from an extensive region, long vigils of prayer, powerful experiences of conversion and confirmation, a number of popular ministers cooperating for extended services over three days or more, a seasonal focus on summer, and unusually large numbers of communicants at successive tables."[37]

In his doctoral work, Leigh Eric Schmidt traces the links from Calvin's reformation to the Scottish communion seasons of the eighteenth century through to the revivals in North America in the mid-nineteenth century.[38] He argues that these communion seasons replaced the high holy festivals and pilgrimages to holy wells of late medieval Catholicism. Many travelled forty or fifty miles to these events, not to "holy sites" of ancient relics of saints, but to the "holy site" of preaching of the Word.

36. See the careful detailed analysis of this in Parker, *Calvin's Preaching.*

37. Leigh Eric Schmidt, quoted in Spinks, *Sacraments, Ceremonies and the Stuart Divines,* 99–100.

38. Schmidt, *Scottish Communions and American Revivals.*

POLITICAL OPPOSITION

I wonder, in fact, how much the abolition of pilgrimage as a spiritual practice was not so much for theological reasons as for political power or for economic control. For example, German princes were reluctant to see movement to Rome; pilgrimages brought financial gain. In England, under the absolute monarchy, this political control in a time of unrest is even more clearly observed. The real condemnation and abolition of pilgrimage in England during the Reformation comes from the political authorities. Henry VIII, we know, went on a personal pilgrimage to Walsingham when he was still married to Catherine of Aragon, walking barefoot the last mile, to pray for a male heir. Some say that this unanswered prayer was his reason for later shutting down pilgrimages, and his particular hatred of Walsingham. Probably a more obvious and pressing reason for Henry's huge distaste for pilgrimage were the large resistance movements of 1534, when some 30,000 peasants from York protested his changes to the Church. They named their march "the Pilgrimage of Grace." Pilgrimage for Henry became synonymous with treason. It is striking that one of Elizabeth's first moves was to stamp out every trace of pilgrimages at the former shrines. The injunctions of 1559 order the destruction of monuments of pilgrimage.[39]

Likewise, a century later, the Anglican monarch Charles I passed an act in Parliament to limit the practice of "communion seasons," citing: "disobedient people, who ordinarlie, when the communion is not ministrat in thair parishes and at all other tymes when their occasions and their humor serves thame, not onelie leaves thair owne parish kirkes bot runnes to seeke the communion at the hands of suche minister as they know to be disconforme to all good order, which is the meanes of their disobedience to his Majesteis laws"[40]

Political leaders are anxious about people on the move, as they cannot be controlled; in the age of absolute monarchy no Tudor or Stewart monarch could tolerate loosening connection to institutions that would happen with pilgrimage. I suggest that this nervousness is because they intuitively knew or feared that movement, the key element of pilgrimage, is destabilizing to institutions, dangerous to order. Victor and Edith

---

39. Hutton, "The Local Impact of the Tudor Reformations," 133.

40. Quoted in Spinks, *Sacraments, Ceremonies and the Stuart Divines*, 100.

Turner, in their classic anthropology of pilgrimage,[41] discovered that although pilgrimage roots someone more deeply in the foundational myths of their faith, at the same time it destabilizes their connection with the current or local institution. Their faith is strengthened in God; and they therefore do not need the church institution to the same extent. Having fewer ties to the institution is deeply threatening to those in authority. What I have discovered, however, is that it also renews peoples' hope in a time of transition in the church, they become less anxious about current threats and changes to the visible church now, and more connected with the whole people of God over time. I am curious about how this sociological phenomena was operative with the shutting down and reclaiming of pilgrimage during the Reformation.

CONCLUSION

It seems there is some innate human need to travel that emerges quickly then after the early years of Reformation, allowed by such redefinition as we saw in Calvin and Vermigli. Although pilgrimage may shift in form, it will reappear because it meets a basic human need for movement. I think Calvin facilitated this reappearance in his time, perhaps because his own experience led him to be less fearful of travel.

I would conclude also that pilgrimage reappears on the scene because it gives people a sense of connection with a wider community over time. I would suggest this is also something of which Calvin and Knox were aware from personal experience. It meets the basic human need for "communitas," belonging to a stronger human community than simply one's local church setting, an expansion of one's participation in "the communion of saints." This need is filled both by an individual's travels, and by the "communion seasons" and "prophesying." The innate wisdom of Calvin, Vermigli, and then Knox in Scotland in encouraging such travel for holy purpose strengthened a Reforming church. Pilgrimage, the Reformation renegade has been, astonishingly, redefined and reclaimed as a respectable Christian practice.

---

41. Turner and Victor Turner, *Image and Pilgrimage in Christian Culture*. See also Edith Turner's insightful preface to the reprinting in 2000.

8

Calvin and the Preaching of the Lively Word

STEPHEN FARRIS

IF YOU UNDERSTAND THE placement of the adjective in the title, remembering always that "lively" in older English did not mean merely "animated" or "exciting" as in modern English but rather "living" or even "life-giving" you will have understood the main thing about this paper.

There was once a professor of Reformed Theology famed both for his learning and for his surpassing grumpiness. Late in his teaching career a certain colleague, the professor of pastoral counseling as the story has it, became dean of the seminary. The new dean mandated that all assignments and examinations should be based on "real life" pastoral situations. You can imagine what the grumpy professor thought of this development. Still, Presbyterians are obedient to all lawful authority so the professor designed a final examination for his introduction to Reformed theology with one question, which obeyed the mandate of the dean:

"You are a Presbyterian minister and you decide to travel to another city by a late night bus. In the darkness you mount the bus and make your way to the one vacant seat. You become aware that you are sitting next to a young woman who is weeping bitterly. As a pastor you turn to her and say, 'Young woman, I am a Presbyterian minister! How may I help you?'

She replies, 'A Presbyterian minister! Oh, thank God! Tell me, I have always wanted to know: what are the seven chief emphases of the Reformed Tradition?'"

I do not know what the other six chief emphases of the Reformed Tradition may be but most certainly one of them is preaching. If this be true and surely no one would question it, the tradition came by this emphasis honestly for Calvin himself was a preacher.

Dawn DeVries wrote: "It is not surprising that a theologian who argued consistently that preaching was the ordinary means appointed by God for the salvation of the elect understood the delivery of sermons as among his most important duties. During his ministry in Geneva (1536–1538, 1541–1564), John Calvin preached well over 2,000 sermons. From 1549, his most characteristic pattern of preaching was twice on Sunday and every weekday of every other week."[1]

If Professor DeVries' depiction of Calvin's activity is accurate, her arithmetic is seriously in error. This may be a conservative estimate even for his preaching from 1549 to his death in 1564 and certainly ignores his preaching in Geneva from 1536–1538 and from 1541–1549. It also does not count his three years preaching to the congregation of French refugees in Strasbourg or any preaching he may have done before his first arrival in Geneva. Moreover it does not take into consideration Calvin's participation in the *congregations,* regular expositions of the Word among the pastors of Geneva, events that could not have not have been very different from sermons. If DeVries' estimate of Calvin's preaching rate also applies with respect to his ministry as a whole, surely the grand total must be more than 4,000.[2] In passing, we may note that Malcolm Gladwell, in *Outliers,*[3] his study of the factors that lead to great success, claims that no one attains superlative excellence in any field without having devoted at least 10,000 hours to that craft. Counting preparation time, Calvin must surely have passed that mark early in his preaching ministry.

It is at least mildly surprising, therefore, that there is no section on preaching as such, in the *Institutes,* though I think it might be fair to call that work as a whole a preaching aid. When he does speak of preaching in the *Institutes,* it is normally in connection with *something else.* Many of the strongest and most vivid statements about preaching come from his sermons or commentaries where, by definition, he is concerned about

1. DeVries, "Calvin's Preaching," 106.

2. This is also the estimate of the total number of sermons in Pitkin, "John Calvin and the Interpretation of Scripture," 351.

3. Gladwell, *Outliers: The Story of Success.*

something *else*, namely the biblical text. The "*something else*" is always his real subject. It appears that Calvin would rather speak about preaching's true subject, the knowledge of God and of ourselves, made known in Scripture, through the illumination of the Holy Spirit, by means of the preached word, rather than about preaching itself. Moreover, as Randall Zachman reminds us, the *Institutes* was intended to be a *Summa*, treating briefly rather than exhaustively a wide range of theological topics.[4] To the best of my knowledge few people, if any, were denying the significance of preaching in his day so perhaps Calvin felt no need to discuss it extensively. In any case, as a Protestant, Calvin was committed to the doctrine of justification by faith. And Calvin affirmed with Paul that "faith comes by hearing." "The ears are the key Protestant organ" as my own former professor, John H. Leith, used to say in class.

There can truly not be any doubt of the absolute centrality of preaching in both Calvin's theology and in his daily life. Calvin names for example, the marks of the true church in a way that I will deliberately though slightly, misquote at this point, as the right preaching of the Word of God and the right administration of the sacraments. You will note which comes first. Calvin balanced very nicely, in two senses of the word, both the requirement of the external ordinance and church practice of attending to the preaching of the word on the one hand, and the necessity of the illumination of the Spirit, on the other. Neither the word preached in our ears nor the Spirit at work in our hearts can rightly be disregarded. Nor, I believe, may one be subordinated to the other. In any case, attending to preaching is a command and that is sufficient for Calvin: "The preaching of the gospel and the meeting of men together to hear the holy Scripture expounded is not something invented by men but . . . God as ordained it and our Lord Jesus Christ has set it down for a law. And we must keep it as a thing inviolable."[5] On the other hand: "But nothing is accomplished by preaching [Christ] if the Spirit as our inner teacher, does not show our minds the way."[6]

---

4. Zachman, *John Calvin as Teacher, Pastor and Theologian*, 86–87.

5. The sermons on Ephesians quoted here can be found in French in *Corpus Reformatorum, Vol. 51*. I will quote them as they are translated by Zachman, *John Calvin as Teacher, Pastor and Theologian*. This quotation is from in Sermon 25, in ibid., 157.

6. Calvin, *Institutes* II.ii.20. All citations from the Institutes are from the Library of Christian Classics edition.

CALVIN@500

Augustine, loosely quoting Cicero, states that the three functions of rhetoric are to delight, to instruct and to persuade.[7] Of those three functions, instruction is clearly primary for Calvin. One of his most used metaphors with respect to both life and worship, is that of the school. As scholars in the school of Christ we are chiefly in need of instruction. Note that this is different from much contemporary homiletical theory where the aim of the sermon is not primarily to convey ideas but to evoke an experience of the gospel.[8]

At this point, it is my intention to consider the preaching of Calvin, not primarily as an historian, a task for which I would not be qualified, but as a student of scripture and a teacher of preaching. I shall do so under three "heads," to borrow a term from Calvin: 1. the preacher, 2. the hearers, and 3. the sermon itself.

THE PREACHER

Andre Resner Jr., in *Preacher and Cross*,[9] a very fine book on the role of "ethos," a technical term in rhetoric for the persuasive faculty of the speaker's character and person, says that when evaluating the importance of the character and gifts of the preacher, we tend to fall into the homiletical equivalent of one of two ancient heresies, donatism or docetism. Donatism was a heresy which asserted that the efficacy of the sacraments rested on the holiness of the priest who presided. Some writers seem, likewise, to make the efficacy of preaching to rest on the character and gifts of the preacher. Docetism, on the other hand, was a christological heresy that undervalues the full humanity of Christ, asserting that he only *seemed* to be human. (The Greek verb "to seem" is "dokeo.") Similarly, it is possible to speak in such a way of the preaching task that the humanity of preachers is swallowed up in the magnificence of the divine word. Calvin would tend strongly towards the latter possibility, at least in theory.

The preacher, says Calvin, is the "mouth of God." "We hear his ministers speaking just as if he himself spoke ... God breathes faith into us on by the instrument of his gospel, as Paul points out that 'faith

---

7. Augustine of Hippo, *On Christian Doctrine*, IV.12.27.

8. This is the conclusion of Robert Reid, David Fleer and Jeffrey Bullock in "Preaching as the Creation of an Experience," 1–9.

9. Resner, *Preacher and Cross*.

comes by hearing."[10] Calvin will, however, speak about the preacher's character and gifts. When doing so, Calvin appears to emphasize, first, the importance of character. He appeals to a saying of Augustine which, he said, "pleases me even more": "When a certain rhetorician was asked what was the chief rule in eloquence he replied 'Delivery'; what was the second rule, 'Delivery'; what was the third rule; 'Delivery'; so if you ask me concerning the precepts of the Christian religions, first, second, third and always I would answer 'Humility.'"[11] That applies to all Christians, of course, but, most definitely, to the preacher also.

Still, the power of preaching does not depend on the character of the preacher. This is said most clearly not in Calvin himself but in Bullinger's Second Helvetic Confession.

> THE PREACHING OF THE WORD OF GOD IS THE WORD OF GOD. Wherefore when this Word of God is now preached in the church by preachers lawfully called, we believe that the very Word of God is proclaimed, and received by the faithful; and that neither any other Word of God is to be invented nor is to be expected from heaven: and that now *the Word itself which is preached is to be regarded, not the minister that preaches; for even if he be evil and a sinner, nevertheless the Word of God remains still true and good.*[12]

The last sentence is an explicit repudiation of homiletical donatism. In fact, one benefit of attending to preaching is that it can engender humility in the listeners if they have to attend to persons less holy and less learned than themselves. (As a professional listener to sermons, I would not like to extend that insight to its logical conclusion.)

Calvin is, however, aware of the value of human gifts, at least when they are absent. In an early letter to Guillaume Farel, he bemoaned the lack of skills of his fellow preachers. "The one best educated had a poor delivery and confused ideas."[13] It would be interesting to know what the very practical Calvin did to help ministers and students to improve poor delivery and to straighten out confused thinking, the task of homiletics proper. Though by all accounts himself a gifted speaker of elegant and eloquent French, Calvin never writes much about what might be called

10. Calvin, *Institutes* IV.1.5–6. See Holton, "Union and Communion," 404.

11. Ibid., II.2.11.

12. *The Second Helvetic Confession of Faith*, chapter 1. The italics are mine.

13. As quoted in Parker, *Calvin's Preaching*, 60.

the mechanics of preaching. It is possible to imagine Calvin in a contemporary seminary teaching Old or New Testament, Patristics, Pastoral Theology or, of course, Systematic Theology. Calvin never says enough about the preaching task and, more specifically, about the human skills involved to judge whether he would be an effective teacher of Homiletics. It would be fascinating to know if the equivalent of homiletics was taught in the Academy of Geneva. Rhetoric was part of the trivium, the educational core of a medieval or renaissance education. Did he assume, therefore, that a university education, the Spirit's aid and the attitude of humility is sufficient for a preacher? If so, is that an adequate understanding of the necessary qualifications of a Reformed preacher? That humility is the human characteristic most necessary to gospel preaching is entirely true, but the advice, "Remember to stay humble," may not be very helpful to the preacher late on Saturday night. The preacher's "Saturday Night Fever" is intrinsically humbling! Some knowledge of technique is useful, then and now. One wonders if Calvin held implicitly an apprenticeship model of homiletics: one learns to preach by listening to good preaching. Calvin never says that, however. What he does say is that preachers must be masters of their subject matter, the content of Scripture, and that they must themselves be obedient to the word they preach. "It would be better for him to beak his neck going up into the pulpit if he does not take pains to be the first to follow God."

The balance between the work of the Spirit and the necessity of human skill and effort may be best stated in a letter to the Duke of Somerset, Lord Protector of England.

> Monsignor, it appears to me that there is very little preaching of a lively kind in the kingdom, but that the greater part deliver it by way of reading from a written discourse. I see very well the necessity which constrains you to that; for in the first place you have not, as I believe, such well-approved and competent pastors as you desire. Wherefore, you need forthwith to supply this want . . .
>
> Now this preaching ought not to be lifeless, but lively, to teach, to exhort, to reprove, as St. Paul says in speaking to Timothy (2 Tim 4:2). So indeed, that if an unbeliever enter, he may be so effectually arrested and convinced as to give glory to God, as Paul says in another passage (1 Cor 14). You are also aware, Monsignor, how he speaks of the lively power and energy with which they ought to speak, who would approve themselves as

good and faithful ministers of God, who must not make a parade of rhetoric, only to gain esteem for themselves, but that the Spirit of God ought to sound forth by their voice, so as to work with mighty energy.[14]

All this is at least slightly refreshing to the spirit of this professor of homiletics. A concentration on technique, exacerbated by that otherwise wonderful aid in preaching class, the video camera can divert student attention from what really matters in preaching. How often I have thought and occasionally said in response to students anxious after watching tapes of their sermons. "Worry less about what you do with your hands and more about what you do with your text." Technique does, of course, matter and Calvin may not have paid sufficient attention to it. But technique is not the heart of preaching. Knowledge of Scripture and what Calvin would call *piety* matter far more.

THE HEARER

It is interesting to note that Richard Lischer in, *The Company of Preachers*,[15] his collection of seminal writings of the homiletical tradition, includes Calvin in the section on the hearer. This is perhaps counterintuitive but profoundly insightful. Preaching is not the work of the preacher alone. Listen to the marks of the church as Calvin actually stated them: "the pure preaching *and hearing* of the Word of God and the administration of the sacraments according the institution of Christ."[16]

Thomas G. Long in his popular textbook, *The Witness of Preaching*,[17] identifies three common models for preaching, one of which is the herald. According to Long, the herald's sole task is to get the master's words right without concern for whether the listeners hear and accept. Though certainly willing to accept the image of ambassador, this is emphatically not Calvin's style. He is, in fact extraordinarily attentive to the listeners.

---

14. Beveridge and Bonnet, eds. *Selected Works of John Calvin: Tracts and Letters, Vol. 5 Letters, Part 2 1545—1552* Letter 229. Online: www.reformed.org/ethics/index .html?mainframe=/ethics/calvin_to_somerset.html. Due to the shortage of trained preachers, preachers were assigned to read sermons from approved books, a practice Calvin understands as a temporary measure but which, he insists, must be rectified forthwith.

15. Lischer, *The Company of Preachers*, 362–68.

16. Calvin, *Institutes* IV.1.9.

17. Long, *The Witness of Preaching*, 19–28.

CALVIN@500

This is shown by what Randall Zachman calls the technique of "imagined interior monologue"[18] but which I will label somewhat differently. Calvin frequently puts words in the mouths of his listeners. For example:

> Some having heard sermons, or having been taught at some lecture, or by some other means, will perhaps say, "It is possible that this may be true and as for me, I will not oppose it, since I am no cleric or divine, it is all the same to me, I will leave it to take is ordinary course," Some other will say, "Ho! I will keep the faith of my forefathers, for it is too dangerous a matter to change." Some other will say thus, "How so?" It is a new doctrine that we have never heard before.[19]

Homiletician David Buttrick calls this kind of preaching move a "contrapuntal."[20] A friend calls it, more memorably, a "Yabbut." In every sermon there are things that make listeners say, "Yeah, but . . ." The frequent yabbuts in Calvin's preaching demonstrate his attentive attitude not only to the Word but to the listener. A preacher attentive to the listeners will attempt imaginatively to identify the likely yabbuts and, with Calvin, address them.

This attention to the hearer is not necessarily because he has a high view of his listeners, certainly as they are in an unregenerate state: In a sermon from Micah on Christmas day, he declared, "Let us remember we are full of nothing but shit and corruption until God purges us. Let us recognize that God must purge us not only or our vices but also beautiful things in order to thoroughly cleanse us."[21] And Merry Christmas to you too!

Still, what is most striking to me is the apparent high expectations Calvin has for his listeners, especially when compared to preachers in our day. If one compares sermons and commentaries on the same passage, Calvin is careful not to introduce Greek or Hebrew words in the sermons; a discussion of the meaning of the word in French suffices.[22]

---

18. Zachman, *John Calvin as Teacher, Pastor and Theologian,* 172.

19. Sermon 14 on Ephesians, as translated in Zachman, *John Calvin as Teacher, Pastor and Theologian,* 160.

20. Buttrick, *Homiletic: Moves and Structure,* 47–48.

21. Calvin, *Sermons on Micah,* 322.

22. This exercise is very carefully and thoroughly carried out by Randall Zachman with respect to Calvin's commentary and sermons on Ephesians in Zachman, *John*

FARRIS—*Calvin and the Preaching of the Lively Word*

Nor does he parade his vast knowledge of the Fathers, the schoolmen, a number of rabbis and of contemporary interpreters, all of whom are engaged in the commentaries. The Bible is a book for the unlearned and when speaking to unlearned audiences it is carrying out its proper task. A homiletical parade of learning must not get in the way of that task. Still, the sermons are as theologically serious and as biblically thorough and detailed as the commentaries. Indeed, in one respect, they are markedly more thorough than the commentaries, as we shall see. Calvin obviously expects the Genevois—"full of shit" though they may be—to listen to serious biblical exposition and theology.

I believe that we preachers overestimate our listeners' knowledge of the Bible but we underestimate their interest and capability. Our listeners do not know the Bible. It is folly to speak casually of even so central a biblical event as the exile assuming that everyone will know what we are talking about. The biblical questions in the basic version of the board game *Trivial Pursuits* are, "What is the first book of the Bible?" and "Who wrote the four Gospels?" Those are supposed to be difficult for most people and the creators of that popular game are probably correct in their judgment. But similarly, we underestimate the capacity and interests of our listeners. We bemoan the effect of the internet and of advertising on the attention span of our listeners. Too often we respond by delivering moralistic little homilies devoid of anything that might stretch the mind or daunt the spirit.

There is a story, possibly apocryphal, about a great Scottish preacher who was called to Southern California to teach preaching. He was, of course, in immediate demand as a guest preacher in the Presbyterian churches of Southern California—he had a Scottish accent, after all. For six months, however, he refused all invitations, choosing rather to attend different services, to assess the state of the church in his new home. After six months he announced that he was ready to accept invitations because he now understood the heart of Christianity in those churches: "It's nice to be nice and it's good to be good." I would not dare say that in our own churches a more profound gospel is always preached and heard.

But our listeners are much better educated than the Genevois and the "God shaped hole" in our hearts is as large as ever, perhaps larger.

Calvin as Teacher, Pastor and Theologian, 147–72. A former student of my own, Carey Nieuwhof, carried out a similar exercise in an unpublished Master of Divinity Thesis, on sermons from Matthew on the passion of Christ.

We are, after all, speaking of the creator of a cosmos far larger and more intricate than the one Calvin knew. Speaking of that creator who is simultaneously our redeemer is *supposed to be a stretch*. Calvin's example encourages us to stretch our own minds and those of our listeners. Our hearers are capable of apprehending big ideas. The real question is whether we are capable of conveying them.

Once again, however, it is not a matter of technique. Richard Lischer, as noted, selects Calvin on the work of the Spirit *in the listener* for his collection. The mere act of listening to sermons is not enough in itself. "Therefore let us not think that it is enough for us to come to a sermon or for each to read God's Word in private, but we must have recourse to God that he may give us increase."[23] Rather, the Spirit is at work through the preached word. "Now then, when we see the holy Scripture truly expounded and applied rightly to our use we know that the Spirit of God bears us testimony that he dwells among us, provided that we learn to receive so excellent a gift and we realize that such is the homage that our Lord Jesus demands from us."[24] It is the Spirit of God who illumines the hearer but it is not right to ignore preaching in favor of private illumination by the Spirit.

THE SERMON

What Calvin does in his sermons is reasonably well known.[25] He preaches *lectio continua* through books of the Bible, expounding a few verses in each sermon. The individual sermons contain exposition of the biblical text and extensive application to the life of the hearers. Randall Zachman would add a third, middle element; exhortation to remember and to keep in mind and heart what has been said of God's mercy and love.[26] What

---

23. Sermon 19 on Ephesians, as translated in Zachman, *John Calvin as Teacher, Pastor and Theologian*, 157.

24. Sermon 25 on Ephesians, as translated in ibid., 159.

25. The standard work on Calvin's preaching remains the excellent discussion in T. H. L. Parker, *Calvin's Preaching*. Shorter but still thorough descriptions of Calvin's preaching can be found in DeVries, "Calvin's Preaching" and Zachman, *John Calvin as Teacher, Pastor and Theologian*. Readers may also wish to consult the sections on Calvin in two very thorough contemporary histories of preaching, Edwards, *A History of Preaching*, 309–26; Hughes Oliphant Old, *The Reading and Preaching of the Scriptures in the Worship of the Christian Church, Vol. 4*, 90–133.

26. Zachman, *John Calvin as Teacher, Pastor and Theologian*, 166–69.

are we to make of this style of preaching in a day of lectionaries, story sermons and LCD projectors?

You will note that I chose to begin this paper with a story, a move typical of our contemporary preaching practice. Calvin, by contrast does not tell stories. In fact, he speaks very negatively of congregations who long for "pleasing stories and buffoonery or old wives tales," and of the preachers who give in to that desire. That criticism is evidence of the fact other preachers of the time did tell stories, even funny ones. In fact, one of the earlier examples in the wonderful anthology, *The Oxford Book of Humorous Prose,* is a story told in a court sermon by Hugh Latimer, contemporary of Calvin and one of the Oxford Martyrs in the reign of Bloody Mary.[27]

If you are tempted to agree entirely with Calvin that stories have no place in preaching, you might remember a figure who is far more important in the homiletical tradition than Calvin and who was famed for his stories. Here is the beginning of one of his stories that may be familiar to you. "A certain man had two sons and the younger of them said to his father . . ." Calvin's disdain for stories need not be imitated. Nevertheless, we are slowly recovering from a period of narrative imperialism in which story has become the dominant mode of preaching. Moreover, in the work of some homileticians, *idea* has become, in two senses, a four letter word. Calvin's theological seriousness and devotion to the text is a useful corrective to these tendencies. Calvin is nevertheless, attentive both in his commentaries and his preaching to the drama of biblical stories and to their narrative structures.

Calvin also used vivid metaphors and lively language in both his writing and preaching. Some of the metaphors in the *Institutes* are justly famous, i.e., his description of the gracious accommodation of God to our weakness in understanding as the nursemaid lisping in a baby's ear. Or we can think of his presentation of scripture as the spectacles through which a clearer vision of the world and all creation can be grasped. That same capacity for vivid, pictorial language is demonstrated in the sermons. "Worldly things are things are like bandages over our eyes. Yet we are unable to follow God one single step of the way because our eyes are bandaged."[28]

---

27. Muir, *The Oxford Book of Humorous Prose.*

28. Calvin, *Sermons on Micah,* 317.

Calvin did not write out his sermons. We know his sermons because, from 1549 to the end of his life, his sermons were taken down in shorthand, chiefly by one Denis Raguenier. Not writing out his sermons must have saved an immense amount of time and is, perhaps, the chief difference between Calvin's preaching and the homiletical practice in our churches today. Rather than write out a sermon, making it a quasi-independent piece of rhetoric, he uses the biblical text as the structure of his sermon. I would not want to make Calvin a model with respect to not writing out sermons. With his great knowledge of the biblical text and his gifts as a speaker of elegant, simple French, Calvin could do what most of us are incapable of doing. Most of us need to write out the sermon as a discipline. I do suggest, however, that allowing the flow and structure of the text to determine the flow and structure of the sermon would be a boon to contemporary preachers.

Much homiletical theory is devoted to finding the right form into which a sermon is to be poured. It might be the old three points and a poem model or the more contemporary six points on the PowerPoint. It may be Eugene Lowry's Homiletical Plot[29] or Paul Scott Wilson's Four Pages of the Sermon.[30] It may even be my own analogical method.[31] These, however, can be impositions on the text that may actually prevent the text from speaking for itself. Moreover, it takes time to master these forms in class and then more time to work them out in weekly sermon preparation. Perhaps it is often more efficient, easier and more faithful to revive what one recent book called, "preaching as running commentary." The book in question, *Preaching Verse by Verse* by Ronald Allen and Gilbert Bartholomew,[32] sank like a stone without, as far as I can tell, much notice, an undeserved fate. Let me hasten to add that preaching as running commentary must not become a new homiletical law nor the only correct form of preaching. Even T. H. L. Parker, surely the most ardent admirer of Calvin's preaching, is forced to admit that if running commentary were the only valid form of preaching one would have to rule as "not really a sermon" Peter's speech on the day of Pentecost, not

29. Lowry, *The Homiletical Plot*.

30. See, among several important works, Paul S. Wilson, *The Four Pages of the Sermon*. The most precise and detailed "formula" for preaching remains that of David Buttrick in his massive work *Homiletic*.

31. Farris, *Preaching that Matters*.

32. Allen and Bartholomew, *Preaching Verse by Verse*.

to mention the Sermon on the Mount.[33] But perhaps as *a* regular and standard form of preaching, it is time for a reconsideration and, indeed, a comeback for preaching as running commentary. It may be faithful to God, edifying to the listener, . . . and humane to the busy preacher.

I do not wish, however, simply and uncritically to hold up Calvin as a model to be emulated. I have noted, after years of listening to sermons and also reading evaluation forms that the greatest strengths of sermons are often simultaneously their greatest weaknesses, So, I believe, it is with Calvin. Calvin's greatest strength as an interpreter of Scripture is a wonderful, imaginative extension of the meaning of the text into the lives of the hearers. Listen, for example, what Calvin says about the commandment, "Thou shalt not steal." Oppressing the poor is theft, surely a lesson Canadians as well as Genevois must hear. Here he is on theft from a poor person:

> 14. *Thou shalt not oppress an hired servant.*
>
> This precept is akin to the foregoing. Moses pronounces that he who has hired a poor person for wages oppresses him unless he gives him immediate recompense for his labor; . . . if a hireling suffers from want because we do not pay him what he has earned, we are by our *very* delay alone convicted of unrighteousness . . . because he sustains his life by his daily labors. Although, however, this provision only refers to the poor, lest they should suffer hunger from the negligence or pride of the rich, still humanity in general is enforced, lest, whilst the poor labor for our profit, we should arrogantly abuse them as if they were our slaves, or should be too illiberal and stingy towards them, since nothing can be more disgraceful than that, when they are in our service, they should not at least have enough to live upon frugally. Finally, Moses admonishes us that this tyranny on the part of the rich shall not be unpunished, if they do not supply their workmen with the means of subsistence, even although no account shall be rendered of it before the tribunals of men . . . Wherefore, although the earthly judge may absolve us a hundred times over, let us not therefore think that we have escaped; since God will always require of us from heaven, whatever may have been unjustly excused us on earth.[34]

33. Parker, *Calvin's Preaching*, 79.

34. It is worth noting here that much of Calvin's commentaries can be found on line now, a considerable boon to the preacher preparing sermons. The quotation comes from Calvin's commentary on Deut 24:14–15 as it appears in online form. URL of this quotation is http://www.ccel.org/ccel/calvin/calcom05.ii.iv.ii.ii.html?bcb=right.

CALVIN@500

That is truly wonderful preaching material, but it is from a commentary not a sermon. A sermon would have been too long and too wordy. Randall Zachman calculates that in Ephesians the average length of a section of commentary is 2,000 words but the average length of the corresponding sermon is 7,000 words![35] This *extra Calvinisticum* is chiefly exhortation. The extensive and intensive applications are also the greatest weakness of Calvin's sermons. They are so strong that, I fear, the law sometimes seems to swallow up the gospel. I hesitate to say this since judging a sermon by its printed form is like picturing the flight of a butterfly by examining a specimen pinned in a museum display case. The tone of voice, the eye contact, the vocal dynamics that can make the difference between sincere, on the one hand, and scolding on the other, are all missing. But still it must be said, lest we become disciples not of Jesus but of Calvin: Calvin does go on.

Calvin has a marvelous theoretical way of uniting law and gospel, the third and principal use of the law. The primary function of the law of God is not the first use, as with Luther, to employ the law to show us how far short we have fallen of the will of God and to prepare us to turn in despair from our own righteousness and to find the mercy of God made known in the cross of Christ. It is not to frighten the evildoer by the threat of punishment. Rather it is a gracious light to the feet of those who have been saved by grace alone and now wish to live a life of grateful obedience. This is what a life of grateful obedience looks like. But in practice, the exhortation is sometimes so fierce that the law as gift is swallowed up in law as denunciation. Perhaps exhortation may even obscure evangel.

Calvin's first biographer, Coladon, admitted Calvin was a man of "*colère*," i.e., he was irritable.[36] Perhaps that irritability was a consequence of his persistent ill health. But that *colère* does seem to come out in his preaching. "It is often impossible to tell from Calvin's sermons which of the three uses (of the law) he was deploying."[37] I suggest that the problem is not the content but the tone. The sermons sound more like the whip to the balky ass than the unveiling of a light for our path. The Lutherans may, in practice, be right in their criticism of Calvin at this point. He is preaching law rather than gospel.

35. Zachman, *John Calvin as Teacher, Pastor and Theologian*, 155.

36. Parker, *Calvin's Preaching*, 119.

37. Ramp, "John Calvin on Preaching the Law," 266.

I remember at the age of ten walking with my church historian father through the old cemetery of Geneva. A trench had been dug, probably to lay a drain, and a human bone, a femur if I recall correctly, was lying exposed in the grass. The sight made me ask my father, "Where is Calvin buried." My father responded, "No one knows. He left instructions that he be buried in an unmarked grave lest anyone come and worship at his tomb." We learn from Calvin but we need not worship even at his homiletical tomb.

Calvin is dead . . . but the word of the Lord endures forever!

And to that Calvin would say, "Amen. *Soli Deo Gloria.*"

9

John Calvin, Refugee

"For here we have no lasting city." Hebrews 13:14

GERALD HOBBS

THE TITLE OF THIS paper may seem if not paradoxical, at least descriptive of only the earlier half of Calvin's life. For even if John Calvin spent his early adult years in the circuit of a number of cities, it is difficult to characterize the mature John Calvin as refugee. He is rather firmly identified with the city of Geneva. Indeed, "John Calvin, tyrant of Geneva." Now we may be thankful that research and writing of the past fifty years has cleared that old smear on Calvin's name, which started in his own day and was revived by historians of the liberal era in the nineteenth century.[1] John Calvin never ran Geneva. He was not even, for all but a handful of years, a citizen. And, in any event, his only formal positions of authority were in the church, not the state. If he had enormous influence, it was through the power of his spoken word as teacher and preacher, his international reputation through his numerous publications, and his presidency of the Company of Pastors. Alas, Calvin's friends have also perpetuated the myth: Calvin, master of Geneva.[2] "Wounded in the house of his friends!" Now this is not the place to argue why this is an unhelpful, and historically misleading epithet. What I pro-

---

1. Although the old canard has remarkable resiliance. Searching the web under "Tyrant of Geneva" still brings one immediately to Calvin, with authors promoting or dismissing the epithet. Pete Wilcox, writing in the *Times* of London, on July 3, 2009, the week of the Calvin 500th anniversary, gave considerable effort to debunking the myth.

2. Title of a novel on the life of Calvin by Gladys H. Barr.

pose here is the thesis that the identification of Calvin with Geneva—his residence of course without interruption from late 1541 until his death in 1564—can cause one to overlook something I want to address in this paper, namely, that Calvin must also be understood as a man profoundly without a *patria*, a homeland, on this earth.

A LIFE ON THE MOVE

Jean Calvin, family name originally *Cauvin*, Latinized by John himself as Calvinus, and so back to French Calvin, was born to a middle-class family in the ancient cathedral city—a town by our standards, with a few thousand people—of Noyon. The city lies in Picardie, the French province lying north-east of Paris (a region scarred by bitter conflict in the First World War). It was astride the great pilgrim road from the Low Countries to Paris and thence to Compostella in Spain. An hour's walk south of town lay Ourscamp, a large Cistercian abbey that welcomed pilgrims. Noyon was a market town of about 5,000 inhabitants, whose proud origins dated back to Roman times. The Church was remarkably visible in Noyon life. Apart from the imposing Cathedral of Notre Dame, built in the early Gothic style, there were ten parish churches and numerous religious houses. With a staff of at least sixty canons, the cathedral establishment was larger even than that of Paris. The ravages of the Wars of Religion and the French Revolution, as well as the occupation by Germany during much of the First World War, have erased a great deal of this visible heritage. Even the cathedral itself is now longer such, but an admittedly spectacular parish church in the diocese of nearby Beauvais.

John Calvin was an extraordinarily private man, and we learn only tiny snatches of his life story from his own writings. Fortunately, his long-time colleague and successor in Geneva, Théodore de Bèze (or Beza) wrote two biographies after Calvin's death, drawing upon the reminiscences of Calvin himself, and of acquaintances, some of whom had followed him eventually to Geneva. Despite the multitude of biographies written since, Beza remains indispensable. John's father was Gérard, a notary who was employed on the large cathedral staff. This was not always a happy working relationship, as we shall see. The family home was on the grain market square, one hundred meters from the Cathedral front. Given, however, the almost total destruction of Noyon in the Wars of Religion, it is likely that the present building housing the

Calvin Museum and presenting itself as his birth home is a structure dating from the next century. John's mother, Jeanne, was a devout believer, and her second son will have known well the cathedral with its soaring stone vaults, its numerous well-decorated altars and ancient statue of the Blessed Virgin and Child. John's mother died when he was only six, leaving him and several siblings. Through his father's influence with the cathedral administration, as was the custom with bright young men, John was received into minor orders and given benefices at age twelve. What was in effect a scholarship for a youth of promise provided some income to support his university studies of arts and eventually theology in Paris.

Thus at twelve or thirteen, the gifted John set off from Noyon to the ancient University of Paris, where he was enrolled first in the Collège de la Marche in an advanced university preparatory program; then, within a year, in the Collège de Montaigu for his first Paris Arts degree in philosophy.[3] Life there was hard, harsh even, as masters believed that to "spare the rod was to spoil the child." At least his church support from Noyon saved him from the worst rigors of poverty. He developed his ability in the Latin language and the arts of rhetoric (the art of speech) and dialectic (the skills of oratory and reasoned argumentation) in particular. Studies continued in Paris, punctuated by the usual vacations, undoubtedly spent in Noyon, until at the age of sixteen or seventeen, he obtained his Master of Arts. At this juncture, Calvin made a dramatic shift of university. For reasons that have aroused speculation, John abandoned the pursuit of theology and a career in the Church for the study of Law, apparently with his father's strong encouragement. The move may have been prompted by his father's increasingly tumultuous relationships with the Noyon cathedral chapter. So Calvin shifted south to Orléans on the Loire, whose ancient university taught only Law. After three years there working essentially on the codes of Justinian, the sixth-century Roman emperor, and his mediaeval commentators, Calvin would have been seriously exposed to church history as well as to law, since, of course, the later Roman Empire was officially Christian, and even much civil legislation evoked church matters. By 1529 he held the bachelor's degree, and was engaging, as customary for a bright student, in some lecturing. The atmosphere in Orléans was much more liberal than in Paris, and

---

3. I will follow here the dating proposed, with considerable cogency, by T. H. L. Parker, in *John Calvin: A Biography,* Appendix 1, 156–61.

he was forming friendships that would continue in the coming years. Two of these probably nudged him toward the evangelical camp, known then in France as "Lutheranism."[4] A cousin from Noyon, Pierre Robert Olivétan, would in 1535 produce the first new French Bible translated from Hebrew and Greek; it was published in Neuchâtel in Swiss territory, funded by the Waldensians of the Savoyard Alps. Melchior Wolmar, a German already known to Calvin in Paris, was under suspicion by this time for "Lutheran" leanings.

In 1529 Calvin switched universities again, this time still further south to the new university of Bourges. There he had Wolmar as a teacher, along with the brilliant Italian jurist Alciati. With Wolmar he also began to learn Greek, and thence to read the New Testament for himself. He remained in Bourges perhaps eighteen months, after which he returned to Orléans long enough to obtain the top law degree, the licentiate. The dating of Calvin's conversion has always been difficult, above all because although he speaks of it once at some length in his *Psalms* commentary to which we shall be referring later, he is utterly and uncharacteristically (for him) imprecise, leaving scholars a broad field for speculation. It was almost certainly, however, accomplished by the Bourges period (i.e., about 1530) when he was twenty-one years of age. We are told that while in Bourges, he preached in a nearby parish church and even in a barn. Given that throughout these years Calvin held different ecclesiastical appointments back home in Noyon without bothering himself with their duties, Parker is probably right in concluding that this preaching was a witness to the new-found evangelical convictions, which required public testimony.[5]

Although Noyon remained throughout Calvin's lifetime a fond memory, it was now a more complicated place for him. Given the emerg-

---

4. Labels can be confusing in this period. The "evangelical" movement was the call to reform the Church in keeping with the gospel (the evangel), and the movement to reform the diocese of Meaux (discussed in the chapter on Gérard Roussel) was "evangelical." The ideas of Martin Luther, circulating in Latin and in French translations, were of course evangelical, and his Reform movement and eventually churches in German lands were and are still called Evangelical, not Lutheran. Ultimately in France what was loosely called "lutheran" would become the movement for evangelical Reform associated with Calvin, and the churches thus organized called themselves "reformed." This would in turn bring the Roman Catholic Church in France to call them "churches that are falsely called reformed"! For the early years I will here use the term Evangelical, and refer to the later Calvinist movement as Reformed.

5. Parker, *Calvin*, 22.

ing evangelicalism of his spirit, his benefices must have been problematic. His father had fallen into serious troubles with the cathedral chapter, and was excommunicated for persisting in the claimed financial malfeasance. A brother was also in conflict with the chapter. Having shifted back to Paris, Calvin was then called home to the deathbed of his father, who passed from this life still excommunicate, and had to receive special dispensation for burial in consecrated ground.

Now to this point the travels of the young Calvin, if frequent, are not unusual. The university scholar then, as still in modern Germany, was peripatetic. Go to university, as it were, and see the world. But by 1533 Calvin's evangelical convictions become the increasing motivation of his travels. In fall 1533 Calvin encouraged his friend Nicholas Cop to offer a frankly evangelical theology in his address as rector of the university. The fallout in Paris, that bastion of reactionary Catholic theology, sent Cop out of France to Basel in order to avoid arrest. Calvin fled south from Paris to Angoulême, to stay at the residence of Louis du Tillet, a friend of evangelical sympathies. After a winter there, he made a short trip to Noyon, finally to resign the church benefices he had held these many years. He moved that summer of 1534 from place to place— Orléans, Poitiers, almost certainly to Nérac in the far south, to the court of the evangelical patron Queen Marguerite of Navarre, sister of King François. Although this last trip cannot be asserted with certainty, it is highly probable. For there he would have encountered the aging Lefèvre d'Étaples, that "grand and godly old man" whose work ten years earlier had first attempted evangelical reform in France, at Meaux not far from Noyon, with a group of colleagues that included Guillaume Farel (of later Geneva and Neuchâtel fame) and Gérard Roussel, to whom a chapter in this book is dedicated.[6] But the events of that October abruptly brought Calvin's days as resident of his native land to an end. Enraged by the Affair of the *Placards*, the spreading of broadsheets or posters all around Paris—even, it is said, in the royal apartments—attacking the Catholic celebration of the Mass in the most violent language, King Francis I ordered the round up, prosecution and eventual death of the suspected culprits, in the event any one known for evangelical convictions. Calvin hastily moved on, with du Tillet his friend from Angoulême, this time on the road east across France, to Strasbourg, to encounter the evangeli-

---

6. Gordon, *Calvin*, 38, is confident the meeting took place, although Calvin does not speak of it.

cal reformers of that city. The meeting, in particular, with Martin Bucer, who would become his mentor at a critical stage in his life, was of capital importance. But he then moved on, into the territories of the Swiss Confederation, at Basel. Calvin had now genuinely become a refugee, in exile from his native land for the sake of the Gospel. He would return only once, briefly.

Over the next two years, he lived for a time in Basel, where the fellowship of other French refugees made life tolerable in the German-speaking city. He renewed contact with his cousin, Olivétan, and contributed at least one, perhaps two, prefaces to the forthcoming Bible. In Basel too, he completed and sent to the presses the first edition of his guide to an evangelical reading of the Scriptures, the *Institution of the Christian Religion*. To it he prefaced an open letter to the King of France, claiming nothing less than that the evangelical faith he and his friends were teaching, not that professed by the Church of Roman, was the *true* form of the Christian religion. This accomplished, Calvin again set forth, this time far south across the Alps to the Italian duchy of Ferrara. The Duke's wife was the princess Renée of France, sister-in-law as well as cousin of King Francis. She was, like Queen Marguerite, openly sympathetic to the evangelical cause—although her husband Duke Ercole D'Esté was distinctly not—and around her gathered a group of exiles from France, as well as Italian evangelicals. In this brief interlude, Calvin will have encountered the poet Clément Marot, who would in future provide the base collection for the Huguenot Psalter. Calvin formed a lifetime friendship with Duchess Renée, and would correspond with her for years; but he did not stay longer than a few months. The Duke had launched a round-up of French evangelicals. So Calvin headed back to Paris, taking advantage of a brief truce offered by the king to the hunted evangelicals, to wrap up financial affairs from his father's estate. Then he took the road east again, leaving his native land for the last time, heading back again to Strasbourg. But political unrest and the movement of troops caused his party to detour to the south. Thus, having turned the southern Jura, he landed for a day or so in Geneva. There, as the well-known account reminds us, he was pressed by a fellow-Frenchman, Guillaume Farel (of the earlier Meaux movement), into giving preaching support in a city seeking its own path religiously, having thrown out their prince-bishop and most of the Catholic clergy some months before.

Calvin the refugee had not, of course, ended his travels. Within less than two years, he and Farel were in conflict with the rule of the Geneva Council, which was at that point being dictated to by the Swiss city of Berne. By Easter 1538, having refused to celebrate communion in the manner required by the City Council at the dictation of Berne, Calvin was on the road again. He turned north, to complete the return to Basel intended in 1536, hoping now to find a lifetime refuge as a quiet scholar living by his publications. Within weeks, instead, Martin Bucer of Strasbourg was soliciting him as pastor of the substantial French refugee community in what was otherwise in the sixteenth century another large German-speaking city. Calvin came downriver to Strasbourg, hesitated, was warned by Bucer of the fate suffered by Jonah when he refused the divine call, and accepted. In September 1538 the city named him city pastor of the French congregation, and appointed him as well professor of New Testament in the newly founded Senior School, where many of evangelical Europe's future leaders and pastors would be trained.

These were, perhaps, the three most settled years of Calvin's adult existence. The Senior School, an ambitious educational enterprise, had just been launched by the City under the headship of Johannes Sturm, the noted educational theorist whom they had lured from Paris.[7] In the Senior School, Calvin was able to launch his career as biblical expositor. His lectures on the epistle to the Romans became the first of his numerous published commentaries on the Bible (1540). He worked closely with the older Martin Bucer in these crucial years of the Catholic-Protestant colloquies that sought unsuccessfully to end the division of Christendom. If Calvin judged Bucer to have been too irenic, too willing to seek words whose ambivalence would enable both sides to confess a common faith, he benefited greatly from Bucer's theological acumen, and his acknowledged skills as church organizer. Bucer appreciated the temperamental, but obviously brilliant younger man; and as he had for other friends, encouraged Calvin to consider marriage. In the event, he found Idelette de Bure, widow of an Anabaptist, and until her death in 1549, their union provided Calvin with a loving home environment. Finally, for Calvin,

---

7. The term Senior School is my own. The institution has been variously termed an Academy and a College. It would evolve through these into the University of Strasbourg in the seventeenth century. It was an advanced Latin school, whose uppermost years taught medicine, law and theology. It quickly drew theology students from all parts of central Europe. Calvin would base his own Genevan Academy upon his experience in Strasbourg (1559).

Strasbourg provided the model for a reformed faith community. On his return to Geneva, he would carry with him the key elements of the future Genevan church liturgy and governance. He would remind his fellow-pastors of this on his deathbed.[8]

Yet despite this centered and settled life, in the end, in September 1541, after a year of negotiations, Calvin accepted the pressing invitation of Geneva, the promises of support for his program, and returned to the city where he would live out the remaining twenty-three years of his life. Now, surely, Calvin's refugee existence was at an end. In one sense, of course. But in another, it is arguable, as I am doing here, that Calvin's psyche was now thoroughly that of the refugee, the exile for the sake of the gospel. And little in Geneva facilitated any settling in. If the magistrates intended to support the program he brought with him from Strasbourg, they soon found themselves in disagreement with him and the pastors on matters of church discipline. The party politics of Geneva were complex, and frankly, some of the most evangelically minded citizen-leaders—the party of the "Artichauds (artichokes)" or Articulants—were those who having created the revolution in the first place, were not much minded to have a foreigner dictate the terms of its settlement. Calvin was French, in exile a welcomed refugee, but nonetheless an exile, not a native in a city where only the native-born could sit on the Petit Conseil, the executive council that ran the city, let alone be magistrates. There was considerable resentment over the attempt of the Consistory, the body of pastors and lay elders appointed by the City, to enforce public morality. As elections came and went, so did the ebb and flow of support for the details of Calvin's ministry. From the late 1540s through to the elections of 1555 which finally swept his opponents permanently from power, Calvin lived with frequent threats of physical violence and a steady stream of resistance to elements of his leadership.

The growth of the community of French refugees whose wealthier members had been able to buy citizenship in Geneva and who were in Geneva precisely as exiles for the evangelical faith, attracted there by Calvin's writings and reputation, meant that public conflict was at an end. Calvin no longer indicated to friends in his correspondence that he expected to be obliged to leave the city and once more take up his travels. Yet his final charge to the Geneva clergy from his deathbed is revealing of an enduring frame of mind. Despite having finally been granted

8. Calvin, *Letters of John Calvin*, vol. 4, 377, quoted in Parker, *Calvin*, 155.

citizenship in 1559—a mere eighteen years after he had been begged to return to the city and set the church in order!—he stated: "I have lived here with continual strife. I have been saluted in derision of an evening before my door with forty or fifty arquebus shots . . . They set dogs at my heels, calling out 'Wretch, wretch.'" After recounting further particular incidents of hostility, he concluded: "You are a perverse and unhappy nation, and though there are good men in it, the nation is perverse and wicked."[9]

Calvin requested a simple burial and an unmarked grave, and this was done. While this may have been one final gesture towards personal modesty, or a demonstration that the Reformed sought to create no new saints, it is possible also, in the light of his last words, to construe this a refusal to allow the city to create a posthumous shrine to one for whom it had been so measured and late in its bestowal of honors.

A COMMUNITY OF REFUGEES

I think I have argued a reasonable case for Calvin as a permanent refugee in this world, having no homeland save perhaps the childhood France to which he could never return in safety. This mindset, this fashion of understanding his life, could only have been reinforced by the experience of so many who surrounded him. Consider his constant engagement with religious refugees. In 1534 Basel, he found his cousin Olivétan at work in exile on a French Bible. In those weeks in Ferrara in 1536, he will have met other French refugees, and in addition had some opportunity to become aware of, and perhaps engage, the lively evangelical movement in Italy. After 1543 Rome installed the Inquisition on Italian soil, he would meet again in Geneva evangelicals like Bernardino Ochino (erstwhile vicar-general of the Capuchins) who chose the life of exile for their understanding of the Gospel. His successor in the Strasbourg Senior School was another of these, Peter Martyr Vermigli. In Ferrara he also experienced the precariousness and vulnerability of the exile's existence, the threat of exposure and persecution. As his deathbed remarks indicate, the first Genevan period left an indelible mark on his memory. Settled in Strasbourg, he was the pastor of a community of refugees from French-speaking lands. A large number of his closest friends were themselves refugees. From his native France, Farel, from the province of

9. Calvin, *Letters of John Calvin*, vol. 4, 377, quoted in, 153–55.

Dauphiné in the French Alps, Clément Marot the poet, who gave him the first installment of French metrical Psalms, Marie D'Entieres, his sometime ally and eventual thorn in the flesh, Théodore de Bèze, his junior colleague, another poet and his eventual successor, Robert Estienne, the great Parisian royal printer who migrated to Geneva with his whole establishment, the family of Guillaume Budé, France's greatest humanist intellectual: the list is long and impressive. Like a magnet Calvin's reputation drew to Geneva French evangelicals, some of whom stayed and constituted his closest community in Geneva, others of whom went back to France, not a few to burn at the stake for their beliefs. The Company of Pastors—the people to whom Calvin addressed his final bitter assessment of Geneva—were to a man (I use the term advisedly) refugees. There would be no Geneva-born pastor until 1573, a decade after Calvin's death. Virtually all the liberal professions were likewise from away. "The total intellectual impact of the French refugee colony upon the history of Geneva, writes William Monter, would be difficult to exaggerate."[10]

Calvin also welcomed refugees from other lands than his own. The community of Italian evangelicals, already mentioned, was of significance. Perhaps best-known to us, however, are the English-speakers— John Knox, William Whittingham, and others—who were welcomed by Calvin as they fled the repression of Queen Mary after 1553, who were given place for an exiles' church, and who with Calvin's encouragement translated the Bible, revised and completed a metrical psalter, and then for the most part in 1558–1559 returned to England, or in Knox' case— *persona non grata* with the new queen Elizabeth because of his misogynous writings—to Scotland. One may even argue that *their* very success in returning from exile may have reinforced Calvin's sense of impermanence, of lifetime refugee status. To these let us add another group—the colleagues known personally or by correspondence, who likewise ended their days in exile: Martin Bucer, his old mentor, struggling unsuccessfully with the damp winters of Cambridge (1549–1551); Peter Martyr Vermigli, in Strasbourg, Oxford, Strasbourg again, and finally Zurich, never to return to his native Italy; Immanuel Tremellius, the Italian Jew who translated the great Geneva Latin Bible from Hebrew, who followed Vermigli to Strasbourg and Oxford, was appointed to the University of Heidelberg, then expelled to Sedan as the result of a regime change. The list is long and impressive. "Here we have no lasting city."

10. Monter, *Calvin's Geneva*, 173.

Moreover Calvin recognized the character of Geneva as a city of refuge for evangelicals. In 1553, while yet his own status in the city still seemed to him in doubt, he dedicated his commentary on the Gospel of John to the Magistrates and Council of Geneva. If hospitality to strangers was an ancient virtue of the classical philosophers, to Geneva, he argued, a much greater honor is due: "In these troublesome and unhappy times, the Lord has appointed you to be the persons whose support and protection should be solicited by the godly and inoffensive banished and driven from their native countries by the wicked and cruel tyranny of Antichrist."

He praises them because they have acted positively to recognize the two gifts Christ has given the city: the establishment of a manner of pure religion, and the opportunity to be city of refuge for, as he puts it, "not of one or a few individuals, but of [Christ's] Church at large." In welcoming these strangers in such abundance, they are, as promised in Matthew's Gospel, receiving Christ himself. They ought to be marked by "a godly anxiety to maintain the church which Christ has placed under the shelter of [their] wings."[11] Here we certainly see Calvin at his political best; cajoling before his Europe-wide readership his political masters in their half-hearted exercise of this virtue of Christian hospitality. I call it half-hearted because, although the city's economy benefitted enormously from the influx of many who were prosperous as well as talented, although at one point more than half the adult population was composed of refugees, only a privileged few were ever allowed to become citizens, and none, as I have already said, could hold top civic office.[12]

A REFUGEE ECCLESIOLOGY

Such a manner of living, such a life-setting, I am now going to argue, contributed significantly to Calvin's mindset, to his theological and ecclesiastical positions, in several ways. In biblical interpretation, arguably Calvin's greatest gift and heritage, this becomes evident at a number of points. Now it is true that the notion of the Christian as *viator*, as a pilgrim or traveler, is an old one. Nowhere is this more evident than in the latter chapters (11–13) of the Epistle to the Hebrews, a point to

11. Calvin, *Commentary on the Gospel according to John*, 15–19.

12. Although the antipathy toward granting citizenship lessened after 1555, still the numbers remained small. On the whole question of the refugee communities in Geneva, see Monter, *Calvin's Geneva*, chapter 7.

HOBBS—*John Calvin, Refugee*

which I shall return. Calvin's role as interpreter of Scripture brought him to engage in this tradition with particular acuity, and to embrace this calling wholeheartedly.

In the flourishing of new publications around the Calvin Quinquecentenary, this theme has been given some prominence. W. Robert Godfray, in his *John Calvin: Pilgrim and Pastor*, uses it as leitmotif for the first half of Calvin's life, that is, until his second coming to Geneva in 1541. In his 2009 biography, the Dutch scholar Herman Selderhuis, assigns the pilgrim motif to the years of wandering 1534–1536, and the refugee theme to the Strasbourg sojourn of 1538–1541.[13] Unfortunately neither of these works was available to me as I wrote this chapter, although the thesis of this chapter differs from both of these. I have been struck, on the other hand, by a small section in Bruce Gordon's biography already cited, where he employs the pilgrim image to interpret one of the earliest and most curious works of Calvin, the *Psychopannia* ("Soul Sleep"). Calvin's exploration of the question of the state of the soul after death and before the Final Resurrection and Last Judgment need not detain us here. What is of interest is how Calvin uses the master-theme of Heb 11 to characterize the life of all believers. "Drawing on his own experience, though never referring to himself, he offered comfort to those who suffered for their faith in God's Word," using figures like Abraham and Job.[14] Interestingly, Gordon points out that Calvin sent his manuscript of the work to, amongst others, Wolfgang Capito in Strasbourg, who was not encouraging. Apart from an illegible handwriting—the curse of more than one Reformation scholar, ancient and modern—Capito seems to have found the work unsympathetic and discouraged its publication. This early Strasbourg assessment—although admittedly Calvin was eventually able to publish it there—may well anticipate the profound differences that emerged in the Nicodemite controversy, to which we shall return.

The chapter in this book by my colleague, Lynne McNaughton, will observe a particular and striking application of this theme around Abraham.[15] I shall not repeat her comments here. Let me offer two others. The most intimate glimpse of his own self that Calvin ever offered us comes in the preface to his Psalms commentary. It is there, for ex-

13. Selderhuis, *John Calvin.*.

14. Gordon, *Calvin*, 42–44.

15. See pages 107–8 of this book.

ample, that he gives one of only two references he makes to his own conversion to the evangelical camp. "Since I was devoted to the superstitions of popery too stiffly ... God subdued my mind to teachableness by a sudden conversion." Alas, this tantalizing reference is without dates, which has left Calvin scholars a field in which to exercise their speculations. Now in this Introduction addressed "To the godly reader," Calvin draws close parallels between himself and David, both as David is recounted in the Samuel narrative, and more importantly, in the many trials, wanderings, false friends, oppositions, of David's life, as these were traditionally understood to be mirrored in the Psalms.[16] Indeed, he finds that the troubles of his own life (I quote) "have been no small help in understanding the Psalms. In them I did not journey as it were in an unknown region." Granted that he does not specifically use the language of exile for the troublous Geneva years, he nonetheless laments openly the constant opposition to him, and consequent unrest for his soul. Like David he has learned to live with ingratitude, threats of violence, slander against both lifestyle and teaching, betrayal by former associates. In all this, "since David shewed me the way by his own footsteps, I experienced no small comfort therefrom ... so I, assailed on all sides, have scarce had one minute's rest from outward or inward fightings."[17]

For a second example within his biblical interpretation, I turn to his sermons preached in 1548–1549, on the book of Jeremiah. It is evident, as generations of my Vancouver School of Theology students have been asked to observe, that Calvin identifies himself with the "weeping prophet," reproaching his people for their unfaithfulness and earning only contempt and even violent opposition. For example, in his sermon delivered June 25, 1549, on Jer 15:6–19, Calvin points out to his hearers that not all clergy are disliked and threatened; there are timeservers and those who associate with the debauched in the citizenry, and they are the equivalent of Jeremiah's false prophets. On the other hand, "here is what men charged with the Word must do ... All those who wish to faithfully bear the Word of God must prepare for war ... The enemy is hidden. The

---

16. An ancient Jewish tradition made David author of the entire Psalter. Calvin stands with the majority of sixteenth-century interpreters, finding that David wrote many though not all, finding occasion for composition of these prayers in the events of his life.

17. Calvin, *A Commentary on the Psalms*, 18–23.

ones are rebels, the others are rogues . . . All the evil will count for nothing against us . . . Nevertheless this battle recommences eternally."[18]

A few days later, preaching on Jeremiah's lament, "Why is my pain eternal?" (Jer15:18), Calvin states: "Let us learn to be patient . . . If God afflicts us for a year or even a whole lifetime without aid, let us expect it after death."[19] Now Jeremiah was of course a citizen of Jerusalem, while Calvin lacked even that cold comfort in 1548–1549. But more to the point, Calvin knew well the tragic end of Jeremiah's ministry, that the prophet who above all had called his people to submit to God's will manifest in the Babylonians, would end his life as an involuntary exile, a refugee in distant Egypt!

Calvin was in the midst of a crisis of doubtful outcome in the case of these last sermons, and one might argue that they reflect his sense of the precarity of his situation. This argument hardly pertains to the Psalms commentary, however, completed and printed in 1557 when, as all Calvin interpreters agree, he had passed the great crisis, and his position was secure. I believe we are on more certain grounds when we see the commonalty that ran through all his life.

His experience of life as an exile and refugee, his certainty that in an inconstant world permanence and constancy would be found only in the unshakeable Word of God and in the hostility it would always arouse, also shaped, in my judgment, Calvin's position in one of the controversies that marked the early decades of the Reformation churches. The Nicodemite, or as Calvin wanted it, the so-called Nicodemite debate took form around the stance to be adopted by persons desirous of evangelical reform, while living in an unreformed church. The problem will have occurred in many territories, but was particularly acute in France, various Italian territories, and the Low Countries, all regions where evangelical literature circulated and won adherents, yet where no state or ecclesiastical authorities had yet openly espoused the Reform. The case of Gérard Roussel, a theme of chapter in this book, is illustrative. Put simply, should persons of evangelical faith conviction abandon their as yet unreformed church community with its celebration of the Latin Mass in a sanctuary adorned with many images? Or conversely, might a person of sincere evangelical conviction stay and work from within to convince the wavering, strengthen the faith of the weak, and hope

18. Calvin, *Sermons on Jeremiah by Jean Calvin*, 46–47.

19. Ibid., 73–74.

thereby to gradually win some of them, even if not the whole community, to a similar evangelical faith? Indeed, was this not the more difficult, but more faithful path to follow, for the sake of the neighbor? Might such evangelicals, scattered throughout the church in France in particular, although Italy and the Low Countries would equally well apply, be the Gospel salt that would season the whole loaf?

Martin Bucer of Strasbourg certainly believed so. He had met Lefèvre d'Étaples, Roussel and others when they fled temporarily to Strasbourg in winter 1525, after the Paris authorities had put a violent end to their attempt at reform in Meaux. He maintained correspondence with them when they returned to France, to live out this role as would-be reformers in an often unfriendly environment. Bucer, in fact, dedicated his 1529 Psalms commentary to the Dauphin (crown prince) of France, and in it he praised the godliness not only of Lefèvre, now enjoying royal favor as chateau librarian and tutor of the younger princes, but of other members of the royal family, including of course Queen Marguerite, to whom moreover Capito had dedicated in 1528 his commentary on Hosea. It is apparent that the Strasbourgers were far from alone among the first generation of reformers in believing that by patient encouragement, perhaps even the kingdom of France might be won to the gospel—as indeed England likewise would be, in their eyes. Persons like Gérard Roussel saw themselves mirrored in the case of Nicodemus, the secret follower of Jesus who retained his membership in the Sanhedrin, and sought to use his influence for good there. He also used his influence to obtain decent burial for Jesus (John 3; 19:38–42). Nicodemus is not enrolled in most calendars of the saints—although he is in French Brittany—but he was viewed as an honorable man.

Now the Nicodemite controversy has itself been subject of differing interpretations, which lie beyond our concern in this chapter, which is the leading role played by Calvin in making the matter subject of intense and virulent comment.[20] For Calvin did not see it in this way. Certainly he had such friends and associates, even in high places. I mentioned earlier the Duchess Renée of Ferrara, with whom he corresponded for years as spiritual adviser. But already in the Ferrara visit, and more so as events unfolded in France, Calvin became convinced that a middle way of compromise—working from within for a Church Catholic whilst

20. A short and helpful overview is given by Higman in "The Question of Nicodemism," 165–70.

being evangelical—was untenable and indeed spiritually unacceptable, if it involved in any way participation in the Catholic Mass, toleration of images and practices like the veneration of relics. He was scathing in his denunciation of the Duchess Renée's temporizing. In 1537 he published two letters addressed to friends well-placed within the Catholic hierarchy. One of these was Roussel, just named Bishop of Oloron. The argument in these two letters is similar: Catholic (what he would call Papist) ceremony and liturgy are full of idolatry and blasphemy. No Christian can participate in these without offense to God. As for accepting any ecclesiastical appointment, this reveals a shameful willingness to compromise for the sake of personal gain. These two letters were probably written in 1536, while he was in Ferrara, and reflect a youthful, even immature fervor. But in 1543, established in Geneva, Calvin wrote a short treatise with the title, *What a faithful person who knows the Gospel Truth, should do while amongst Papists*. Beneath this title, he printed the text from Elijah's combat with the prophets of Baal in 1 Kgs 18: "How long are you going to hobble along between the two sides?" Within the treatise, he endeavored to show some sympathy for those finding themselves caught and unable easily to flee; but the message was clear. God's commandments against all forms of idolatry leave no room for compromise with what is a false form of Christian faith. The next year, Calvin returned to the charge. He had received considerable criticism for his uncompromising stance. Now he entitled his work *A Justification of John Calvin to my lords the Nicodemites*. Here the title page bore the even clearer text from Isa 30: "They are a rebellious people and hypocrites, a people who refuse to obey the Lord's Law." The persons he addresses are not justified in claiming a model in Nicodemus, they are in fact giving themselves a false label. Only cowardice and a preference for the soft life, the leeks and garlics of Egypt, the wealth of the Catholic Church, could hold them back from the duty they owe to Christ.[21]

Francis Higman has recently observed that in this matter Calvin failed utterly to understand the driving passion of a number of these people for the unity of the Church.[22] I am reminded of Erasmus, who could not bear to tear in pieces the seamless robe of Christ, to break

---

21. Bernard Roussel and Francis Higman have just published, in a magnificent volume in an up-dated French translation, these two treatises, with excellent annotation: Calvin, *Ouevres*, 504–72.

22. Higman in Calvin, *Ouevres*, 1274.

the unity of the Church, however much he might deplore its faults. With the wisdom of hindsight, it is permitted to wonder whether the kingdom of France might have gone a different way had more of Calvin's students stayed in place and worked from within. Quite possibly not. The French royal family turned out to be passionately attached to the traditional Roman Mass, and once Henri II came to the throne (1547), he firmly committed to its defense by the shortest route, the attempted extermination of the Protestant heresy. What does seem clear to me is that in condemning as hypocrites such evangelical Catholics as Roussel, Calvin's judgment was influenced by two factors, intimately linked. The first was clearly personal, profoundly shaped by the experience of exile he himself was living out. But also theologically, we must recognize that, as Bruce Gordon has underlined, Calvin did not consider the Roman Church to be a true church. It was not bound to the Word and the right administration of sacraments. Instead it was bound to a substitute, a false word that encompassed the traditions of the church that were allowed in practice to outweigh the voice of Scripture. Its sacraments were numerous, and cluttered with human inventions, even, Calvin would say, blasphemous claims that overrode the clear injunctions of Scripture. Now we cannot ask of Calvin a tolerant if not ecumenical spirit such as we would hope to practice in our day. Moreover, among the factors that certainly also shaped him were the reports of the martyrdoms at the stake being imposed by authorities here and there in Catholic France. To understand him is not, however, to excuse the intolerance and the harsh language in which it was couched. We could wish he had absorbed less of the vitriol of his friend Farel, and more of the spirit of his mentor Bucer, who wrote in a plea for an irenical spirit, and with a perspicuity remarkable in that age: "God does not grant that everyone sees the same things at the same time."[23]

A HOLY ROOTLESSNESS

I want now to make a proposal by way of conclusion to this study of Calvin the refugee. Calvin firmly embraced the metaphor of the Christian life as pilgrim journey. As he wrote in his commentary on Heb 11, "we

---

23. Calvin, *Psalms Commentaries* (1529) at the conclusion of his exposition of Psalm 1.

are to conclude that there will be for us no inheritance in heaven, except we become pilgrims on earth . . . we who have no promised habitation in this world." And on 1 Pet 2:11, "we are not in bondage to the flesh, when we pass as strangers through this life." One can read this last, and the commentaries themselves permit it, simply as a warning against the attractions of the flesh, understood in the Pauline sense of the values of this world. I want to suggest, however, that Calvin's life experience as exile or refugee, as I have outlined it here, enabled him to maintain a certain detachment from the cords of location, culture, and home that typically bring churches into a cultural captivity. A certain detachment, I say; not entire of course. That would be too much to expect. But Calvin's willingness to entertain experiment, to try to hold to the freedom that a sense of *adiaphora*, of non-essentials, can give, even if as Bruce Gordon has suggested, he could contradict himself on this, is certainly grounded also in the exile's sense of holy rootlessness, an unwillingness, even an inability, to settle down. Here we have no permanent city. But we look for that city. Calvin the refugee may have bequeathed to the Reformed tradition some sense of the relativity of so much of human thinking, a willingness to imagine beyond the bounds of what now is, to what the church might and should be.

Ecclesia reformata, semper reformanda—a Reformed church must always be about being re-formed.

10

A Comment on Calvin's
The Necessity of Reforming the Church (1543)

VICTOR SHEPHERD

SETTING

CHARLES V, EMPEROR OF the Holy Roman Empire, was aware that the disputes the Reformation had engendered were unsettling on many fronts. He was anxious lest the multi-faceted upheaval distract Protestant princes from his war with France. Wishing to maximize the probability of his triumph, Charles V called for a Diet in the German city of Speyer,[1] wherein he would plead his case; namely, that Protestant doctrinal zeal, with its concomitant divisiveness, should be suspended in the interest of maintaining a united ecclesiastical front against France.

Martin Bucer (the Reformer in Strasbourg whose theology had influenced Calvin[2] when Calvin had been harassed out of Geneva and had been afforded refuge in Strasbourg from 1538 to 1541) had considered writing a document that would set forth the Reformation's case,[3] therein reminding (if not informing) the emperor as to why the Reformation church could not surrender theological conviction or suspend theological activity regardless of social, political, or military consequences.

1. Speyer had been the site of two previous Diets, 1526 and 1529. The former recognized Protestantism, while the second rescinded the recognition; thereafter the Reformers were labelled "Protestants." Charles scheduled the third Diet for February 1544, several months away.

2. See Wendel, *Calvin.*

3. See Reid, "Introduction," 183; and Greschat, *Martin Bucer,* 195–97.

146

The Reformers were iron-fast in their intransigence and its defensibility: their theological convictions, after all, pertained not to theological *adiaphora* or religious frippery but rather to the eternal well-being of humankind. In other words, the Reformers were convinced that the Reformation, however collaterally disruptive on however so many fronts, was essential to the recovery and promulgation of a gospel apart from which humankind was ultimately lost before God.

The document Bucer considered writing would assure the emperor that Protestants were not politically treacherous or even politically indifferent. At the same time, Protestants could never be expected to surrender theological conviction for the sake of a united, extra-theological front.

Bucer, however, came to doubt whether such a document would be effective.[4] He declined to write it. Yet where Bucer appeared immobilized, Calvin was inflamed. By the end of 1543 he had penned a tract that would subsequently assist the theological self-criticism and gospel-reorientation of the Protestant church for centuries thereafter.

In light of Reformation writings extant by 1543, why was such a document needed? Luther had already written much and disseminated it widely. Melanchthon had published his *Loci Communes*, the first systematic theology of the Reformation, a work that Luther had deemed subordinate only to Scripture. Calvin himself had already published his 1536 *Institutes*, the tome for which he would chiefly be known thereafter. In addition he had hugely expanded the Latin edition of 1536 into the Latin edition of 1539, and then had translated the latter into French in 1541, thereby assuring a much wider readership. Moreover, while he was working alongside Bucer in Strasbourg, Calvin had written his iconic commentary on Romans in 1539 and had published it in 1540. Had not the Reformation's cause and course been announced, driven and defended in all such publications? Had not Calvin's convictions been exposed adequately in his own writings to date, together with what he had produced since the Romans commentary (e.g., *Draft Ecclesiastical Ordinances*, 1541)?

Plainly Calvin was aware that the church has to be producing at least two types of theology. One type is the sort exemplified in Melancththon's *Loci Communes* or Calvin's *Institutes*; namely, that theological construct

---

4. Reid, "Introduction," 183.

which explores the "whole counsel of God"[5] in such a way as to identify the essential "building blocks" of the faith (e.g., creation, fall, calling of Israel, incarnation, atonement, resurrection, bestowal of the Spirit, eschatology) and relates them internally to each other, indicating a logical connection wherein the neglect of any one of them denatures all the remaining. The second type of theological writing is "occasional" in that it addresses a crisis or opportunity that has appeared unanticipated; i.e., what the turning of the wheel of history has exposed on a singular occasion should be seized and dealt with before the same wheel, turning relentlessly, eliminates such an opportunity. Calvin knew that the *ecclesia* was not merely *reformata* but also *semper reformanda*, always being reformed because always needing to be reformed. *Reformanda* remains essential since the Word of God must be brought to bear remorselessly on the anti-gospel accretions that haunt the church, and since, in the second place, *reformanda* characterizes the church's mission to a world whose challenges appear in different dress in different eras. For this reason Calvin leapt at the opportunity to address the princes of the Reformation territories on the necessity (i.e., the non-negotiability and the non-postponement) of reforming the church.

DOCTRINE

Calvin addresses the tract under discussion to the emperor and to the princes "that they seriously undertake the task of restoring the church, presented in the name of all those who wish Christ to reign."[6] On the one hand Jesus Christ, declared victor in his resurrection, has been installed as ruler in his ascension and session. As such he is impregnable, and reigns regardless of what anyone wishes or does not wish, the reign of Christ not being determined by creaturely acknowledgement. On the other hand, Calvin boldly asserts that unfaithful guardians of sound doctrine "banish Christ and the truth of his gospel."[7] (Two decades later Calvin will be found making the same bold point: where doctrine is distorted "God's remedy for rescuing mankind from death is rendered useless."[8]) When doctrine is distorted Christ cannot be called upon and

---

5. Acts 20:27 (RSV).

6. Calvin, "The Necessity of Reforming the Church," 184.

7. Calvin, cited in ibid., 209.

8. Calvin, *Sermons on the Book of Micah*, 369.

known. For this reason the recovery of sound doctrine is essential to the salvific accessibility of Christ—and therefore reason enough for the Reformers' preoccupation.

How urgently does sound doctrine need to be recovered and the church restored? Calvin maintains that the issue is not whether the church is afflicted with disease, but whether the disease is of such a nature that waiting upon "too slow a remedy"[9] inexcusably imperils people. For this reason Calvin rejects the accusation that he and his fellow-Reformers are guilty of "rash and impious innovation."[10] In fact he denies that the Reformation is innovation at all; it aims at restoring the church, not re-inventing it. As for the suggestion of rashness, Calvin presupposes an understanding of the human predicament that forfends any imputation of indiscretion. In this regard he refers to Luther, whom, along with others, "God raised up as a torch ... that lifted people into the way of salvation."[11] Evidently Calvin assumes that sinners are at risk before the all-holy God. People need to be *lifted* into the way of salvation inasmuch as they are not in that "way" at present, are imperiled as long as they are not, and are unable to raise themselves from death to life. Salvation, for all the Reformers, is that act of God whereby God-in-his-mercy saves people from God-in-his-condemnation. There is no suggestion anywhere in the Reformers of the existentialism that laps contemporary theology; namely, that the gospel is God's remedy of a predicament that humankind has brought upon itself; i.e., alienation or estrangement. To be sure, humankind *is* alienated—from God, from each other, from self—but all of this not because of human disobedience, rebellion, or folly but rather on account of God's *reaction to and judgment upon* such inexcusable disobedience, outrageous rebellion and culpable folly. (Adam and Eve, it should be noted, did not wander out of the Garden of Eden but rather were expelled from it by a judicial act of God.) Ultimately, the threat to humankind is none other than God; only God can rescind the threat that he is. He has done so by rendering himself "propitiatory" (a word that Calvin uses on almost every page of *Institutes* and Commentaries) in the cross, the truth of which is attested by doctrine. The recovery of doctrine must proceed without tarrying for any consideration, including the emperor's, lest the day of grace be foreclosed. For this reason Calvin tells

9. Calvin, "The Necessity of Reforming the Church," 185.

10. Ibid.

11. Ibid.

the emperor and other political leaders that regardless of the urgency of their causes, the Protestant cause, and with it the writing of his tract, is of the "*highest* necessity."[12]

Essential to God's urgent, relentless "search and rescue mission" is a repristination of the "heads of doctrine,"[13] or to use an expression mentioned earlier, the building blocks of the faith. Such heads of doctrine setting forth the "pure of worship of God" and comprehending "the salvation of men [*sic*],"[14] had been rendered "in a great sense obsolete."[15] Had they been rendered utterly obsolete, of course, the faith would have disappeared, and with it the salfivic availability of Christ. Still, Calvin does not hesitate to say that essential doctrines have "in a great measure"[16] been lost to sight.

What renders anything obsolete at any time? Novelty does. What is novel renders what is current obsolete. Theological novelty—i.e., what is non-scriptural (and therein necessarily non-catholic)—has rendered obsolete the truths without which the church crumbles. Reformation theology, Calvin wants everyone to know, so far from exemplifying novelty renounces faddism in any form.

In anticipating and denying the charge of theological innovation Calvin everywhere insists that Jesus Christ is Truth (in the sense of the apostle John's *aletheia,* "reality"). In accord with Scripture and the church fathers he insists no less on soundness of doctrine in that he is aware at all times of the relationship between Truth and the truths (doctrine) that point to reality and articulate it. Truth is a living person; *truths* are statements that describe this reality. *Truth* and *truths* are categorically distinct and must therefore always be distinguished. Yet even as they must be distinguished they may not be separated. Theology is concerned with both insofar as theology (i) has to do with reality; (ii) formulates statements that aim at speaking provisionally, to be sure, yet speak *truthfully* and *adequately* of this reality without pretending to speak *exhaustively.* Not to be concerned with sound doctrine is to "banish Christ" in the sense that one is asserting (i) that there is no Truth, or (ii) Truth (i.e., the reality of the living God) is not knowable, or (iii) Truth is of such a

---

12. Ibid. Emphasis added.

13. Ibid.

14. Ibid., 186.

15. Ibid.

16. Ibid.

nature that while it may be intuited it cannot be articulated (by means of truths) and therefore cannot be commended. Either sound doctrine (truths in the service of Truth) is recovered or Christ remains effectively "banished."

Calvin avers that apart from doctrinal pronouncement the Lord of such pronouncement does not operate salvifically within the economy of the church and its mission. In a word, while Jesus Christ infinitely transcends all that the church can say or think concerning him, nevertheless human witness to him and articulation of him as God's redemptive event remain the means of his acting upon humankind to the latter's eternal blessing. The Lord of all such witness and articulation assured the apostles that as they enacted their ministry in his name, *he* would speak to and act upon the recipients of the apostles' witness. "Whoever hears you, hears me"[17] is Christ's promise to do nothing less than this without thereby collapsing himself into the apostles or claiming to act apart from them.

In his *Necessity of Reforming the Church* Calvin returns relentlessly to the cruciality of doctrine that is Scripture-normed and Scripture-informed just because he is aware of the ineluctable connection between doctrine and the reality that transcends it. Here, however, Calvin is far from the Calvinistic scholasticism that arose after him and with which he is identified incorrectly. All forms of scholasticism, Reformed as surely as Roman, tend to identify statements (truths) with the Truth they are deemed to express.[18] Such inappropriate identification is to be avoided even as doctrine is ever to be refined by the Word of God for the sake of intimacy with the One whose mercy must always justify the sinner, and justify as well every aspect of the sinner, including doctrinal formulation.

In light of the intrinsic relation among doctrine that de-obscures the gospel, the self-magnification of the One who adopts and uses such doctrine, and the restoration of a church that is nothing less than the earthly-historical manifestation of that One's body, Calvin claims that he speaks for himself, for several European princes and untold numbers of devout people who deplore the corruption of the church and who, for this reason, will not apologize for the Reformation.[19]

17. Luke 10:16 RSV.

18. See Torrance, *Reality & Evangelical Theology*, 49.

19. Calvin, "The Necessity of Reforming the Church," 185.

Essential to this doctrinal recovery is an unremitting attention to Scripture. Such attention, however, does not entail an uncritical or illogical Biblicism—an approach to Scripture that Calvin does not endorse. At the same time, where Scripture does not norm, form, and inform theology, the church, now fast departing from the faith "once for all delivered to the saints"[20] is left either with listening to little more than "old wives' tales and fictions equally frivolous,"[21] or submerging the Word of God in the fanciful vagaries of speculation[22]—or as he says in a related tract, "the fictions of our reason."[23]

WORSHIP

Worship is always at the forefront of Calvin's theological consciousness. God is honored only as the gospel constrains the church's thinking so as to conform the church's mind to the mind of Christ. At the same time, Calvin characteristically eschews a one-sided cerebralism that upholds the head but neglects the heart.[24] When Calvin speaks of worship he appears to mean more than what the congregation does corporately on Sunday. Worship, for Calvin, appears to include the formal, public praise of God as well as the attitude or disposition that characterizes every aspect of the Christian's thinking and doing. Such worship, says Calvin, should be marked by

1. a manner that is neither cold nor presumptuously chummy, the latter being "careless";[25]

2. a magnification of the glory of God (this is bedrock for Calvin, for worship must be preoccupied with discerning and adoring God's inherent splendor now visited upon the church; worship is always other-directed, the congregation's glory appearing only as the congregation aspires to renounce all claim to glory and live to serve the glory of God);

20. Jude 4 RSV.

21. Calvin, "The Necessity of Reforming the Church," 187.

22. Ibid., 188.

23. Calvin, *Best Method of Obtaining Concord*; cited in Reid, *Calvin: Theological Treatises,* 330.

24. Calvin's concern with the heart, the affective response of the whole person to the gospel, looms everywhere in his theology.

25. Calvin, "The Necessity of Reforming the Church," 187.

SHEPHERD—*Calvin's* The Necessity of Reforming the Church   153

3. the making known the perfections in which God's glory shines; (Calvin, eschewing empty theological clichés, wants worshippers to know precisely what it is in God that is nothing less than glorious);

4. the setting forth of the "benefits" vouchsafed to believers ("benefits", for Calvin, always refers to the two benefits that jointly exhaust the gospel; namely, justification and sanctification, or remission of sin and newness of life); these benefits are to be lauded "as eloquently as we can," naturally enough, since they gather up the totality of Christ's work on behalf of his people and within them;

5. the incitement to reverence God's majesty; (it is to be noted that Calvin characteristically speaks of the majesty of God—i.e., the grandeur of God; Calvin does not speak in this tract—if he speaks anywhere—of the sovereignty of God; throughout the *Institutes* Calvin speaks *nowhere* of the sovereignty of God);

6. an atmosphere that moves people to "render due homage to his [i.e., God's] greatness;"

7. a felt gratitude for God elicited by God's mercies;

8. a oneness of heart and mind in the showing forth of God's praise.[26]

The outcome of the foregoing is that there is "infused into their [i.e., worshippers'] hearts that solid confidence which afterwards gives birth to prayer."[27] People who are the beneficiaries of Christ through faith in him and who possess assurance concerning their union with him are constrained to "confide in his power, trust in his goodness, depend on his truth . . . turn to him with the whole heart, rest on him with full hope . . . resort to him in necessity, that is, at every moment, and ascribe to him every good thing enjoyed, and testify to this by expressions of praise."[28]

Undeniably, according to Calvin, doctrine is always intimately related to life. Only as doctrine is re-developed so as to allow the gospel's inherent brightness to shine forth are people able to call upon God, know God, mirror God's glory, and "enjoy" the One who alone gladdens

26. Points 1–8 are found in ibid., 187.
27. Ibid.
28. Ibid.

the heart of those made in his image and likeness. Doctrine, categorically distinct from the human person's intimacy with God-in-person, is nonetheless essential to it, and therefore essential as well to believers' enjoyment of such intimacy.

CATHOLICITY

The Protestant Reformers, ceaselessly accused of unconscionably sundering the unity of the church, replied as often they had done no such thing. Throughout one of his earliest tracts, *Reply to Sadolet* (1539) Calvin maintained that sectarianism could not be charged against the Reformers. When Cardinal Sadolet had charged the Genevan church with schism Calvin had maintained that the Reformers' dispute with Rome was not that the Church of Rome was "too catholic" but rather that it was insufficiently catholic.[29] Roman Catholicism, the Reformers insisted, had obscured aspects of the gospel vouchsafed to the church and found, for instance, throughout the Patristic era. As the Roman See had gained primacy, catholicity had weakened, rendering the Church of Rome sectarian in several respects. So far from espousing sectarianism the Reformers, in reforming the church, were underlining catholicity as essential to the definition of the church. Once again Calvin is adamant: the theological non-negotiables of the Reformers are no invention. While the Reformers, for instance, have insisted that preaching accompany every celebration of the sacraments lest the latter degenerate into an "empty spectacle"[30] (the spectacle soon becoming worse than empty as superstition takes over and idolatry dishonors the One of whom a sacrament is meant to be effectual sign), the church fathers had earlier stipulated as much.[31] Similarly, when the Reformers, perusing Scripture, noted that *episkopos* and *presbyteros* have the same denotation, their conclusion that monarchical episcopacy could not pertain to the *esse* of the church was manifestly supported by Patristic authorities.[32] The ancient church maintained, as the Reformers have come to insist, that presbyters are to be examined with respect to both their doctrine and

---

29. See Calvin, "Letter to Sadolet."
30. Calvin, "The Necessity of Reforming the Church," 188.
31. Ibid., 203.
32. Ibid., 207.

their life.[33] In the same vein, ancient authorities support the Reformers' insistence on a worship whose substance and style are governed by a zeal for hearing and heeding Scripture.[34]

A major point here is Calvin's emphasis on tradition's witness to the un-normed normativity of Scripture. Tradition, Calvin notes, does not attest the primacy of tradition. Unquestionably tradition is authoritative; tradition, however, remains a normed norm, self-acknowledged to be Scripture-normed. The Reformation can never be accused of rejecting tradition; it can be thanked, however, for recovering tradition's self-understanding on behalf of the church. Calvin, supported by tradition, maintains that if tradition is elevated above Scripture the gospel will be submerged and "gross idolatry" will surface; such "gross idolatry" will be evident, e.g., in "divine honors paid to dead men's bones."[35]

Calvin's point here is telling; his warning pertains to the church in every era. We must be sure to note the contemporary Protestant equivalent of his criticism of sixteenth-century Roman Catholicism. In 2001 I was asked to attend the World Methodist Council. The theme of the 2001 Council was the Aldersgate event (1738) wherein Wesley felt his "heart strangely warmed." Throughout the conference Wesley's experience was both romanticized and left unprobed. As a result, despite the conference's veneration of Wesley in the birth and development of Methodism it failed to mention (i) that the Aldersgate heart-warming found Wesley thereafter repudiating the mystical moralism that had rendered his ministry ineffectual for fifteen years; (ii) that the same event was the springboard for an evangelistic ministry whose foundation was justification by faith; (iii) that Wesley unhesitatingly and uncompromisingly declared thereafter that justification by faith was "the very foundation of our Church [i.e., Anglican] . . . and indeed the fundamental [doctrine] of the Reformed Churches;"[36] (iv) that Wesley's ministry after 1738 presupposed an understanding of the human condition under God that was nothing less than catastrophic regardless of unbelievers' ignorance of it; namely, the sinner's condemnation already enacted and merely awaiting manifestation on the Day of Judgment, which condemnation could be relieved only as the sinner exercised Spirit-wrought repentance and

33. Ibid.

34. Ibid., 190.

35. Ibid., 188.

36. Wesley, Sermon #150, "Hypocrisy in Oxford"; *Works of John Wesley*, 395.

faith. Despite the adulation of Wesley there was no recognition of what impelled the man to travel 250,000 miles on horseback, preach 40,000 times, endure ice-cold downpours and abusive mobs and denominational opposition and a criminal justice system that abetted injustice. There was no examination of Wesley's gospel concerning either its substance or its urgency. What else was such misbegotten veneration except "divine honors paid to dead men's bones?"

SACRAMENTS

Calvin's chief complaint is that the "signs" (water, bread, wine) of the sacraments are one-sidedly attended to, thereby befogging the One whose action the sacraments attest, Jesus Christ.[37] The result is that people come to trust not the Lord to whom the signs point but the signs themselves. The twofold outcome of this latter misapprehension is idolatry of the elements and the veiling of Christ.[38]

In a seeming paradox, Calvin avers that once Christ is collapsed into the sacrament and is deemed to inhere it (this is one of the Reformers' objections to transubstantiation), Christ is obscured by the sacrament;[39] i.e., that once the sacrament is held to "contain" Christ, the rite renders Christ inaccessible. The confusing of sign with signified finds people venerating elements (here Calvin has in mind such practices as the reservation and adoration of the host.) Once rendered "content with gazing upon them [i.e., the elements] and worshipping them," worshippers "never once raised their mind to Christ."[40]

The same confusion may be present in Protestant denominations today, especially in those that are declining precipitously. As nervous observers watch an institution decline, it is recalled that Christ has guaranteed that the powers of death will not prevail against the church.[41] Frequently forgotten is the fact that Christ's promise pertains to his people; he has guaranteed that the community of his faithful people will never perish. He has made no such promise to institutions. History is littered with the debris of long-dead denominations and congregations.

---

37. Calvin, "The Necessity of Reforming the Church," 203.

38. Ibid.

39. Ibid., 205.

40. Ibid.

41. Matt 16:20.

It appears that false confidence has arisen through the notion that Christ has collapsed himself into the church and now inheres it. Overlooked is the truth that while the most intimate relationship obtains between Christ and his people, the relationship is between Christ and his *people*, not between Christ and any institutional structure as such. Overlooked as well is the truth that while head and body cannot be severed (i.e., Jesus Christ is not a severed head), Christ ever remains *lord* of the relationship between him and his people, *lord* of the church. In other words, even as Christ remains indissolubly bound to the church he infinitely transcends it, has not collapsed himself into it, and must not be thought to inhere it. Any suggestion that he does inhere the church, in the seeming paradox Calvin noted concerning the sign and signified in the elements, renders the church idolatrous, the gospel obscure, and Christ "inaccessible." The peril of misunderstanding and misapplying Christ's pledge concerning the indefeasibility of the church is precisely what Calvin found concerning the misunderstanding of the sacraments; namely, that as soon as Christ is thought to inhere the church, Christ is obscured by the church. No institution that obscures Christ should comfort itself with a promise that the Lord whom no one can "capture" has made to the church.

Continuing with his defense of the Reformers' theology of the sacraments, Calvin objects to the practice of sundering command and promise.[42] The command is "Take, eat, drink;" the promise, "You eat my body and drink my blood."[43] Whenever the elements are reserved and adored but not consumed, command and promise have been sundered.[44] Disobedience to the command forfeits the blessing of the promise.

Calvin does not relate explicitly his point about command and promise in connection with the Lord's Supper to Abraham and Isaac on Mount Moriah, but the connection is undeniable in view of the fact that Calvin recognizes Gen 22 to be the paradigmatic test, as attested in both older and newer testaments, of holding command and promise together.[45] Abraham has been promised that he will have descendants as numerous as the sand on the seashore. Abraham, the prototype of faith, must persevere in faith and Isaac must survive. If Abraham surrenders faith in God, Abraham can have no descendants *in faith*. If Isaac

42. Calvin, "The Necessity of Reforming the Church," 205.

43. Ibid.

44. Ibid.

45. See Calvin, *A Commentary on Genesis*, 561–72.

perishes, Abraham will have no *descendants* in faith. The dilemma is stark: if Abraham obeys God and offers up Isaac, the promise has been cancelled since Isaac has not survived; if Abraham second-guesses God (i.e., disobeys God) and spares Isaac in order to "ensure" the promise, the promise has been cancelled by a disobedience that exemplifies Abraham's unfaith. What is Abraham to do? Replete with knife and flame and firewood the anguished man resolutely trudges up Mount Moriah, determined to obey God immediately and trust God to fulfill God's promise to him even though his obedience appears to void the promise. In other words, Abraham will obey God in an act whose outcome he cannot deny and trust God to fulfill God's promise to him in a manner he cannot foresee. The conclusion of the trial of Abraham (and no less of Isaac, old enough to carry sufficient wood to consume his remains and deemed, by rabbinic tradition, to be thirty-seven years old)[46] is glorious: because of Abraham's refusal to sunder command and promise all the nations of the world will be blessed.[47]

In his insistence on the simultaneity of command and promise Calvin challenges the church today. The church is commanded to declare the gospel and to live by it alone. God has promised that his word does not return to him fruitlessly, that as the church obeys the command, the promise will be fulfilled. Yet the command appears to vitiate the promise as the church dwindles (at least in some places) week after week. The gospel appears too specific in an era that prefers religious generalities, too narrow in an age of inclusiveness, too confident of its effectiveness in a time of polite opinions, too sharply delineated for those who prefer the softer contours of romanticism. It appears that as the church attempts to live by the gospel it will die by the gospel. Then what is the church to do? Like Abraham of old it must obey God even as it trusts God to fulfill his promise concerning the church in ways that the church at present cannot anticipate. To do anything else is to abandon Abraham, faith's prototype; to do anything else is to sunder command and promise, a divorce that Calvin deems to render Christ an idol and worship superstition.

---

46. For an expanded exposition of Gen 22, including the exegesis of both Calvin and Luther, see Shepherd, "Abraham and Isaac in Genesis 22."

47. Gen 22:18.

SPIRITUALITY

Calvin's emphasis on doctrine, worship and sacrament never eclipses his awareness that the Word must transmogrify and indwell the human heart. In holding Word and Spirit together Calvin insists that what has been done outside of us yet for us (*extra nos, pro nobis*) in Christ must also be done in us (*in nobis*) by the Spirit—or else all that Christ has achieved on our behalf fails to profit us.[48] No caricature of Calvin is less accurate than the notion that he is a one-sided theologian of the "head" while neglecting the "heart." Consider, e.g., "with *experience* as our teacher we find God just as he declares himself in his Word";[49] "God openly reveals what he has proclaimed and promised in his Word, and enables us to *experience* it."[50] The knowledge of God's benevolence toward us that is essential to faith must be both revealed to our minds and *sealed upon our hearts*."[51] Similarly Calvin does not hesitate to announce that "the enjoyment of Christ kindles a new desire for him,"[52] and that spiritual need can be remedied only when such need is "really felt," those who are "insensible" of their need remaining "incurable."[53] Only in those who "cheerfully" embrace the teaching of Christ is our election in Christ sealed upon us "visibly"[54]—election, cheerful faith and visible seal are necessary in view of the fact that the Fall ensures that we are born "bears and lions and tigers."[55] As crucial as the cognitive aspect of faith is, it always subserves the affective aspect; e.g., "knowledge of faith consists in assurance rather than in comprehension," such assurance alone allowing us "with tranquil hearts to stand in God's sight."[56] Again, while faith is certainly knowledge of God, the heart is deeper than the head, with the result that while believers "feel the divine power of the gospel"[57] faith

---

48. Calvin, *Institutes*, 3.1–2 *passim.*

49. Ibid., 1.11.2. (Emphasis added.)

50. Calvin, *Sermons on the Book of Micah*, 406. (Emphasis added.)

51. Calvin, *Institutes*, 3.2.7. (Emphasis added.)

52. Calvin, *Commentary on John* 7:38.

53. Ibid., 9:41.

54. Ibid., 8:47.

55. Ibid., 10:8.

56. Calvin, *Institutes*, 3.2.14; 3.2.15.

57. Ibid., 3.2.10.

160 CALVIN@500

cannot "comprehend what it feels."[58] The ethos Calvin's theology generates is not at all hostile to the contemporary concern with spirituality.

Calvin, of course, does not use the word "spirituality," the word entering the theological vocabulary centuries later through a Jesuit agenda fostered by Ignatius Loyola's *Spiritual Exercises*. Calvin speaks frequently of "godliness" and "piety." Godliness, obviously, is other-engendered. Piety, for Calvin, is "that reverence joined with love of God which the knowledge of his benefits induces."[59] Calvin customarily speaks of faith, since faith presupposes Jesus Christ (who bears and bestows the Spirit) as faith's author and object. Calvin always suspects a devaluation of gospel vocabulary wherein biblical words with precise meanings are reduced to religious commonplaces devoid of gospel content. In this regard Calvin reminds readers in *Necessity* that gospel substance is jettisoned whenever gospel words are retained but gospel significance lost. Merely to deploy "faith" and "repentance" is no guarantee of spiritual adequacy.[60] Today he would cringe at the way "guilt" has been altered from one's situation before God to how one happens to feel; i.e., from a divine-judicial category to a psychological category.

As eager as he is to recognize the place of spiritual experience Calvin warns us against a contemporary concern with spirituality that often appears unable to recognize and resist rampant subjectivism. Drift is always more dangerous than decree. Few denominations decree a repudiation of doctrinal standards; most, however, drift imperceptibly.

It appears that drift may be evident where not expected. Whereas Calvin maintains that there is found in us "nothing but sin and death,"[61] a widely-used book on Christian spirituality asserts, "Augustine, like us, sought for an external God, a God separate from himself. He discovered, however, that God is to be found and loved within the depths of our being."[62] Augustine aside, Calvin would insist that God *is* external to us, even as God has come among us in his Son and indwells us by his Spirit; not only do we not find God in the depths of our being, we do not find God at all since God finds us as God overtakes us and

58. Ibid., 3.2.14.

59. Ibid., 1.2.1.

60. Calvin, "The Necessity of Reforming the Church," 193.

61. Ibid., 197.

62. Mulholland, *The Deeper Journey*, 143.

arrests us in our headlong flight from him. Ransacking our "depths" will never yield God.

If it is true that the church, in the past few decades or in the Reformation tradition generally, has one-sidedly emphasized the head to the detriment of the heart, the way forward is not by means of an uncritical subjectivism; the way forward is the recovery of the emphasis Calvin makes in *Necessity* and throughout his work. Calvin's characteristic deployment of "feel" and related words recalls Charles Wesley's hymn wherein he asks, "Depth of mercy, can there be mercy still reserved for me? Can my God his wrath forbear, me the chief of sinners spare?" only to answer, "God is love; I know, I *feel*; Jesus lives, and loves me still."[63] In eighteenth-century English "feel" meant "prove by lived experience." The affective dimension is upheld while a self-referential mentality is denied. Two hundred years earlier Calvin had as much in mind when he wrote that believers are to "feel due gratitude for his [i.e., God's] mercies."[64] Calvin remains a theologian of the heart no less than a theologian of the head. Recovering his theology will satisfy the church's legitimate quest for spiritual experience without courting religious romanticism.

In penning and promulgating his tract *The Necessity of Reforming the Church* when Charles V preferred him to postpone it for political considerations, Calvin was aware that he would likely be accused either of folly or presumption. In self-extenuation he pleaded, "If a thing is done honestly and from pious zeal, we deem it worthy of praise; if it is done under the pressure of public necessity, we at least deem it not unworthy of excuse."[65]

The spiritual descendant of Calvin who expounds the Reformer's tract can only plead the same.

63. Quoted in Wesley, *Works of John Wesley*, Vol. 7, 284–85.
64. Calvin, "The Necessity of Reforming the Church," 187.
65. Ibid., 184.

11

"Everyone's a Part of the Line of Production"

STEPHEN ALLEN

INTRODUCTION

IN THIS CHAPTER I hope to do four things: (1) Focus on some of Calvin's insights into social and economic matters—more broadly Calvin's theology on how Christians are called to live in the world. In this regard, I have found Andre Bieler's *Calvin's Economic and Social Thought* especially helpful; (2) Situate Calvin historically—what was happening in Geneva, Europe, and the world beyond Europe? (3) Identify some parallels between Calvin's time and today. Indeed many issues that challenge us today find their roots in Calvin's world; (4) Remind us of important documents in The Presbyterian Church in Canada that have been influenced by John Calvin and more broadly, Reformed theology.

I am not a Calvin scholar, but this 500th anniversary is an opportunity for me to learn about Calvin and his influence on The Presbyterian Church in Canada. An ecumenist can do no less (I am an Anglican) than seek to appreciate the abundant riches available across the Christian community. As someone who has joyfully served The Presbyterian Church in Canada since September 1997, it is important for me to deepen my understanding and appreciation of The Presbyterian Church in Canada and Reformed theology.

Let me begin with a simple statement: the Reformed tradition and Calvin's insights have much to offer us today as we struggle to live faithfully on this planet. The title of my chapter is "Everyone's a part of the line of production." My hope is that it will become clear to you why I chose this title. And if it is not clear by the end of my chapter, then alas, I will have failed!

JOHN CALVIN AND JUSTICE

John Calvin had much to say about how Christians should live in the world. Calvin's influence is felt all over the world today. This theologian, jurist, philosopher, and political thinker has left his mark on the universal church. Calvin is often portrayed as the father of modern capitalism. I do not find this observation helpful. I believe Calvin's influence on capitalism is more complicated and nuanced. Thomas Wipf, President of the Swiss Protestant Churches asserts that Calvin contributed to economic ethics. Wipf argues that Calvin believed that business should serve the common good.[1] Economy—from the Greek *oikos* + *nomos*—means the law or management of the household and in its ancient sense, as Douglas Meeks suggests, is about access to what it takes to live and to live abundantly.[2]

Over 75 million people are members of the World Alliance of Reformed Churches. In the not too distant future, WARC will come together with the Reformed Ecumenical Council which represents 12 million people. One perhaps should not give too much weight to numbers—what is important to note is that the Reformed community is a global church.

Pre-industrial Europe of the sixteenth century is a world away from our age of globalization, micro-chip technologies, exploration of outerspace and the human genome and the ever-present threat of nuclear annihilation. Many of us live longer and enjoy material pleasures that people in the sixteenth century could not even dream about. This must be qualified, however, by noting that the church knows through its ministries locally, nationally, and globally, that not all of God's people enjoy the fruits of God's creation. Human flourishing is denied to many.

Calvin instructed and exhorted Christians in the purpose for which they were created—to know, to love, to serve the triune God—Father, Son, and Holy Spirit—who creates, redeems, and gives faith. This purpose is also its greatest good, the fulfillment and meaning of human life.

---

1. Wipf, *Where God is Known, Humanity Also Flourishes*, 6.
2. Meeks, *The Economy of Grace and the Market Logic*.

Social and economic themes are "interwoven with the fundamental character of Calvin's theology." Consider the following statement from Calvin's Commentary on the five books of Moses regarding Exodus 16:19: "A fair distribution can become reality if the rich do not greedily swallow up whatsoever they can get together; if they do not rake up every side of what belongs to others to satisfy their greed; if they do not gorge themselves upon the hunger and want of the poor, if they do not, as far as in them lies, stifle the blessing of God . . . And surely, we often see that what the greedy collect by theft, rapine, fraud, cruelty, trickery or meanness often becomes rotten."[3]

A central truth for Calvin, and one that needed no evidence, was this—God is good and just and that what God wills is good and right by definition. Neither the worship of God nor love of neighbor can be done without the other. Love of neighbor, the second great commandment is evidence of love of God. According to Calvin, what Christians did in the everyday world was not cut off from the liturgical experience on Sunday, but a vital part of the worship of God. Each day Christians are in God's presence and are called to live responsibly. Calvin emphasizes that Christians are to live in right relationship with God and in ways that do not harm their neighbors.

Elsie Anne McKee in her essay "The Character and Significance of John Calvin's Teaching on Social and Economic Issues," says: "for Calvin, the wonder of God's generosity and the beauty of God's creation, together with God's will for human good, give us many reasons to delight in that divine goodness which lavishes gifts on all human beings." There is a caveat—these gifts from God are to be used to glorify God and not result in harm to others. When harm is done to others through our own greed, we abuse God's generosity.[4]

I note here two theological principles that Calvin felt were vital to Christian faith: (1) the Sovereignty of God; (2) *imago Dei*. God is Sovereign—the authority of state and church and other human institutions are limited. I quote here from my colleague and friend, Michael Hogeterp, when he states that "compassion and the pursuit of the public good are integral to Reformed theology—accepting these assertions is

---

3. WARC & the John Knox International Reformed Centre, *The Legacy of John Calvin*, 28; Calvin, *Commentary on the Five Books of Moses*, Exodus 16.19, 28.

4. McKee, "The Character and Significance of John Calvin's Teaching on Social & Economic Issues," 7.

SOME KEY HISTORICAL MOMENTS IN THE LATE FIFTEENTH AND SIXTEENTH CENTURIES

based on the fact that God is Sovereign and God's Reign extends to all of life."[5] Calvin believed that humans are created in God's image. Imago Dei implies that we have responsibilities to each other. Through God, we are social beings.

SOME KEY HISTORICAL MOMENTS IN THE LATE FIFTEENTH AND SIXTEENTH CENTURIES

Let us briefly turn to Calvin's time. John Calvin was born July 10, 1509 and died May 27, 1564. This was a formative period not just in European but in world history. By the late 1400s, Columbus had already made several trips to the Americas. The European expansion to the Americas, Africa, and Asia was beginning. This expansion would lead to a scale of plunder difficult to imagine, to slavery and then colonization. Once the military had paved the way, the church, in some instances, often followed.

In 1516, Spain received its first shipment of slave-grown sugar from the Caribbean and in 1518, a ship in Spanish service carried the first cargo of Africans directly from the Guinea Coast to the Americas. For the next three and a half centuries, some 10 to 12 million Africans were shipped across the Atlantic. Untold millions more died along the way.[6] Once the Spanish and the Portuguese became involved in the slave trade, England followed. Queen Elizabeth put her ship, named "Jesus" at the disposal of slave traders.[7]

Calvin condemned slavery. He compared slavery to killing: "to deprive a man of such a great good [freedom] is almost like cutting his throat."[8] I have not done an exhaustive study of what Calvin thought about European expansion to Africa, Asia, and the Americas, but Bieler suggests that Calvin was not opposed to European expansion and colonialism because of the opportunity this presented for mission and evangelizing. Readers more familiar with Calvin may have insights on these issues.

The treasuries of Indigenous peoples in Mexico and Peru were looted. The silver mine in Potosi, Bolivia, discovered in 1545 by the

---

5. Hogeterp, "Calvin, Reformed Faith and the Passion for Social Justice."

6. Davidson, *Africa In History*, 207.

7. Bieler, *Calvin's Economic and Social Thought*, 145.

8. Cited in ibid., 149.

Spaniards along with gold, contributed to transforming the economies in Europe, including Geneva.[9]

Andre Bieler in his *Calvin's Economic and Social Thought*, writes that the towns and the markets were the sites of social emancipation and the cradle of the Reformation. As the economies of the towns developed, a merchant class emerged. The development of the capitalist economy provided the material conditions for European expansion.

The influx of precious metals (gold and silver) had a profound impact on local and national economies. The number of banks increased. Bankers, writes Bieler, became the new nobility. Currency speculation was more prevalent. This has a familiar ring to it. Gold and silver contributed to price increases in grain, manufactured goods, and the price of land in Europe.[10] Bieler notes that the church ignored the growing practice of banks charging interest on loans because churches needed the bankers.[11] Calvin argued for a ceiling on interest—5 percent for investment loans. In a letter to Claude de Sachin, Calvin wrote: "We must be concerned that the contract [of usury] helps rather than harms the common good."[12]

The first joint stock companies in Europe were set up in 1554, precursors to the multinational corporation. Stock exchanges were established in Antwerp in 1531 and shortly after in Lyon. This was a period of gambling, speculation, and the expansion of economies in Europe.

FAST FORWARD TO 2009

Decisions made in Calvin's time have some influence on our own times. I want to spend a few moments on the multinational corporation. It is a creation of the twentieth century, although its roots can be traced back to the period of colonization and the search for raw materials to feed European economies. Today, the global corporation is pre-eminent. No major decisions are made concerning global trading rules, bi-national trade agreements, investment policies, patent issues, etc. . . . without significant input from the corporate sector.

---

9. Galeano, *The Open Veins of Latin America*, 30–35.

10. Bieler, *Calvin's Economic and Social Thought*, 127.

11. Ibid., 127.

12. Wipf, *Where God is Known, Humanity Also Flourishes*, 6.

Of the 100 largest economies in the world, fifty-one are global corporations and forty-nine are nation states. There are over 40,000 corporations in the world whose activities cross national boundaries. These firms carry out their activities through 250,000 affiliates. But only 200 corporations account for 28 percent of the world's economic activity, expressed in sales (equivalent to GDP). Fully one third of world trade consists of transactions among various units of the same corporation. Nike buys from Nike. Microsoft sells to Microsoft. Much has been written about these intra-firm transfers that allow companies to reduce taxation—by, for example, selling high so that the purchasing affiliate declares losses and reduces its tax level.[13]

186 of the top 200 are headquartered in just seven countries—France, Germany, Japan, the Netherlands, Switzerland, United Kingdom, and United States. Brazil and South Korea are the only countries from the global south to break into the top 200. Half of the total sales of the top 200 are in trading, automobiles, banking, retailing, and electronics. The concentrated economic power in these sectors is enormous.

A full 5 percent of the top (in the world) 200 corporations' combined workforce is employed by Wal-Mart, a company notorious for union-busting and widespread use of part-time workers to avoid paying benefits. The discount retail giant is the top private employer in the world, with 1,140,000 workers, more than twice as many as No. 2, DaimlerChrysler, which employs 466,938. If Wal-Mart was a country, it would be the eighth largest importer of products from China.

Today 85 percent of the world's GDP is controlled by the wealthiest 20 percent of humanity, while the poorest 80 percent control 15 percent.[14] We live in a very unequal world, yet it is a world that is abundantly rich. There is more than enough food to eliminate hunger. The Globe and Mail reported on July 31, 2009, that 5,000 Wall Street bankers received bonuses of at least one million each in 2008—that is over $5 billion. The total bail-out of U.S. and European banks is in the range of $9 trillion.[15]

13. Anderson and Cavanagh, *Top 200: The Rise of Global Corporate Power*, online: www.globalpolicy.org.

14. Ibid.

15. Dillon, " Forum on Faith and a Sustainable Economy."

CALVIN@500

COLONIZATION AND COMMODITIES

I would now like us to consider some products that are familiar to us. Coffee and sugar are two commodities with roots in slavery and/or colonialism. These household products tell a story about our world today.

Whose Coffee?

Coffee is indigenous to Ethiopia where the beans were first consumed around 500 AD.

The coffee plant, which originated in Ethiopia, produces cherry-like fruit. These cherries were eaten by slaves who were transported from present day Sudan into Arabia and Yemen. Yemen acquired and began cultivating coffee trees sometime around the fifteenth century, and began brewing coffee as a beverage. The coffee drink was promoted by Yemen authorities as a superior alternative to the traditional stimulant: eating the buds and leaves off the "Kat" shrub, which induced extreme side effects.

Many other countries coveted coffee plants, but Arabic law prohibited the export of the fertile beans. The Dutch succeeded in smuggling out live coffee trees in 1616. The subsequent spread of the coffee plant around the world occurred mostly through European colonizing countries who had the plants cultivated by indigenous peoples in their foreign territories. The Dutch spread the plant to its colonies in India, Indonesia and parts of Central and South America.

Sugar—Not Such A Sweet Story

In 500 BC in India, raw sugar was extracted from sugarcane. The technology for sugar production slowly spread around the globe. An estimated 4 to 7 million Africans were taken to Brazil and the Caribbean as slaves on sugar plantations until the United Kingdom's abolition of slavery in the nineteenth century.

Sugar is a commodity that fluctuates widely in price. Sugar prices plummeted 76 percent in real terms between 1980 and 2000. Any change in international sugar supply or demand can cause a sharp jump in sugar prices. For example, in the early 1980s the Coca Cola Company decided to substitute a corn base for sugar in its soft drinks. This proved to be a real boost for corn producers in the U.S. At the time, Coca Cola was consuming 600,000 tons of sugar annually and was the most important consumer of sugar in the world. The change in demand made by this single company plunged the sugar industry into a long and deep crisis. Wild fluctuations play havoc for countries that depend on a few commodities. Sugar makes up 70 percent of Cuba's total exports and 40 percent of Belize's exports.

I have briefly referred to the history of these products not for the purpose of asking: "did Calvin have anything to say about these products?" but to remind us that these commodities have a long history and they provide a window on the complex relationship between the global north and the global south today.

THE GLOBAL FAIR TRADE MOVEMENT—BUILDING FOR THE REIGN OF GOD

Coffee and sugar producers benefit from the fair trade movement. Today there are 632 certified producer organizations, from fifty-nine countries throughout Latin America, the Caribbean, Africa, and Asia. There are over 1.5 million producers directly involved in Fair Trade and over 7.5 million individuals directly impacted. In the early days of the fair trade movement, the only products available were coffee and tea. Today hundreds of products are now certified.[16]

The global fair trade movement involves hundreds of thousands of people. Many congregations in The Presbyterian Church in Canada use fair trade coffee and other products. Coffee co-ops involved in fair trade earn three to five times more than they would by selling their coffee on the "open market."

Sugar co-ops in Costa Rica, Ecuador, Kenya, Malawi, Peru, Paraguay, and Zambia represent over 10,000 families. Canada sells 1 percent of globally available Fair Trade sugar.

The annual growth of Fair Trade Certified products in Canada is 48 percent. The approximate retail value for all products in 2007 was $116M (2007). There are over 250 TransFair licensee companies selling Fair Trade Certified products including: coffee, tea, sugar, cocoa, bananas, fruit, rice, sports balls, quinoa, cut flowers, cotton, wine, spices, and shea butter.

The fair trade movement is a global movement. Fair trade makes a positive difference in the lives of thousands of people and perhaps more importantly, points the way to a different order, a different kind of eco-

16. For further information, see Transfair Canada, www.transfair.ca.

nomics. When we feel that there is so much hopelessness and despair in the world, we need to celebrate initiatives that are life giving and which offer a glimpse of what the Reign of God might look like.

TOMATOES AND CONTEMPORARY SLAVERY

The third product is the tomato. The tomato originated in Central America and was taken to Europe by the Spanish in the sixteenth century. I do not know if permission was given to the Spanish to take the tomato plant to Europe. The fruits were likely orange-yellow in color giving rise to one of their early names *pomodoro*, Italian for "golden apple."[17] You may have noticed grape tomatoes that come in a plastic container and are grown in Immokalee, Florida. There are many large tomato farms in this region of southern Florida. There have been and there continue to be serious human rights violations on some of these farms.

The Coalition of Immokalee Workers struggles for fair wages, an end to indentured servitude in the fields, better working and living conditions and stronger enforcement laws against those who violate workers' rights. The Coalition, with support from Christian denominations, such as the Presbyterian Church USA, has struck agreements with Yum! Brands, Burger King, Subway, and McDonald's to address ill-treatment of those who work in the fields.

These large companies buy from tomato growers and so these companies have a lot of influence with the growers. Because of the agreements with these companies, conditions are improving for some agricultural workers involved in tomato production and harvesting. Sadly, problems persist.

In December 2008, farm labor supervisors in Florida were sentenced in federal court for enslaving tomato pickers. The pickers had been beaten, chained and locked in a truck at night.

Sally Rausch—a high school student in Columbia, S.C., and a member of Spring Valley Presbyterian Church—said this when she learned about the treatment of some fruit and vegetable pickers, many of whom are migrants. "We feel like everything bad happens out there," she said. But, "everyone eats fast food and everyone's a part of the line of production. Something on the dollar menu may be good for me, but what does it mean for other people?"[18]

17. Wells, *The World in Your Kitchen*, 100.

18. Furkin, *Coalition of Immokalee Workers*.

THE PRESBYTERIAN CHURCH IN CANADA

The Holy Bible guides and shapes our lives. There are two documents, both subordinate standards of The Presbyterian Church in Canada that I would like to refer to. The first is *The Declaration of Faith Concerning Church and Nation*, ratified by General Assembly in 1955. I would like to quote parts of three sections:

> 1. The one holy triune God, sovereign Creator and Redeemer, has declared and established His kingdom over all powers in heaven and earth.

> 5. . . . and he demands that we obey Him against all authorities, whether civil or ecclesiastical, whenever they claim absolute power, especially the power to control [men's] thinking on right and wrong.

> 9. . . . Nevertheless, no citizen is thereby relieved of [his] constant responsibility to work for the remedy of any unjust statute, or iniquitous assessment, or violation of conscience.[19]

The second is *Living Faith*. The 110th General Assembly (1984) approved the following motion: "The document *Living Faith* be received by General Assembly and be commended to our Church as an acceptable statement of faith and as useful in worship and study." *Living Faith* was approved as a subordinate standard in 1998. I will quote the opening section on Justice:

"God is always calling the church, to seek that justice in the world which reflects the divine righteousness revealed in the Bible."[20]

Neither of these documents provides specific direction nor clear answers to complex issues the church might be grappling with. What these documents do, inspired by the Holy Bible, is call the church to proclaim the gospel of Jesus Christ and to be a vital presence in the world. How the church responds to specific issues is the responsibility of General Assembly, guided by the Holy Spirit. On a day to day, week to week basis, preaching and bible study are essential in nurturing and

---

19. The Presbyterian Church in Canada, *The Declaration of Faith Concerning Church and Nation*.

20. The Presbyterian Church in Canada, *Living Faith*, 25.

challenging the faithful. How do we make sense of the world? How do we live faithfully as disciples of Jesus Christ?

I would also like to draw the readers' attention to a document called "The Accra Confession—Covenanting for Justice in the Economy and the Earth." The Accra Confession was adopted by delegates to the World Alliance of Reformed Churches' 24th General Council held in 2004 in Accra, Ghana.

The Accra Confession[21] challenges Reformed Christians around the world to engage injustices in the world as an essential part of their churches' witness and mission. The Accra Confession is the culmination of a fifteen year long process that began at the World Alliance of Reformed Churches' General Council in 1989 in Seoul, Korea.

We are an Easter people. We are called to be actively engaged in this world, to bring hope, a hope that is made possible through God's eternal love.

CONCLUDING REMARKS

I conclude with these observations by Andre Bieler:

> The political stance of Christians is too generally commensurate with action inspired by class and too often dependent on ideologies that are to a vague degree, religious, but are alien to the Christian faith. To emerge from these two blind alleys, only one road is possible. We have to rediscover the biblical realism that encompasses the whole of existence. For every age, the discovery made by the Calvinist Reformation must be made afresh. It had perceived that the Word of God has to do with the whole range of human activity, and it had resolutely accepted letting itself be guided by it. Each new generation is responsible for making the discovery afresh, allowing for the continuously evolving changes in historical situations.[22]

Sally Rausch reminds us that we are more than consumers when she says: "Everyone's part of the line of production." I think John Calvin would agree.

Soli Deo Gloria (Only to God be the Glory).

---

21. The Accra Confession is available on the World Communion of Reformed Churches' (WCRC) web site: www.wcrc.ch WCRC was established following the merger between the World Alliance of Reformed Churches and the Reformed Ecumenical Council, in June 2010.

22. Bieler, *Calvin's Economic and Social Thought*, 459.

Bibliography

Abrams, M. H. *The Mirror and The Lamp: Romantic Theory and Critical Tradition*. Oxford: Oxford University Press, 1960.

Allen, Robert, and Gilbert Bartholomew. *Preaching Verse by Verse*. Louisville: Westminster John Knox, 1999.

Anderson, Sarah, and John Cavanagh. *Top 200:The Rise of Global Corporate Power*. Online: www.globalpolicy.org.

Asbridge, Thomas. *The First Crusade: A New History*. London: Free Press, 2004.

Augustine, *The City of God*. Translated by Marcus Dods. New York: The Modern Library, 1950.

————. *On Christian Doctrine*. Translated, with an introduction, by D. W. Robertson, Jr. New York: Bobbs-Merrill, 1958.

Babington Macaulay, Thomas. *The History of England from the Accession of James the Second*. New York: AMS, 1968.

The Barna Group, Ltd. *Most American Christians Do Not Believe that Satan or the Holy Spirit Exist*. April 10, 2009. Online: www.barna.org.

Barr, Gladys H. *Calvin Master of Geneva*. New York: Holy, Rinehart, and Winston, 1961.

Beeke, Joel R. "Calvin on Piety." In *The Cambridge Companion to John Calvin*, edited by Donald K. McKim, 125–52. New York: Cambridge University Press, 2004.

Bieler, Andre. *Calvin's Economic and Social Thought*. Edited by Edward Dommen. Translated by James Greig. Geneva: WARC & WCC, 2005.

Bouwsma, W. J. *John Calvin: A Sixteenth-Century Portrait*. Oxford: Oxford University Press, 1988.

Bregman, Lucy. "Religious Imagination: Polytheistic Psychology Confronts Calvin." *Soundings* 63 (Spring, 1980) 36–60.

Brown, Susan Tara. *Singing and the Imagination of Devotion: Vocal Aesthetics in Early Modern Protestant Culture*. Studies in Christian History and Thought. Colorado Springs: Paternoster, 2008.

Brueggemann, Walter. *The Book that Breathes New Life*. Minneapolis: Fortress, 2005.

Buttrick, David. *Homiletic: Moves and Structure*. Philadelphia: Fortress, 1987.

Calvin, John. *A Commentary on the Psalms*. Edited by T. H. L. Parker. London: James Clarke, 1965.

————. *Advertissement contre l'astrologie judiciaire*. Edited by Olivier Millet. Geneva: Droz, 1985.

————. "Avertissement contre la censure." In *Œuvres*. Bibliothèque de la Pléiade. Edited by Francis Higman and Bernard Roussel, 435–44. Paris: Gallimard, 2009.

————. "Briève instruction . . . contre les erreurs de la secte commune des anabaptistes," Vol. II. In *Series IV Ioannis Calvini Scripta didactica et polemica*, edited by M. Van Veen, 33–142. Geneva: Droz, 2007.

Bibliography

———. *Calvin: Theological Treatises*. Library of Christian Classics 22. Translated with introductions and notes by J. K. S. Reid. London: SCM, 1954.

———. *Commentaries on the Epistle of Paul the Apostle to the Romans*. Translated and edited by John Owen. Edinburgh: Calvin Translation Society, 1849. Reprint, Grand Rapids: Eerdmans, 1955.

———. *Commentaries on the First Book of Moses Called Genesis*. Translated by John King. Grand Rapids: Eerdmans, 1948.

———. *Commentaries on the First Book of Moses called Genesis, Vol. First*. Grand Rapids: Baker, 2005.

———. *Commentary upon the Book of The Acts of the Apostles*. 2 Vols. Translated by Henry Beveridge. Edinburgh: Calvin Historical Society, 1844. Reprint. Grand Rapids: Eerdmans, 1965.

———. *Commentary on The Epistles of Paul the Apostle to the Corinthians*. 2 Vols. Translated by John Pringle. Edinburgh: Calvin Translation Society, 1848. Reprint, Grand Rapids: Eerdmans, 1948.

———. *Commentary on the Gospel according to John*. Translated by the Calvin Translation Society, 1847. Reprint, Grand Rapids: Eerdmans, 1956.

———. *Commmentary on the Gospel of Matthew*. Translated by William Pringle. Edinburgh: Calvin Translation Society, 1846.

———. "Contre les libertines spirituelz." In *Series IV Ioannis Calvini Scripta didactica et polemica, Vol. 1*, edited by Mirjam Van Veen, 43–163. Geneva: Droz, 2005.

———. *Daniel I*. Calvin's Old Testament Commentaries. Translated by T. H. L. Parker. Grand Rapids: Eerdmans, 1993.

———. *The Epistles of Paul to the Romans and Thessalonians*. Calvin's New Testament Commentaries. Edited by David W. Torrance and Thomas F. Torrance. Translated by R. Mackenzie. Grand Rapids: Eerdmans, 1973.

———. *Epistolae, Vol.1*. Edited by C. Augustijn and F. P. Van Stam. Geneva: Droz, 2005.

———. "Epistre contre un Cordelier." In *Series IV Ioannis Calvini Scripta didactica et polemica, Vol. 1*, edited by Mirjam Van Veen, 173–96. Geneva: Droz, 2005.

———. *Institutes of the Christian Religion*. Library of Christian Classics, Vols. 20 and 21. Edited by John T. McNeill. Translated by Ford Lewis Battles. Philadelphia: Westminster, 1960.

———. *Institutes of the Christian Religion, 1536*. Translated and edited Ford Lewis Battles. Grand Rapids: Eerdmans, 1995.

———. *Institutes of the Christian Religion*. Translated by Henry Beveridge. Peabody, MA: Hendrickson, 2008.

———. *Institutes of the Christian Religion of John Calvin, 1539: Text and Concordance*. Edited by Richard F. Wevers. Grand Rapids: Meeter Center for Calvin Studies, 1988.

———. *Institution de la religion chrétienne (1541)*. Edited by Olivier Millet. Geneva: Droz, 2008.

———. *Ioannis Calvini opera quae supersunt omnia*. Edited by William Baum, Edward Cunitz, and Edward Ruess. 59 Vols. *Corpus Reformatorum*, Vols. 29–87. Brunsvigae: Schwetschke, 1863–1900.

———. *John Calvin: Tracts and Treatises*. Translated by Henry Beveridge. 3 vols. Grand Rapids: Eerdmans, 1958.

Bibliography

———. "Letter to Sadolet." In *Calvin: Tracts and Treatises*. Library of Christian Classics, Vol. 22, translated with introductions and notes by J. K. S. Reid, 221–56. London: SCM, 1954.

———. "The Necessity of Reforming the Church." In *Calvin: Tracts and Treatises*. Library of Christian Classics, Vol. 22, translated with introductions and notes by J. K. S. Reid, 184–216. London: SCM, 1954.

———. "Remarks on the Letter of Paul III." In *Calvin's Tracts and Treatises*, Vol. 1, translated by Henry Beveridge and edited by Thomas F. Torrance, 255–86. Edinburgh: Oliver & Boyd, 1958.

———. "Response a un certain holandois," In *Series IV Ioannis Calvini Scripta didactica et polemica, Vol. 1*, edited by Mirjam Van Veen, 197–273. Geneva: Droz, 2005.

———. *Romans and Thessalonians*. Calvin's New Testament Commentaries. Translated by T. H. L. Parker and edited by David W. Torrance and Thomas F. Torrance. Grand Rapids: Eerdmans, 1963–1974.

———. *Selected Works of John Calvin: Tracts and Letters, Vol. 5: Letters, Part 2. 1545–1552*. Edited by Henry Beveridge and Jules Bonnet. Reprint, Carlisle, PA.: Banner of Truth, 2009.

———. *Sermons on Jeremiah*. Texts and Studies in Religion, Vol. 46. Translated by Blair Reynolds. Lewiston, NY: Mellen, 1990.

———. *Sermons on Micah*. Translated by Blair Reynolds. Lewiston, NY: Mellen, 1990.

Cheng, Yang-en. "Calvin on the Work of the Holy Spirit and Spiritual Gifts." *Taiwan Journal of Theology* 27 (2005) 173–206.

Chung, Paul. "Calvin and the Holy Spirit: A Reconsideration in Light of Spirituality and Social Ethic." *Pneuma* 24 (2002) 40–55.

Cottret, Bernard. *Calvin: A Biography*. Translated by M. Wallace McDonald. Grand Rapids: Eerdmans, 2000.

Crouzet, Denis. *La genèse de la Réforme français, 1520–1560*. Paris: Sèdes, 1996.

Davidson, Basil. *Africa in History*. London: Phoenix, 2001.

De Greef, Wulfert. *The Writings of John Calvin: An Introductory Guide*. Translated by L. Bierma. Grand Rapids: Baker, 1993.

De Koster, Lester. *Light for the City: Calvin's Preaching, Source of Life and Liberty*. Grand Rapids: Eerdmans, 2004.

Descartes, René. *Meditations on First Philosophy: With Selections from the Objections and Replies*. Translated with an introduction and notes by Michael Moriarty. Oxford: Oxford University Press, 2008.

Detmers, Achim. "Calvin, The Jews And Judaism." In *Jews, Judaism, and the Reformation in Sixteenth Century Germany*, edited by Dean Phillip Bell and Stephen G. Burnett, 197–217. Leiden: Brill, 2006.

DeVries, Dawn. "Calvin's Preaching." In *The Cambridge Companion to John Calvin*, edited by Donald K. McKim, 106–24. Cambridge: Cambridge University Press, 2004.

Dillon, John. "Forum on Faith and a Sustainable Economy: The Financial Crisis." Presentation hosted by the Commission on Justice and Peace of the Canadian Council of Churches on Parliament Hill, Ottawa, May 12, 2009.

Dryness, William. *The Reformed Imagination and Visual Culture: The Protestant Imagination from Calvin to Edwards*. Cambridge: Cambridge University Press, 2004.

Edgar, William. "Ethics: The Christian Life and Good Works According to Calvin (3.6–10, 17–19)." In *A Theological Guide to Calvin's Institutes: Essays and Analysis*, edited by David W. Hall and Peter A. Lillback, 320–46. Phillipsburg, NJ: Presbyterian & Reformed, 2008.

Bibliography

Edmondson, Stephen. *Calvin's Christology*. Cambridge: Cambridge University Press, 2004.

Edwards, .O. C., Jr. *A History of Preaching*. Nashville: Abingdon, 2004.

Elwood, Christopher. *The Body Broken: The Calvinist Doctrine of the Eucharist and the Symbolization of Power in Sixteenth-Century France*. Oxford: Oxford University Press, 1999.

Erasmus, Desiderius. "*De votis temere susceptis, 1522.*" In *Collected Works of Erasmus, Vol. 39: Colloquies*. Translated by Craig R. Thompson, 35–43. Toronto: University of Toronto Press, 1997.

———. "In Psalmum Quartum Concio." In *Collected Works of Erasmus*, Vol. 63: *Expositions of the Psalms*. Translated by Dominic Baker-Smith. Toronto: University of Toronto Press, 1997.

Farge, James K. *Orthodoxy and Reform in Early Reformation France: The Faculty of Theology of Paris, 1500–1543*. Leiden: Brill, 1985.

Farris, Allan L. "Calvin's Letter to Luther." In *The Tide of Time: Historical Essays by the Late Allan L. Farris, Professor of Church History and Principal of Knox College, Toronto*, edited by John S. Moir, 61–73. Toronto: Knox College, 1978.

Farris, Stephen. *Preaching that Matters: The Bible and Our Lives*. Louisville: Westminster John Knox, 1998.

Fitzmyer, Joseph A. *Romans: A New Translation with Introduction and Commentary*. Anchor Bible 33. New York: Doubleday, 1993.

Flood, John L. "The Book in Reformation Germany." In *The Reformation and the Book*, translated by Karin Maag and edited by J.-F. Gilmont, 21–103. Aldershot, UK: Ashgate, 1998.

Fredriksen, Paula. *Augustine and the Jews: A Christian Defense of Jews and Judaism*. New York: Doubleday, 2008.

Furkin, Bethany. *Coalition of Immokalee Workers to Submit Petition Signed by Faith Community to Florida Governor*. Presbyterian News Service, March 6, 2009.

Galeano, Eduardo. *The Open Veins of Latin America*. New York: Monthly Review, 1974.

Gardiner, S. R. *History of the Commonwealth and Protectorate*. London: Longmans, Green, 1894.

Gay, Peter. *The Enlightenment: An Interpretation—The Rise of Modern Paganism*. Vol. 1. New York: Norton, 1977.

Gladwell, Malcolm. *Outliers: The Story of Success*. Boston: Little, Brown, 2008.

George, Timothy. "Calvin's Biggest Mistake: Why He Assented to the Execution of Michael Servetus." *Christianity Today* 53 (September 2009) 32.

Goering, Joseph. "The Internal Forum and the Literature of Penance and Confession." In *The History of Medieval Canon Law in the Classical Period, 1140–1234: From Gratian to the Decretals of Pope Gregory IX*, edited by Wilfried Hartmann and Kenneth Pennington, 379–428. Washington, DC: Catholic University of America Press, 2008.

Gordon, Bruce. *Calvin*. New Haven, CT: Yale University Press, 2009.

Graf, Friedrich W. "Calvin im Plural: zur Vielfalt moderner Calvin-Bilder." Plenary paper presented at the conference *Calvin et son Influence, 1509–2009*. Geneva, 24–27 May 2009.

Green, Garret. *Imagining God: Theology and the Religious Imagination*. New York: Harper and Row, 1989.

———. *Theology, Hermeneutics and Imagination*. Cambridge: Cambridge University Press, 2000.

Bibliography

Greidanus, Sidney. *Preaching Christ from the Old Testament: A Contemporary Hermeneutical Method*. Grand Rapids: Eerdmans, 1999.

Greschat, M., *Martin Bucer*. Translated by Buckwalter. Philadelphia: Westminster, 2004.

Habermas, Jürgen. *The Structural Transformation of the Public Sphere: An Inquiry into a Category of Bourgeois Society*. Translated by Thomas Burger. Cambridge: MIT Press, 1991.

Hancock, Ralph C. *Calvin and the Foundations of Modern Politics*. Ithaca, NY: Cornell University Press, 1989.

Harink, Douglas K. "Spirit in the World in the Theology of John Calvin: A Contribution to a Theology of Religion and Culture." *Didaskalia* (Spring 1998) 61–81.

Harkness, Georgia. *John Calvin: The Man and His Ethics*. Nashville: Abingdon, 1958.

Hedley, Douglas. *Living Forms of the Imagination*. London: T. & T. Clark, 2008.

Helm, Paul. *John Calvin's Ideas*. Oxford: Oxford University Press, 2004.

Hesselink, I. John. "Calvin, the Holy Spirit, and Mystical Union." *Perspectives* (January 1998) 15–18.

Hexham, Irving. "Protestant Reformers, Travel, and Pilgrimage." http://www.christiantravelers-guides.com/culture/pilgrimreform.html.

Higman, Francis. *Censorship and the Sorbonne: A Bibliographical Study of Books in French Censured by the Faculty of Theology of the University of Paris, 1520–1551*. Geneva: Droz, 1979.

———. "The Question of Nicodemism." In *Calvinus Ecclesiae Genevensis Custos*, edited by W. H. Neuser, 165–70. Frankfurt: Lang, 1984.

———. "Premières réponses catholiques aux écrits de la Réforme en France, 1525–c.1540." In *Lire et Découvrir: La circulation des idées au temps de la Réforme*, 497–514. Geneva: Droz, 1998.

———. "Ideas for Export: Translations in the Early Reformation." In *Lire et Découvrir: La circulation des idées au temps de la Réforme*, 531–44. Geneva: Droz, 1998.

———, and Roussell, Bernard. "Les deux lignes de force de toute la carrière de Calvin—*enseigner* et *lutter*—sont déjà présentes dans cette première *Institutio*." In *"Introduction" to Calvin. Œuvres*. Bibliothèque de la Pléiade, xi–xli. Paris: Gallimard, 2009.

Hogeterp, Michael. "Calvin, Reformed Faith and the Passion for Social Justice." Paper presented at the Rediscovering Calvin Conference, University of Toronto, June 20, 2009.

Holt, Mack P. *The French Wars of Religion, 1562–1629*. Cambridge: Cambridge University Press, 1995.

Horton, Michael. "Union and Communion—Calvin's Theology of Word and Sacrament." *International Journal of Systematic Theology* 11 (2009) 389–414.

Hotchkiss, Valerie R., and Jaroslav Pelikan, eds. *Creeds and Confessions of Faith in the Christian Tradition*. Vol. 2. New Haven: Yale University Press, 2003.

Huntston Williams, George. *Radical Reformation*. 3rd ed. Kirksville, MO: Sixteenth Century Essays & Studies, 1992.

Hutton, Ronald. "The Local Impact of the Tudor Reformations." In *The English Reformation Revised*, edited by Christopher Haigh, 114–38. Cambridge: University Press. 1987.

Imbart de la Tour, Pierre. *Les Origines de la Réforme, Tome III, L'Évangélisme (1521–1538)*. Paris: Hachette, 1944.

Johnson, Luke Timothy. "Imagining the World Scripture Imagines." *Modern Theology* 14 (1998) 165–80.

Bibliography

Jordan, W. K. *The Development of Religious Toleration in England: From the Accession of James 1 to the Convention of the Long Parliament, 1603–1640.* London: Allen, 1936.

Kant, Immanuel. *Critique of the Power of Judgement.* Edited by Paul Guyer. Cambridge: Cambridge University Press, 2000.

Kaplan, Benjamin J. *Divided by Faith: Religious Conflict and the Practice of Toleration in Early Modern Europe.* Cambridge, MA: Belknap, 2007.

Kearney, Richard. *The Wake of Imagination: Toward a Postmodern Culture.* New York: Routledge, 1998.

Kelly, Douglas F. *The Emergence of Liberty in the Modern World: The Influence of Calvin on Five Governments from the 16th through 18th centuries.* Phillipsburg, NJ: Presbyterian and Reformed, 1992.

Kelsey, David. *Imagining Redemption.* Louisville: Westminster John Knox, 2005.

Kerr, Fergus. "The Self and the Good: Taylor's Moral Ontology." In *Charles Taylor*, edited by Ruth Abbey, 84–104. Cambridge: Cambridge University Press, 2004.

Kirby, Torrance. *Richard Hooker, Reformer and Platonist.* Aldershot, UK: Ashgate, 2005.

Kolb, Martin. *Martin Luther: Confessor of the Faith.* Oxford: Oxford University Press, 2009.

Labbe, Phillipe, and Gabriel Cossart. "*Sacrorum conciliorum, nova et amplissima collectio.*" In *Graz: Akademische Druck- u. Verlagsanstalt.* Tom. IV, Col. 562. Graz: Adeva, 1960–61.

Landa, Paul Joseph. "La Familière Exposition du symbole, de la loi et de l'oraison dominicale found in, The Reformed Theology of Gerard Roussel, Bishop of Oloron (1536–1555)." In *Familiere Exposition du simbole, de la loy et de l'oraison dominicale en forme de colloque and his Forme de visite de diocese (c. 1548).* PhD diss., Vanderbilt University, 1976.

Lassman, Peter and Velody, Irving. "Max Weber on Science, Disenchantment, and the Search for Meaning." In *Max Weber's "Science as a Vocation,"* edited by Peter Lassman, Irving Velody, and Herminio Martins, 159–204. London: Unwin Hyman, 1989.

Lischer, Richard. *The Company of Preachers: Wisdom on Preaching, Augustine to the Present.* Grand Rapids: Eerdmans, 2002.

Locher, Gottfried. "Calvin spricht zu den Juden." *Theologische Zeitschrift* 23 (1967) 180–96.

Long, Thomas G. *The Witness of Preaching.* 2nd ed. Louisville: Westminster John Knox, 2005.

Lowe, Walter. "Hans Frei and Phenomenological Hermeneutics." *Modern Theology* 8 (1992) 133–44.

Lowry, Eugene. *The Homiletical Plot: The Sermon as Narrative Art Form.* 2nd ed. Louisville: Westminster John Knox, 2000.

Luther, Martin. *Luther's Works, Vol. 25: Lectures on Romans: Glosses and Scholia.* Edited by Hilton Oswald. General series editors Jaroslav Pelikan and Helmut Lehmann. St. Louis: Concordia, 1972.

———. *Selections from his Writings.* Edited and with an introduction by John Dillenberger. Garden City, NY: Anchor, 1961.

———. *Luther's Works, Vol. 31: Two Kinds of Righteousness.* Translated by Lowell J. Satre and edited by H. J. Grimm. Philadelphia: Concordia, 1957.

Marsh, Christopher. *Popular Religion in Sixteenth-Century England: Holding Their Peace.* Basingstoke, UK: Macmillan, 1998.

Bibliography

Matheson, Peter. *The Imaginative World of the Reformation*. Minneapolis: Fortress, 2001.

McGrath, Alistair. *Iustitia Dei: A History of the Christian Doctrine of Justification*. Cambridge: Cambridge University Press, 2005.

McKee, Elsie Anne. "The Character and Significance of John Calvin's Teaching on Social and Economic Issues." In *John Calvin Rediscovered: The Impact of His Social and Economic Thought*, edited by Edward Dommen and James D. Bratt, 3–24. Louisville: Westminster John Knox, 2007.

McLeod, Don. "A Taste of Pure Religion." *The Presbyterian Record* (August 2009) 31–32.

McNaughton, Lynne. *Pilgrimage Leadership: Facilitating Liminality for Transformation. A Case Study*. D.Min., Columbia Theological School, 2007.

Meeks, M. Douglas. *The Economy of Grace and the Market Logic*. Presented at Churches' Consultation on Globalization, Stony Point, New York: January, 2004.

Migliore, Daniel L. *Faith Seeking Understanding: An Introduction to Christian Theology*. 2nd ed. Grand Rapids: Eerdmans, 2004.

Millet, Olivier. *Calvin et la dynamique de la parole: étude de rhétorique réformée*. Paris: Champion, 1992.

Monter, William. *Judging the French Reformation: Heresy Trials by Sixteenth-Century Parlements*. Cambridge: Harvard University Press, 1999.

Mostaza, A. "Forum internum—forum externum (En torno a la naturaleza juridica del fuero interno)." *Revista Española de derecho canonico* 23 (1967) 253–331.

Muir, Frank. *The Oxford Book of Humorous Prose: From William Caxton to P. G. Wodehouse: A Conducted Tour*. Oxford: Oxford University Press, 1990.

Mulholland, R. Jr. *The Deeper Journey: The Spirituality of Discovering Your True Self*. Downers Grove, IL: InterVarsity, 2006.

Müller, Friedrich. "Georg Nigrinus in seinen Streitschriften: 'Jüdenfeind, Papistische Inquisition und Anticalvinismus.' Ein Beitrag zur Charaketristik des Luthertums am Ende des 16. Jahrhunderts." In *Wilhelm-Diehl-Festschrift*, 105–52. Darmstadt: Historischer Verein für Hessen, 1941.

Niesel, Wilhelm. *The Theology of Calvin*. Translated by Harold Knight. London: Lutterworth, 1956.

Oberman, Heiko A. *The Roots of Anti-Semitism in the Age of Renaissance and Reformation*. Translated by James I. Porter. Philadelphia: Fortress, 1981.

O'Loughlin, Thomas. *Journeys on the Edges: The Celtic Tradition*. Maryknoll, NY: Orbis, 2000.

Opitz, Peter. "Calvin's Appeal to Scripture." Online: www.calvin09.org.

Parker, T. H. L. *Calvin's Preaching*. Edinburgh: T. & T. Clark, 1992.

Pelikan, Jaroslav. *The Christian Tradition, Vol. 1: The Emergence of the Catholic Tradition (100–600)*. Chicago: University of Chicago Press, 1971.

Pettegree, Andrew. *Reformation and the Culture of Persuasion*. Cambridge: Cambridge University Press, 2005.

Pitkin, Barbara. "John Calvin and the Interpretation of the Bible." In *A History of Biblical Interpretation, Vol. 2: The Medieval through the Reformation Periods*, edited by Alan Hauser and Duance F. Watson, 341–71. Grand Rapids: Eerdmans, 2009.

Placher, William. "Paul Ricoeur and Postliberal Theology: A Conflict of Interpretations?" *Modern Theology* 4 (1987) 35–52.

Pope, Paul III. "To the Emperor Charles V." In *Calvin's Tracts and Treatises, Vol. I*, translated by Henry Beveridge and edited by Thomas F. Torrance, 237–53. Edinburgh: Oliver & Boyd, 1958.

Potter Engel, Mary. "Calvin and the Jews: A Textual Problem." *The Princeton Seminary Bulletin*, Supplementary Issue I (1990) 106–23.

The Presbyterian Church in Canada. "Declaration of Faith Concerning Church and Nation." In *The Book of Forms*, Appendix E, 2007.

———. *Living Faith: A Statement of Christian Belief.* Winfield, BC: Wood Lake, 1984.

Ramp, Stephen. "John Calvin on Preaching the Law." *Word & World* 21 (2001) 262–69.

Reagan, Charles E. *Paul Ricoeur: His Life and Work.* Chicago: University of Chicago Press, 1996.

Reid, J. K. S. "Introduction—The Necessity of Reforming the Church." In *Calvin: Theological Treatises*, 183. Philadelphia: Westminster, 1954.

Reid, Robert, David Fleer, and Jeffrey Bullock. "Preaching as the Creation of an Experience: The Not-So-Rational Revolution of the New Homiletic." *The Journal of Communication and Religion* 18 (1995) 1–10.

Renaudet, Augustin. *Préréforme et Humanisme à Paris pendant les premières guerres d'Italie (1494–1517).* 2nd ed. Paris: Librairie D'Argences, 1953.

Resner, Andre Jr. *Preacher and Cross: Person and Message in Theology and Rhetoric.* Grand Rapids: Eerdmans, 1999.

Rice, Howard. *Reformed Spirituality: An Introduction for Believers.* Louisville: Westminster John Knox, 1991.

———, and Lamar Williamson Jr. *A Book of Reformed Prayers.* Louisville: Westminster John Knox, 1998.

Rice, Oliver. "Calvin's Theology of the Holy Spirit." *Evangelicals Now* (July 2009). Online: http://www.e-n.org.uk/4705-Calvin%27s-theology-of-the-Holy-Spirit.htm.

Ricoeur, Paul. "Phenomenology and Hermeneutics." In *Hermeneutics and the Human Sciences*, edited and translated by John B. Thompson, 101–30. Cambridge: Cambridge University Press, 1981.

———. "Philosophical Hermeneutics and Biblical Hermeneutics." In *From Text to Action: Essays in Hermeneutics*, edited by Kathleen Blamey and John B. Thompson, 89–101. Evanston: Northwestern University Press, 1991.

———. "Preface to Bultmann." In *Essays on Biblical Interpretation*, edited by Lewis S. Mudge, 49–72. Philadelphia: Fortress, 1980.

———. "The Bible and the Imagination." In *The Bible as a Document of the University*, edited by Hans Dieter Betz, 49–79. Chico, CA: California Scholars', 1981.

———. "The Summoned Subject in the School of the Narratives of the Prophetic Vocation." In *Figuring the Sacred: Religion, Narrative and Imagination*, edited by Mark I. Wallace, 262–75. Translated by David Pellauer. Minneapolis: Fortress, 1995.

———. "Theonony and/or Autonomy." In *The Future of Theology: Essays in Honour of Jürgen Moltman*, edited by Miroslav Volf, Carmen Kreig, and Thomas Kucharz, 284–98. Grand Rapids: Eerdmans, 1996.

———. "Thou Shalt not Kill: A Loving Obedience." In *Thinking Biblically: Exegetical and Hermeneutical Studies*, translated by David Pellauer and edited by Andre LaCocque and Paul Ricoeur, 111–38. Chicago: University of Chicago Press, 1998.

———. "Toward a Hermeneutic of the Idea of Revelation." In *Essays on Biblical Interpretation*, edited by Lewis S. Mudge, 73–118. Philadelphia: Fortress, 1980.

———. "Two Essays by Paul Ricoeur: The Critique of Religion and the Language of Faith." *Union Seminary Quarterly Review* 28 (1973) 203–24.

Roelker, Nancy Lyman. *One King, One Faith: The Parlement of Paris and the Religious Reformations of the Sixteenth Century.* Berkeley: University of California Press, 1996.

Bibliography

Rogers, Eugene F. "The Mystery of the Spirit in Three Traditions: Calvin, Rahner, Florensky or, You Keep Wondering Where The Spirit Went." *Modern Theology* 19 (2003) 243–60.

Salmon, J. H. M. *Society in Crisis: France in the Sixteenth Century.* New York: St. Martin's, 1975.

Schmidt, Charles. *Gérard Roussel, Prédicateur de la Reine Marguerite de Navarre: Mémoire servant a l'histoire des premières tentatives faites pour introduire la reformation en France.* Reprint, Genève: Slatkine, 1970 (Originally published in Strasbourg, 1845).

Schmidt, Leigh Eric. *Scottish Communions and American Revivals: Evangelical Ritual, Sacramental Piety, and Popular Festivity from the Reformation through the Mid-nineteenth Century.* PhD diss., Princeton, 1987.

Schner, George. "Metaphors in Theology." In *Theology after Liberalism: A Reader,* edited by John Webster and George P. Schner, 3–51. Oxford: Blackwell, 2000.

Seeberg, Reinhold. *Texbook of the History of Doctrines, Vol. II.* Grand Rapids: Baker, 1952.

Selderhuis, Herman J. *Calvin's Theology of the Psalms.* Grand Rapids: Baker Academic, 2007.

———. *John Calvin: A Pilgrim's Life.* Downers Grove, IL: InterVarsity, 2009.

Shepherd, Victor. "Abraham and Isaac in Genesis 22: Hope as the Reconciliation of Promise and Command." In *Teach Me Your Path: Studies in Old Testament Literature and Theology,* edited by Jeffrey P. Greenman and John Kessler, 9–38. Toronto: Clements, 2001.

Shute, Daniel. *Peter Martyr Vermigli and the European Reformations: Semper Reformanda.* Edited by Frank A. James III. Leiden: Brill, 2004.

Skinner, Quentin. *The Foundations of Modern Political Thought: The Reformation.* Cambridge: Cambridge University Press, 1978.

Snodgrass, Klyne. "Introduction." *Ex Auditu* 12 (1996) v–vi.

Spinks, Bryan D. *Sacraments, Ceremonies and the Stuart Divines: Sacramental Theology and Liturgy in England and Scotland 1603–1662.* Aldershot, UK: Ashgate, 2002.

Stevenson, William R. Jr. *Sovereign Grace: The Place and Significance of Christian Freedom in John Calvin's Political Thought.* New York: Oxford University Press, 1999.

Taylor, Charles. "Introduction" to Marcel Gauchet's *The Disenchantment of the World: A Political History of Religion.* Translated by Oscar Burge. Princeton: Princeton University Press, 1997.

———. *A Secular Age.* Cambridge, MA: Belknap, 2007.

———. *Sources of the Self: The Making of the Modern Identity.* Cambridge: Cambridge University Press, 1989.

Taylor, Larissa. *Soldiers of Christ: Preaching in Late Medieval and Reformation France.* Oxford: Oxford University Press, 1992.

———. "Dangerous Vocations: Preaching in France in the Late Middle Ages and Reformations." In *Preachers and People in the Reformations and Early Modern Period,* edited by Larissa Taylor, 91–124. Leiden: Brill, 2003.

Topping, Richard R. *Revelation, Scripture and Church: Theological Hermeneutic Thought of James Barr, Paul Ricoeur and Hans Frei.* Aldershot, UK: Ashgate, 2007.

Torrance, Thomas F. *Reality & Evangelical Theology.* Downers Grove, IL: InterVarsity, 1982.

Tucker, Ruth A. "John Calvin and the Princess." *Christian History and Biography.* Online: http://www.christianitytoday.com/ch/bytopic/women/johncalvinandtheprincess.html.

Bibliography

Turner, Edith and Victor. *Image and Pilgrimage in Christian Culture: Anthropological Perspectives*. New York: Columbia University Press, 1978.

Tylenda, Joseph N. "Christ the Mediator: Calvin versus Stancaro." *Calvin Theological Journal* 8 (1973) 5–16.

Van Drunen, David. "The Two Kingdoms: A Reassessment of the Transformationist Calvin." *Calvin Theological Journal* 40 (2005) 248–66.

Van Raalte, Theodore, and Jason Zuidema. *Early French Reform: The Theology and Spirituality of Guillaume Farel*. Aldershot, UK: Ashgate, 2011.

Venard, Marc. "Un catéchisme offert à Marguerite de Navarre." *Bulletin de la société de l'histoire du protestantisme français* 142 (1996) 5–32.

Vermigli, Peter Martyr. *The Commonplaces of the Most Famous and Renowned Divine Doctor Peter Martyr*. London, 1583.

Vial, Marc. *The Importance of the Holy Spirit and Its Role in Salvation*. Online: www. calvin09.org.

Vissers, John. "The Forgotten God: Rediscovering the Holy Spirit." *The Presbyterian Record* (June 2009) 37–38.

Wanegffelen, Thierry. *Ni Rome Ni Genève: Des fidèles entre deux chaires en France au XVIe siècle*. Paris: Honoré Champion, 1997.

WARC and the John Knox International Reformed Centre. *The Legacy of John Calvin: Some Actions for the Church in the 21st Century*. Geneva: WARC, 2008.

Warfield, Benjamin B. *John Calvin the Theologian*. Electronic Edition by ReformationInk (www.markers.com/ink) 1909.

Warnock, Mary. *Imagination and Time*. Oxford: Blackwell, 1994.

Weber, Max. *Lectures on the Philosophy of History*. Translated by Henry Sibree. London: Bohn, 1857.

———. *The Protestant Ethic and the Spirit of Capitalism with other Writings on the Rise of the West*. Translated by Stephen Kalberg. New York: Oxford University Press, 2009.

Wells, Troth. *The World in Your Kitchen*. Oxford: New Internationalist, 1993.

Wendel, François. *Calvin: The Origins and Development of his Religious Thought*. New York: Harper & Row, 1963.

Wesley, John. Sermon #150, "Hypocrisy in Oxford." In *Works of John Wesley*, Vol. IV, edited by Albert C. Outler, 392–407. Nashville: Abingdon, 1987.

Willis, E. David. *Calvin's Catholic Christology*. Leiden: Brill, 1969.

Wilson, Paul S. *The Four Pages of the Sermon: A Guide to Biblical Preaching*. Nashville: Abingdon, 1999.

Wipf, Thomas. *Where God is Known, Humanity Also Flourishes*. Berne, Switzerland: Federation of Swiss Protestant Churches, 2008.

Witte, John Jr. *The Reformation of Rights: Law, Religion, and Human Rights in Early Modern Calvinism*. Cambridge: Cambridge University Press, 2007.

Wolin, Sheldon S. *Politics and Vision: Continuity and Innovation in Western Political Thought*. Princeton, NJ: Princeton University Press, 2004.

Wolterstoff, Nicholas. *Divine Discourse: Philosophical Reflections on the Claim that God Speaks*. Cambridge: Cambridge University Press, 1995.

Wright, N. T. *The Last Word*. New York: HarperCollins, 2005.

Zachman, Randall C. *The Assurance of Faith: Conscience in the Theology of Martin Luther and John Calvin*. Minneapolis: Fortress, 1993.

———. *John Calvin as Teacher, Pastor and Theologian: The Shape of His Writings and Thought*. Grand Rapids: Baker, 2006.

Printed in the USA
CPSIA information can be obtained
at www.ICGtesting.com
LVHW011515211023
761548LV00002B/34